# PUBLIC SPEAKING TODAY

# PUBLIC SPEAKING TODAY

## GORDON I. ZIMMERMAN
University of Nevada, Reno

**WEST PUBLISHING COMPANY**

St. Paul    New York    Los Angeles    San Francisco

COPYRIGHT © 1979 By WEST PUBLISHING CO.
50 West Kellogg Boulevard
P. O. Box 3526
St. Paul, Minnesota 55165

**Library of Congress Cataloging in Publication Data**

Zimmerman, Gordon I.
  Public Speaking Today.
  Bibliography;  p.
  Includes index.
  1.  Public speaking  I.  Title.
PN4121.Z488        808.5'1          79-4455 9-13-82
ISBN 0-8299-0259-7

To my mentor and friend
DR. KENNETH E. MOSIER

# Contents

# Preface

The purpose of *Public Speaking Today* is to improve communication skills in an increasingly important activity—the public or presentational speech. This book is a practical guide to developing and presenting messages to contemporary audiences. It is designed as a text for a beginning public speaking class, as a companion volume to an interpersonal communication text in a broad introductory speech communication course, or as resource material for adult learning workshops in public speaking.

Several factors influenced my approach in this text. In general, these factors are a product of my several years as an instructor and practitioner of public speaking and reflect my review of current public communication literature and courses.

**1.** *Training in public communication has become increasingly important.* More and more college-trained people are discovering that audience presentations are essential in their careers. As women and minority people find new opportunities in the business and professional arena, the pool of potential public speakers increases. The electronic media further enhance the importance of public speaking by exposing the speaker to larger and more diverse audiences. And perhaps most important, training in public speaking aids in the development of intelligent, reasoning, articulate people. It has been argued that the increasing impact of television and the decline of training in verbal skills have combined to breed a nation of semiliterates. Whether that is accurate, it is certainly true that verbal competence—writing, reading, speaking, and listening—is crucial to one's professional success and personal well-being. And it is also true that public speech training can help develop not only one's confidence in an audience setting but also one's ability to think quickly, clearly, and analytically, and to apply that thought to everyday tasks through fluent, articulate speech.

**2.** *Textbooks in public speaking are best oriented toward real-world communication activities.* Certainly the materials should assist the student in fulfilling the requirements of the basic public speaking class. But the text should go one step further; it should help the student understand and adapt to typical speech activities in everyday living. The rationale for various principles and suggestions for the public speaker lies not only in communication theory and research but also in the practical life facts of real communication events in which the students will be involved. Thus this book will help the beginning student to understand public speaking and to practice it in classroom exercises. But it will do so in the context of typical people in typical situations.

There are three reasons for this applied approach. First, I want to avoid giving beginning speakers the impression that classroom speaking, usually to a captive audience of other beginners who are nervously awaiting their turn to speak, is typical of public communication generally. It is not. While classroom projects are crucial in developing raw skills, I believe that a textbook should go beyond that laboratory environment and identify specific applications of these skills.

Second, in providing in real life focus, this text explores topics not usually included in books that concentrate more narrowly on speaking in the classroom. For example, this text includes sections on negotiating the speech, managing the speech environment, enhancing two-way communication, speaking in special situations, and coping with ethical dilemmas, all crucial factors in contemporary public communication. They expand the students' awareness of the variety and complexity of speech-making.

Most important, by using real examples and applications, I have attempted to promote the students' motivation to learn. Human beings seek information more avidly, acquire it in more depth, and retain it longer and more completely when they can see specific uses for that information. For example, why should a student want to read a chapter on visual aids and then carefully prepare and practice using them for a classroom project? Because it will help her satisfy course requirements and get a good grade? Perhaps. But a potentially stronger motivator is that it may someday save her from embarrassment and help her achieve tangible benefits.

In general, the applied focus of *Public Speaking Today* not only provides guidelines for doing well in a speech class, but also adds depth and practicality to the learning process.

**3.** *A significant decrease in the number of full-time students who spend most of their time on campus* was a third factor that influenced my approach in this book. The growth of community colleges with commuter students, the increase of part-time students with outside jobs and families, the popularity of off-campus housing, the return of many older students who are seeking new careers, and the growing reliance on adult training programs in business and government, all suggest that a textbook should not be written primarily for "resident unmarried students between 18 and 22 who have not yet embarked on a career."

Though the language of a textbook should be simple and clear, the examples relevant and interesting, the content should not be too accommodating toward the campus scene. Yet some texts include comments like "Someday you will be looking for a job," or "A beginning speaker may be nervous because that cute sorority girl he's dating is also in the class," or "A good topic for a humorous speech is 'Life in the Dormitory.'" Comments that presume the reader's age, interests, and campus involvement may alienate many students and suggest limited relevance to real public-speaking situations. This text develops ideas and examples in ways that most adult readers can appreciate.

**4.** *Teachers and students in a basic public-speaking class prefer a text that emphasizes practical suggestions, the "doing" of public communication.* The book should not be a treatise on communication theory and research. Students do not take a public speaking course primarily because they want to become speech majors, nor do departments teach the course as an introductory survey of the speech communication discipline. Instead, the major motive is skills improvement. While this text has been written in congruence with modern theory and research, and while occasional citations have been necessary, this information has been blended into the practical focus of each chapter. Except for some theoretical frameworks in Chapter 1 and an ethical perspective in the concluding chapter, every chapter emphasizes the "how-to-do-it" of public speaking.

**5.** *Public speaking training should be based on a receiver-centered approach.* The suggestions for the speaker's audible and visual style, message development, and speech environment should all be presented in the context of "Who is the audience, what are their characteristics and expectations, and what response do I want from them?" Some texts devote a special chapter to "Audience Adaptation" and usually discuss selected strategies for persuading diverse groups. I believe that this is too narrow a view of *audience*. Instead, I have argued that the audience participates in an interpersonal, two-way communication process. The speaker must be aware of the audience at every stage of the communication event. Rather than telling the reader, "Now we come to Chapter 9 and it is time to think about who will be listening to your speech," I have focused on the receivers throughout the book. It is time to begin thinking about the audience from the moment one even considers the possibility of presenting a speech.

In general, I have intended this text as a serious, practical, task-oriented book for students who view public communication as a serious, practical task. Some special features include:

A major discussion of nonverbal communication, an important factor in a public speaker's effectiveness.

A chapter on deciding to speak publicly, including the process of negotiating the speech with agents of a potential audience.

A chapter on introductions and conclusions.

A chapter on speech anxiety, providing suggestions for what many speakers report to be their most difficult speech problem.

A chapter on two-way communication, on interaction with the audience before, during, and after the presentation.

A major section on maintaining interest and attention, one of the greatest problems for public speakers today.

A major section on adapting to the physical setting in public communication, including potential seating arrangements.

A discussion of special types of public-speaking events that are typical of real world communication activities.

A chapter on listening, often ignored as a concomitant of effective speaking.

A concluding section on the ethics of public speaking, on developing responsible public communication.

In general, the guiding principle for including materials in this text has been: "Is this information useful for the kinds of public speaking situations the student is likely to encounter in everyday living?"

After an *Introduction* that provides an overview of public speaking and the communication process, *Part One* explores the preliminaries to the actual presentation—the techniques of speech preparation. *Part Two* covers some essentials of the actual presentation—delivering the speech, using audiovisual aids, and managing speech anxiety—that beginning speakers report to be among their most difficult tasks. *Part Three* also involves essentials, but is a more adanced treatment of ways to improve the presentation, including tasks that speakers do not confront until they feel fairly confident in their basic preparation and presentational skills.

The outline at the beginning of each chapter provides a preview of the key ideas. The "Learning Objectives" help students understand what is expected of them. The questions for study at the end of each chapter will, if answered thoroughly, assure students that they have understood the essential information in that chapter.

I wish to thank several people who were instrumental in the completion of this book. Kathryn Landreth was primarily responsible for the materials in Chapter 10 on informative speaking and in Chapter 12 on listening. She also provided many useful suggestions based on her several years experience teaching public speaking. Clyde Perlee, Editor-in-Chief of the College Division of West Publishing, first conceived of this project and provided invaluable direction and impetus throughout. My family was especially patient and cooperative as I wrote this book, and my wife Roslyn typed the final manuscript and provided constructive criticism that improved its quality. Several professionals in speech communication provided incisive manuscript reviews. Betty Ghiglieri, secretary of the Speech and Theatre Department at the University of Nevada–Reno, assisted me in my chairmanship duties with her usual thorough efficiency, so that I had sufficient time to complete the manuscript. Finally, many former students and consulting clients gave me valuable feedback about the kinds of public-speaking activities in which they regularly participate; many of their examples have been incorporated in this book. To all the people noted above, I express my deepest appreciation.

Gordon I. Zimmerman

# part one

## SPEECH PREPARATION

# chapter 1

# THE COMMUNICATION PROCESS AND PUBLIC SPEAKING

**LEARNING OBJECTIVES**

After reading this chapter, you should be able to:
1. Understand your own public speaking efforts as a part of a larger model of human communication.
2. Define "nonverbal communication," note some of the various types, and explain their relevance for the public speaker.
3. Explain why public speaking is an interpersonal, dyadic, two-way communication process with practical implications for our daily lives.
4. Define public speaking as a receiver-centered (audience-centered) process.

# 1

When Suzanne Jacobs became assistant personnel manager for Northwest Gas and Electric, the last thing she expected to do was to give public speeches. Though she enjoyed interviewing job applicants and chatting informally with employees, the thought of speaking to larger groups frightened her. But when the company decided, because of energy shortages and rapidly increasing power bills, that it needed better communication with the public, and thus developed a Speakers' Bureau to provide programs on energy use and conservation for various audiences, Suzanne's supervisor "strongly recommended" that she participate. Suzanne complied reluctantly, but was soon surprised to find that she not only did a good job but that she enjoyed the rather heady experience of being appreciated by a variety of audiences. She now gives three or four speeches a month in the highly successful Speakers' Bureau program, and as a result is seen by her superiors as one of Northwest's more active and committed employees.

Alec Wilson had never been involved in politics, but when a friend decided to run for the state legislature, Alec agreed to help. After some early advance work making arrangements for the candidate's public appearances, Alec began to speak to groups of volunteers about the candidate's position on issues and the kinds of things they could do during the campaign. He also made presentations at neighborhood coffee hours, to groups of business people who were potential contributors to the campaign fund, and to church groups. Near the end of the busy campaign, Alec spoke at televised press conferences. After the election, Alec realized that though his speeches were usually shorter and less formal, he had spoken to nearly as many audiences as the candidate himself had.

Elena Ramirez became a teacher because she loved children and was committed to improving the educational opportunities of children from the inner city, particularly the *barrio* where she had been raised. She loved teaching but became increasingly dissatisfied with the overcrowded classrooms, inadequate supplies, and low salaries—but she found the leadership of the local teachers' association inarticulate and apathetic. Elena began speaking out at the monthly meetings and, not surprisingly, was soon elected president. In that capacity, she made regular presentations to the school board and the PTA chapter; her finest hour was a speech before the education committee of the state legislature that led to passage of a law limiting class size. Several people have suggested that she run for public office, but Elena is happy being a teacher. She continues to make several speeches each month and commands respect in the educational community.

Richard Baxter worked his way through college as a salesclerk for a department store. He seemed to have a knack for selling, and upon graduation became sales agent for a manufacturing firm. He visited hundreds of retail stores and explained the company's product line to individual dealers. But his company decided that his method of selling should be supplemented by presentations to larger groups of prospective buyers, and asked Richard to set up meetings at markets and conventions. Richard now travels throughout the region making day-long presentations, including demonstrations and audiovisual materials, to groups of business people. He has learned that his skills at selling in a one-to-one situation are even more successful when he deals with audiences.

All the examples above are true stories. None of these people were lawyers, ministers, politicians, or show business personalities; they were all fairly normal, everyday sorts of people who became active public communicators inadvertently. They did not enter a career called "public speaking" or think that it would become an important part of their everyday lives, but their willingness and ability to speak to audiences were instrumental in their professional satisfaction and success. Finally, these examples are typical of many people who are discovering that speaking to an audience is a fairly frequent and necessary communication event in their lives, that if they are active in their careers or in community activities they will be called upon to give speech presentations at least several times a year.

But these examples may still seem somewhat remote from your own experience. Perhaps as a student in a public speaking class you will find the following cases more relevant. Students X, Y, and Z have just enrolled in a first course in public speaking. Student X is an education major who is required to take the class for graduation. Student Y is an engineering student who has always been fearful of speaking to audiences, but he recognizes the importance of being able to give presentations in his chosen field and has resolved to take the course to become more fluent and confident in public settings. Student

© Howard Harrison 1978

Z has been away from college for several years and has returned to finish a degree in business. Having seen and experienced many situations in the "real world" that required effective speaking, she has decided that this class will help her better achieve her career goals. Perhaps you can identify with one of these three people. But whatever your motives for enrolling in this course, you will have generally the same experience as others in the class—the challenging opportunity to *do* public speaking, to grow as a communicator, and to prepare for everyday communication events. This book is designed to help you, the beginning speaker, maximize that learning process.

## COMPONENTS OF THE HUMAN COMMUNICATION PROCESS

This is a book about contemporary public speaking. We shall explore many strategies and skills that will help people become more effective in informing or persuading others in an audience setting. Terms like

*public speech*, *public communication event*, *presentational speaking*, *audience presentation*, and *one-to-many communication* will be used interchangeably throughout the book. But before discussing the public speech, let us first examine the larger communication model of which it is a part.

### Major Elements—A Simple Model

David Seibert defines communication as *the process in which persons assign meanings to events and especially to the behavior of other persons* (Zimmerman et al., 1977, p. 6). He identifies six major elements of this process (see Figure 1):

**1.** The *sender* (source, speaker) is a person whose behavior, both verbal and nonverbal, is perceived by one or more people.

**2.** The *receiver* (listener, auditor, interpreter) is one who perceives the sender's behavior, like hearing speech sounds or seeing bodily movement, and assigns meaning to it.

**3.** The *message*, then, is that portion of the sender's behavior that is perceived and given meaning.

**4.** The message must obviously be carried from sender to receiver via some medium, called a *channel*. In face-to-face communication, the channels are usually vision and hearing (light and sound), but could also include touch and smell. Sometimes electronic channels (television, radio, telephone, etc.) affect one's perception of another's message behavior.

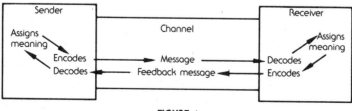

**FIGURE 1**

**5.** *Feedback* in this model denotes a receiver's verbal and nonverbal response to the sender's message, response that affects the behavior of the original sender. Thus feedback can be viewed as closing the circular communication process. Two people are both senders and receivers as they each engage in communication behavior and perceive behavior of the other. Seibert is careful to note that not all receiver responses (behaviors) are feedback, just as not all sender behaviors are messages. Only those responses that are perceived by the sender and affect subsequent behaviors are considered feedback. Further, Seibert explains:

> Feedback need not be intentional. For example, if you are giving a speech and someone in the back row is lulled to sleep by your talk, you may or may not notice. If you notice and adjust by raising your voice to awaken the sleeper, you are responding to feedback. If you don't notice, there is no feedback from the sleeping audience member (Zimmerman et al., 1977, p. 10).

**6.** The *context* is the situation or environment in which the communication transaction occurs. Context might include the physical location or setting of the communication event, the attitudes and expectations of the participants, the purposes of each participant in the transaction, the time available for the interaction, the particular mix of participants, the kinds of channels available, and any other factor that may affect the ways in which people behave, perceive the behavior of others, and give meaning to that behavior. Because any context includes a large set of interdependent elements, and because these elements converge at a particular point in time that will never be repeated, communication events are always unique; no two are ever identical.

## The Concept of Meaning

The concept of *meaning* is crucial to our understanding of this model. It is important to note that words and behaviors have meaning only insofar as people assign it to them. A commonly held premise in communication theory is that "meanings are in people, not in words." Words don't "mean"; people mean. The sender of a message cannot

confidently assume that "This is what my words mean" or "This is what the dictionary says they mean." A more realistic statement is, "I have created a set of meanings in my own mind that I choose to express with a set of verbal symbols that I hope will cause you, the receiver, to create similar meanings." A useful way to think about meaning, then, is as a *response* to a message. We can only know what a message means to receivers by observing how they respond to it. What do they say, how do they look, how do they act in response to what we have just said? One reason why feedback is so important in the communication process is that it is a response that tells us how the receiver has assigned meaning to our behavior.

One indicator of effective communication is the degree to which meaning is shared by both sender and receiver. It may be true that perfectly shared meaning, in which both sender and receiver understand a message in precisely the same way, is an impossibility. Even in the simplest messages, like "Put the book on the table," subtle distinctions in meaning are possible, depending in part on the way in which the message is spoken, the communicators' prior experience in using those language symbols, and the relationship and feelings between the communicators. When the receiver responds by putting the book on the table, we can reasonably assume that *essentially* shared meaning exists between sender and receiver. But we cannot be absolutely certain, because part of the response is intrapersonal—it occurs within the person. This mental or psychological response may include what the receiver thinks or feels about the sender or about the act of putting the book on the table. Nor will perceptible responses like a shrug of the shoulders, a smile or frown, or even comments like "Sure" or "Okay" assure us that absolute shared meaning has occurred. But as communicators we can move toward the ideal of shared meaning. We can evoke responses from others that suggest, in general, that the *intended* response sought by the sender is very similar to the *actual* response given by the receiver. Movement toward shared meaning is sometimes especially difficult in the public speaking setting, where there may be less chance to observe the behavior (responses) of all the receivers and to get verbal feedback from them. Hence we shall later develop strategies for improving shared understanding between speaker and audience.

## THE IMPORTANCE OF NONVERBAL COMMUNICATION

In many of our everyday activities we tend to be word-oriented. The legal and political arenas stress precise wording and careful recording of verbal proceedings. The business world continually tries to improve its "word processing" with computers, high-speed printing and typewriting, and information storage and retrieval systems. And in interpersonal transactions we are frequently concerned with "saying the right thing" (i.e.—using the right words). Our school systems have been criticized for failing to develop verbal competence in the students and are beginning to reemphasize reading and writing. It is not surprising, then, that when most of us think of "communication" or "sending messages" or "public speaking," we think of using words—spoken or written language symbols.

But this verbal orientation gives us a distorted view of the communication process, because it ignores many of the messages (behaviors) of senders and receivers. In this section, we shall identify some of the common types of nonverbal messages. Mark Knapp uses *nonverbal* as a term that describes "all communication events which transcend spoken or written words" (Knapp, 1972, p. 20). To this we add that, to be part of the communication model in the previous section, nonverbal communication includes only those events, behaviors, and characteristics *that we perceive and give meaning to*. Some of the characteristics and behavior of the sender will not be noticed by the receiver, and vice versa. These therefore are not part of the message.

### Types of Nonverbal Communication

As a convenient way of understanding nonverbal communication, let us identify several different types. The purpose of the following list is not simply to improve your understanding of the communication process. The primary objective is to set the stage for *the many different ways in which nonverbal factors will affect your success as a speaker*. The public speaking student who says "I just want to present my message as smoothly and accurately as possible" may be surprised when listeners become confused or distracted by nonverbal elements that impede verbal communication. Hence, under each of the points below, try to think of ways in which the factors could affect your own presentations, regardless of the quality of your spoken words. You should also remember that in an actual communication transaction, nonverbal features and behaviors combine and overlap to present a total image that we perceive as a unified whole. Unlike verbal messages that we can dissect to examine each word, the nonverbal message is more difficult to analyze in parts, to understand why we are assigning meaning to some elements and ignoring others.

*Physical features of the human body.* It is often unfortunate that we ascribe important meanings to physical features over which a speaker has little control. Yet being short or tall, fat or thin, shapely, muscular, dark-skinned or pale, hairy or bald, husky or frail, or even physically crippled can and does affect the ways in which others interpret our behavior. Evidence exists that the meanings we associate with physical features significantly influence our judgments of credibility, intelligence, attitudes, personality, and ability (Knapp, 1972, pp. 63–79).

*Bodily movement and posture.* The term *kinesics* is used to denote the broad category of observable physical motion that communicates— that is, to which people give meaning. One type of kinesics is *facial expression*, perhaps the most obvious feature in our perception of a speaker's behavior. Facial cues may be the most precise and valid indicator of a person's inner feelings. The features themselves may be important (we notice, for example, how people may look gruff or shy or happy or worried simply by the way their faces are shaped), and the way senders manipulate those features (smile, frown, smirk, leer, grimace) supplies many cues from which receivers may interpret literally hundreds of meanings. Eye behavior is usually the focal point of facial expression (shifty eyes, sexy eyes, sleepy eyes, happy or sad eyes). *Eye contact*, in general American culture, is one of the key indicators that we are attending to (perceiving) another person. It is thus a normal part of most interpersonal communication and crucial to good public speaking. *Length of gaze*, or the duration of uninterrupted eye contact, can also be an important cue. What different meanings might we assign to people who stare at us for more than a couple of seconds? And what might we conclude from the opposite behavior— like a public speaker who avoids any eye contact with us at all?

A second type of kinesics is *gesture*. Often thought of as arm and

© Howard Harrison 1968

hand movement, gestures also include such bodily movement as shrugging the shoulders, cocking the head, tapping fingers or toes, kicking motions, swaying, and pacing back and forth. Arm and hand movements are common in normal conversation; one of the indicators of one's improvement as a public speaker is the use of natural, comfortable gestures when communicating in an audience setting.

A third type of kinesics is *posture,* or one's body position and stance. Posture is often characterized by the receiver as formal, relaxed, rigid, defensive, aggressive, suggestive, sexy, slouched, awkward, casual, etc. Shifts in posture can also be meaningful. Notice, for example, how people in relaxed conversation develop a more rigid, formal posture when a person with authority or high social status enters the communication setting.

*Vocal inflection.* The human voice is an instrument for uttering language symbols, or words, but it is also part of the nonverbal domain. We use it to give special forms and patterns of inflection to verbal sounds. The term *paralanguage* refers to the vocal (audible) cues that accompany spoken language. Paralanguage does not refer to words themselves, but rather to everything that we can hear about the *way* in which the words are spoken. Paralanguage becomes nonverbal *communication* when we perceive the sound and assign meaning to it.

Vocal inflection includes such factors as *pitch* (the highness or lowness of the voice), *force* (the loudness, emphasis, or volume), *rate* (the speed with which consecutive sounds are uttered), and *quality* (acoustic or resonant characteristics of the voice—raspy, breathy, nasal, hoarse, etc.). The *pause*, sometimes silent and sometimes audible (um, uh, er), is also an important element of paralanguage. The receiver may assign meaning when a sender hesitates, such as assuming that the pause means forgetfulness, uncertainty, deviousness, or ignorance. And other vocal sounds—groaning, laughing, crying, sighing, burping, yawning, throat-clearing—may suggest meanings far more potent than the speaker's actual words. As with bodily movement, vocal inflection factors combine in characteristic patterns; they interact with each other and with physical movement to evoke a particular response or meaning from the receiver.

*Touch and smell.*   Human beings often assign meanings to touching behavior (*tactile communication*) and to odors (*olfactory communication*). Both are primitive forms of messages that we experience from birth. In American culture we tend to minimize touching, especially in public, except between family members, lovers, or close friends. Formal or impersonal touching that is socially acceptable seems to be confined to handshakes, pats on the back, or kisses on the cheek. Similarly, we tend to cover up natural body odors in our culture with scented soaps and perfumes. Touch and smell are the least relevant types of nonverbal communication in the public speaking setting, though the speaker who refuses to shake hands with audience members or who has offensive body odor should not be surprised if the intended verbal message is received poorly or with unintended responses.

*Object language.*   Unlike the previous categories that refer to the sender's bodily characteristics and behavior, *object language* refers to the material things in our environment that become nonverbal cues. *Artifacts* are clothing, jewelry, and other accessories that we use to present and describe ourselves to others. *Status symbols* are objects to which we expect the perceiver to assign favorable meanings. Objects in a communication situation frequently define who we are and what we expect in the transaction. At the same time, the objects may actually prompt us to behave in certain ways. For example, a judge's robe and a police officer's uniform certainly affect communication transactions and the kinds of messages that people receive; at the same time, those artifacts affect the ways in which judges and police actually behave. That is, the style and content of the message may differ significantly depending on which of our various "uniforms" are being worn.

*Space.* The distances between ourselves and others, as well as the space around us, frequently become important nonverbal messages. The term *proxemics* (think of *proximity*) is used to describe our perception and use of personal and social space for communication. Distance between people may suggest their attitudes and expectations about certain situations. For example, how might we as receivers respond differently to a public speaker who stands several feet away from us on a raised platform and behind a podium, as compared to a speaker who stands on the same level and is closely surrounded by the group of listeners? And in a social situation, what meanings might we take from a person whom we have just met who "violates our space" by moving in only a few inches away to speak with us?

Size of space can also be important. What meanings might be assigned to someone who has a large, carpeted, exquisitely furnished office overlooking the city versus someone in a windowless cubicle surrounded by other desks? And how might our communication behavior differ with the occupant of each office?

The degree to which we can manipulate and modify the space around us, including the placement of objects within that space, may determine our communicative effectiveness in a variety of contexts, including the public speech.

*Time.* Time as nonverbal communication is important in two respects. First, time as *a specific point on the clock* can suggest important meanings. Often when we notice what time it is, we become sleepy, get hungry, become impatient (as when we notice that a speaker has gone past the time he was supposed to have concluded), or change our behavior in various other ways. Our perception of clock time causes us to assign meaning. A second way to think about time is *duration*, or time span. Closely related to clock time, duration of various events like a public speech, conversation with a new acquaintance, or completion of a project may affect our evaluation of those events. And the time between events, like the number of weeks since someone has written or spoken to us, can also suggest important meanings.

*Silence.*  As if nonverbal communication were not complex enough, the mere *absence* of audible messages in a face-to-face situation may also be meaningful. When a person who could communicate orally chooses to remain silent, either briefly or at some length, that choice is a kind of behavior with message content. For example, the pause in conversation or public speaking can have emotional impact on the receiver, or it can suggest a sender's confusion, anger, indifference, boredom, thoughtfulness, distraction, or any number of other interpretations. In American culture we are frequently intolerant of the silent person, assigning negative meanings to silence and demanding that reticent people participate more actively in oral communication.

## Premises about Nonverbal Communication

Let us conclude this section with several premises about nonverbal communication.

**1.**  *Nonverbal and verbal communication are interdependent.*  All perceived messages are part of an interrelated whole to which the receiver assigns meaning.

**2.**  *Nonverbal messages are often more accurate and important than verbal ones, especially at the subjective (emotional) level.*  As receivers, we may assign meaning and rely more on verbal symbols when the messages involve logical, factual, or physical information. But when messages deal primarily with feelings or relationships, nonverbal elements may be more reliable bases for developing shared meaning. For example, if the verbal message is "I like you [*feeling*] and want to be your friend [*relationship*]," but negative nonverbal behavior of the sender suggests just the opposite, the receiver will tend to assume the latter.

**3.** *In speech communication events, nonverbal messages are inevitable.* If we can be seen or heard, receivers will assign meaning to the visual or audible cues.

**4.** *Nonverbal messages often have low reliability of meaning between receivers.* That is, similar nonverbal behaviors and characteristics, when perceived at different times or by different people, may result in widely varied meanings. We selectively perceive some elements, filter out others, and attribute greater significance to some perceptions over others. Thus, disagreement between people about what the nonverbal message means is quite common, just as with verbal communication, even when all receivers have perceived the same communication event, as in a public speech.

**5.** *The meanings of (responses to) nonverbal messages vary significantly between cultures.* In communication transactions between people of different racial, ethnic, or geographical backgrounds, the language barrier (verbal communication) may be significant. But even more bothersome may be elements like eye contact, gesture, facial expression, clothing, vocal inflection, and distance between people. Many of the "rules" and "meanings" we have learned through interaction in our own culture are not shared by people in other cultures. Thus, creating shared meanings in crosscultural communication settings may be especially difficult.

Throughout this book we shall refer back to this section, because of the importance of nonverbal communication in the public speaking process. For example, in Chapter 5 we shall discuss in depth various elements of *paralanguage* or vocal inflection, as well as the *kinesic* or visual elements of a speaker's posture and movement. In Chapter 6, we explore visual aids, part of the *object language* of nonverbal communication. In Chapter 8, we note that the meanings that audience members take in the two-way communication transaction with the

speaker are based to a large extent on nonverbal factors. In Chapter 10, we discuss the persuasive effectiveness of the speaker as a person —including general physical appearance. And Chapter 11 explores the language of space or *proxemics* in terms of the ways in which a speaker adapts to the context or environment. Students who begin now to understand and deal with the many nonverbal factors described in this section will find it progressively easier to control later, more challenging public speaking situations.

## THE PUBLIC COMMUNICATION EVENT

*The public communication event typically involves a sender who, in a relatively active role, initiates verbal and nonverbal messages to a group of relatively passive receivers who, depending on group size and composition and on the communication setting, provide varying amounts and types of feedback.* Of course, public speaking events are so numerous and diverse that it is difficult to understand the transaction with a single-sentence definition. Instead, we shall probe the term "public speaking" (public communication, presentational speaking, one-to-many communication) in more depth with several points explained below.

### Interpersonal Communication

*Public communication is a type of interpersonal communication.* "Interpersonal communication" is sometimes thought of as a separate category from "public speaking." For example, a common definition of interpersonal communication is "the face-to-face interaction between people who are consistently aware of each other. Each person assumes the roles of both sender and receiver of messages, involving constant adaptation and spontaneous adjustment to the other person" (Giffin and Patton, 1976, p. 11).

With this definition we may think of one-to-one or small group settings that include relatively informal conversation. But notice that a public speech generally conforms to this same definition. It is usually face-to-face (except when radio or television is the sole channel); the participants "interact" and in varying degrees are "consistently aware

© Howard Harrison 1971

of each other"; all participants are behaving and perceiving behavior and are thus both sending and receiving messages; and all are making either overt or subtle adjustments to other people. Of course, some public speakers may not be as aware of or adapt as much to the receivers as they might in some communication situations. After hearing a boring lecture, sermon, or political speech, we might suggest that the speaker is not adapting to us at all!

But we argue that some spontaneity, some response exists, even if it only involves the speaker's adjusting vocal volume or audience members' shifting in their seats. Both sender and receivers are at least aware of the other's presence. So the public speech differs perhaps in form but not in substance from other kinds of communication transactions. It is a special type of communication between people; but it is nevertheless interpersonal.

## Dyadic Communication

*Public communication is* dyadic—*it is a series of one-to-one relationships and transactions.* A common but misleading way to describe a public speech event is to think of a speaker initiating messages to a mass of humanity called the *audience.* Depending on the situation, this mass could be viewed as having various dimensions—number, seating arrangement, personal background, beliefs, attitudes, values, and so on.

The speaker's task in this situation is presumably to identify the ways in which the audience is homogeneous, the common characteristics its members share that permit some adaptation of the message to the receivers. For example, a political speaker might conclude, "My audience consists primarily of Caucasian business and professional women who are generally politically conservative and suspicious of interference by big government in free enterprise." The speaker has done nothing wrong by making that candid assessment of "audience" (see Figure 2).

However, any public communicator must recognize that rarely does an audience respond uniformly, despite common characteristics in the group. Each person is unique and thus interprets or assigns meaning to the message in separate ways. Hence the realistic speaker

will recognize that this blob of humanity called "audience" is actually a *series of dyads*, each of which will be different in some respects from all others (see Figure 3).

The message, including every verbal and nonverbal element in the presentation, will be selectively perceived differently by each receiver, who will respond in unique ways. The speaker, in perceiving feedback, will likewise notice that each receiver responds differently to the initial message. Though collective audience feedback such as laughter or applause may give the appearance that the message is the same for everyone, each receiver creates personal meanings, provides personal feedback, and establishes a personal dyad with the speaker.

The notion of public communication as dyadic is especially important because it helps determine a public communication strategy with a particular audience. If a speaker views the audience as a "bunch of people," he may perceive what seems to be a unified response as evidence that he has achieved his communication goals. "They are applauding and smiling; I think they understood me and liked me as a speaker." However, if the speaker views the audience as a "series of separate dyads," he will be more cautious about interpreting group or collective response and will seek more specific feedback from various audience members. This speaker might think, "A couple of people appeared to be confused; I'll leave some time for audience questions." Note, incidentally, that dyads between two audience members are also possible.

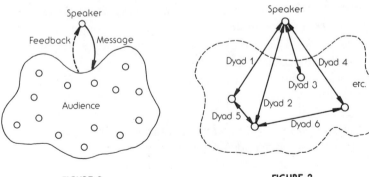

FIGURE 2                    FIGURE 3

Whether two listeners exchange nonverbal greetings across the room from each other or carry on a whispered conversation while the speech is in progress, they are participants in dyadic communication separate from that which each shares with the speaker. Though these dyads can sometimes be distracting, the public speaker who recognizes and accepts the inevitability of these transactions can develop ways of either ignoring or dealing with them. And that speaker will be less surprised or confused by wide variations in audience responses to the message.

### Two-way Communication

*Public speaking is usually two-way communication. One-way communication* occurs when a sender perceives and interprets no feedback from the receiver. *Two-way communication* occurs when a receiver initiates feedback (verbal and nonverbal) that is perceived and interpreted by the sender. Public speaking, like other forms of interpersonal communication, usually involves the simultaneous sending and receiving of messages. The audience behaves in various ways (nod, laugh, fall asleep, ask questions, interrupt, talk to neighbors, walk out, shift posture, etc.), and the degree to which the speaker notices, interprets, and responds to these behaviors indicates the quantity and quality of two-way communication.

There are two situations in which public speaking tends to be virtually one-way. The first is when an audience is not physically present with the speaker. For example, a presentation that is taped and played back to an audience at a later time, or the live radio or television broadcast, have no simultaneous feedback. (Even this situation could include two-way communication if the speaker receives delayed feedback such as newspaper reports of the speech, public opinion polls, or letters from people who heard the message.)

A second type of one-way communication occurs when the sender avoids any perception of or response to audience behavior. The proverbial professor droning on with eyes buried in notes, seemingly oblivious to the responses of student-listeners, is a good example. But in most situations, even aloof, unperceptive speakers have some awareness of audience behavior.

The best public speakers are those who recognize the two-way communication process, watch and listen for audience responses, and adapt to those responses in ways that improve the receivers' understanding and appreciation of the message.

### Boundaries of Communication Events

*The boundaries of the public communication event are often difficult to determine.* When does the public speech begin and end? With the first and last words that the speaker utters? Does the event begin when receivers first see and assign meaning to the speaker's appearance and behavior? Does it end only when the receivers stop thinking about what has just been seen and heard, meaning that the event could last indefinitely?

Suppose an international crisis prompts the President to schedule a televised speech to the American people. Previews in the news media prompt us to speculate about what the President might say. Already we have begun to assign meanings that may affect how we interpret the eventual speech. Perhaps the communication event has already begun, even though the President has not yet spoken. Then suppose that the actual verbal message has significant implications and far-reaching consequences such that we remember it for weeks and months afterward, continually refining and modifying the meanings we first assigned to the message. If so, the communication event did not end when the President finished speaking.

The public communicator who believes that a speech begins with an introduction and ends with a conclusion will be less effective than one who accepts the idea that the boundaries are not fixed. The latter person will attempt to understand how pre-speech and post-speech events and behaviors can affect good public communication.

### "Public" Audiences

*Public speeches are not always "public" in the strict sense of the word.* In this book we use the term "public speaking" because it is convenient and popularly understood to mean any one-to-many communication event. But these events are usually selective and specific in terms of audience; *they are not available for anyone who wants to listen.*

We see a few situations in which the audience might be a representative and voluntary group of citizen-listeners—the political speech in a park, a sermon at a revival meeting, a public lecture on a college campus, a Presidential message on radio or television. But the speaking that most of us will do most of the time will involve a more selective group of receivers. They might be co-workers in our business or profession, members of a club or society, volunteers in political campaigns, or a group of potential customers in a sales presentation. In public speaking today we are dealing with relatively narrow "publics."

The implications of this fact are varied. The speaker may find it easier to identify common receiver characteristics and interests if the group is more specific and their reason for attending is readily apparent. On the other hand, such an audience may have much higher expectations about the speaker's quality and quantity of information and about the care with which it is adapted to their unique interests.

If a political candidate, for instance, is speaking to a truly "public" audience, like a random group of people at a shopping center, she can discuss her platform in more general terms. But when she speaks to the Cattle Ranchers Association, or a chapter of the National Organization for Women, or the Black Caucus, or a trade union local, or the Chamber of Commerce, she had better have very detailed information about and good understanding of the specific issues that most concern the receivers. Thus, while responses from these specialized audiences may be easier to predict, message preparation for selective, well-informed receivers may also be more challenging.

## Increasing Usefulness

*Public speaking is an increasingly useful form of communication.* It might perhaps be argued that public speaking is slowly becoming obsolete. We don't seem to have the great orators anymore, and people appear to be more interested in watching a ball game or going to a movie than in attending a speech presentation. Even political campaigns utilize catchy slogans and brief television ads. But it might be more realistic to say that the age of public speaking is just beginning. Electronic media, especially public and closed-circuit television, now provide for greatly expanded audiences. An executive in a corporation can be heard and seen by all employees simultaneously. A presidential speech can reach well over *one billion* people around the world via satellite communication.

Furthermore, many more people now have the opportunity to speak publicly. Speakers of the past were typically white males, most of whom had wealth and education. With today's wider educational opportunities, legislation, and changing social consciousness, women and minority people are assuming more leadership positions that regularly put them in the speaker-to-audience setting. Public speaking is also becoming common in more and more situations—social movements and public demonstrations, labor union meetings, business conferences, public information and instruction, professional conventions, and service club programs are but a few of the arenas that increasingly demand effective presentational speaking.

## Speech Competence and Success

*Our willingness and ability to speak publicly will often be an important factor in our professional or career success.* It would be comforting to think that the accountant, the electrical engineer, the doctor, the teacher, the editor, the home economist, the marriage counselor, the personnel manager, the farmer, the housing contractor, the basketball coach, the scientist, or any other business or professional person could be evaluated and reap rewards solely on the basis of specific knowledge and competence. Wouldn't it be nice—and fair—if we could depend totally on our technical proficiency to determine our advancement, our salary, our self-esteem and recognition? Why should we be penalized because we don't happen to have the "gift of gab" like our colleague who is no smarter or more competent than we are?

We have two responses to this concern. First, a life fact of most careers is that people who can communicate well, especially in one-to-many settings, *get noticed*. We remember their names. We think of them when we are seeking help or information. And we also think of them when it is time to distribute the rewards of the system. Recall the example that opened this chapter. Suzanne Jacobs not only gave speeches. She indirectly told her superiors, "I am the kind of employee whom you can count on to help with whatever needs to be done." But

the reverse can also be true. The person who regularly avoids or declines opportunities to give speech presentations may be saying to colleagues, "I am not the kind of person whom you can depend on to adapt to the needs of the organization. I do what I am trained to do; it is unreasonable to ask me to do something else." We have all seen verbally competent people get rewarded and reticent people get overlooked. That trend, whether justified or not, will likely continue.

Second, it may be legitimate to reward people in part by their ability to speak publicly. That ability makes them more valuable in some settings. Maybe two people who are *equally skilled* in a specific task (like, say, computer programming or bookkeeping) are not *equally competent* in the business or profession if one person can more effectively participate in various communication tasks like orienting new employees, representing the organization in meetings and conventions, or talking with public groups. Thus we make no apology for the fact that public speaking skill may help determine career success. We think that in many situations it is not an unfortunate fact of life but rather a valid way of evaluating people.

## A RECEIVER-CENTERED APPROACH

In an earlier section we identified several components of a communication event—the *sender*, the *receiver*, the *message*, the *channel*, *feedback*, and *context*. Any effective speaker must be aware of all these components. However, we usually tend to view at least one of them as the most critical in achieving communicative effectiveness. The three most commonly emphasized components are the *sender* (speaker), the *message* (speech), and the *receiver* (audience).

### Sender- and Message-Centered Approaches

The *sender-centered approach* exists when the speaker is primarily concerned with the delivery or presentation of the message. The speech is a *performance* that can be appreciated as such by an audience. The sender-oriented speaker is most satisfied when the polished performance comes off without a hitch, when the audience perceives no awkward gestures or disfluencies, when all its members are impressed by the artistry with which the speaker kept them interested, amused, entertained.

There is certainly nothing wrong with pleasing or impressing an audience with one's presentational style. The absence of nervous physical mannerisms and other delivery flaws may improve a receiver's ability to attend to the message without distraction. The speaker must always be concerned with her own communication behavior. But the problem comes when she is so preoccupied with the performance dimension that she gives less emphasis to the message and to the receivers' responses. Has shared meaning occurred? Does the audience *understand* what the speaker intended? Are they *convinced* of her point-of-view? Will they *do* what she has suggested? The sender-oriented person does not always concern herself with these questions. Instead she asks, "Do they like me? Do they think I am a good speaker? Did I impress them? Did I make any mistakes that bothered them?"

The *message-centered approach* means that the speaker is primarily concerned with the verbal or linguistic content of the communication transaction. Regardless of how well it was presented, and regardless of how the audience received and assigned meaning to that presentation, the information itself must be precise, logical, and accurate. A speaker with a message orientation sometimes views himself and his listeners as incidental parts of the communication process. The message is the thing, and it seems to have an existence of its own irrespective of who happens to be speaking or hearing it. The speaker emphasizes careful word selection, precise phrasing and structuring of information, and accurate, logical progression of ideas. The speech message is prepared much as one might write an essay that is intended to be read and reread as a separate entity existing apart from whoever happened to write it and whoever happens to read it.

Again, we cannot quarrel with a speaker's attempt to develop a message that is clear, concise, and persuasive. Several sections of this book will offer suggestions for effective message preparation and content. But our concern is that the speaker will fail to recognize the important premise that words don't have meanings—people have, and assign meanings to words. Therefore, the message *does not exist* independently, but rather exists in the minds of the speaker and the listeners. The message-centered speaker may forget that carefully prepared language and information is useless except as it is perceived and interpreted. That speaker may thus be surprised that all the hard work of message preparation has not yielded the intended response. When misinterpretation results, the sender may say "But I told you so," while the listeners reply "Why didn't you say so?" We can usually agree about what *words* the speaker uttered. Our memory, tape recordings, or written transcripts can verify that. But we cannot know what the *message* was unless we can learn what the sender intended when he encoded his ideas into words, and what meanings the receivers assigned when they decoded those words. Like the sender-centered perspective, the message-centered approach does not focus directly enough on what we think is the major objective of public speaking— the development of shared meaning between sender and receiver.

## Receiver-Centered Approach

The basis of this book, then, is the *receiver-centered approach*. With this perspective, everything the speaker does to prepare and deliver a message, to utilize appropriate channels, to enhance the speech context or situation, and to receive feedback is designed to improve shared meaning with the audience. A good delivery is not a performance but a means to an end, improved audience comprehension and acceptance of ideas. The same is true for a clear, well-organized message.

The receiver-centered approach demands that the speaker ask such questions as "Who are the receivers? What are their expectations of me and of this situation? What do I want them to understand, to believe, to do? What responses from them do I want to obtain? How can I learn from my listeners whether I have succeeded in my communication goals?"

The receiver-centered speaker is concerned about the well-being of the people who have given of their time and energy to participate in the communication event. He is willing to *accommodate* them, not by flattery or by saying only those things that they want to hear, but rather by demonstrating that he cares about their responses, about the ways in which they have received and can use the information he provides. If receivers want to enjoy a performance, they can go to the theatre or concert hall. (The exception, of course, is a speech to entertain, as might be appropriate at a party or banquet.) If receivers simply want to absorb information, they can read a newspaper or magazine or punch a button for a computer printout. But if they participate in a public speech setting, they have a right to expect significant adaptation by the speaker to them and their unique situation.

The distinctions we draw here are not nitpicking; rather, they are important assumptions that help determine the communication strategies that each speaker will use. We shall refer to the receiver-centered approach throughout the rest of this book.

## SUMMARY

*Public speaking* (also called *public communication*, *presentational speaking*, *audience presentation*, or *one-to-many communication*) is one type of communication, the process in which people assign meanings to the events and behaviors they perceive. The communication process includes a *sender*, a *receiver*, a *message*, a *medium* or *channel*, *feedback*, and *context* or *setting*. The concept of *meaning* is important in this process and refers to a response to a message; we know what the message means only when we perceive how someone responds to it. An important objective of communication is to elicit essentially shared meaning—similarity between the intentions of the sender and responses of the receivers.

The *verbal message (language symbols)* has an important counterpart in *nonverbal characteristics and behaviors*. These include the human body, movement and posture (*kinesics*), vocal inflection (*paralanguage*), touch and smell (tactile and olfactory communication), object language, space (*proxemics*), time, and silence. Nonverbal factors become a part of the communication process only when we perceive and assign meaning to them. They are interdependent with verbal factors, are inevitable in any speech communication event, and may evoke widely varied responses depending on the perceiver's background and culture.

Public speaking is best conceptualized as *dyadic (one-to-one) inter-*

*personal communication*. It is essentially two-way in nature according to the degree to which the speaker perceives and responds to audience behaviors. The public speaking event (the boundaries of which are sometimes difficult to determine) is becoming a more frequent and useful form of communication, but perhaps also more challenging as audiences become more selective and well-informed. People who can speak well in audience settings may legitimately be more successful professionally than those who cannot.

This book is written from a *receiver-centered* perspective. A *speaker-centered* orientation (that focuses on a speech as a performance with carefully developed vocal and visual style) and a *message-centered* orientation (that focuses on the specific verbal message irrespective of speaker and listeners) miss the most important rationale for participating in a public communication event—the development of shared meaning between the sender and receivers. Hence, the receiver-centered orientation (that focuses on intended audience response to speaker and message) is the most valid for assuring that speech purposes will be achieved.

## QUESTIONS FOR STUDY

1. What do we mean by "meaning"? Explain the phrase "Words don't mean; people mean."

2. What are the basic elements or components of the communication model? Explain each component in terms of a student presentation in your speech class.

3. In terms of a public speaker whom you have seen and heard, how did nonverbal factors affect the ways in which you received his or her message?

4. What difference does it make whether a speaker thinks of the audience as a "group of people" rather than as a "series of dyads"?

5. What is the difference between sender-oriented, message-oriented, and receiver-oriented approaches to public speaking?

# chapter 2

# DECIDING TO SPEAK PUBLICLY

**LEARNING OBJECTIVES**

After reading this chapter, you should
be able to:

1. Identify several factors that should
   be present before one decides to
   deliver a speech.
2. Explain the speech negotiation
   process, its importance, and the
   potential factors that can be
   negotiated.
3. Apply several of the "negotiation
   variables" to public speaking
   assignments in the classroom.
4. Narrow a general speech topic and
   select a speech purpose for classroom speaking assignments.

Both public speakers and audience members often encounter problems such as these:

### Speakers

*"I wish I hadn't agreed to speak to the Employee's Association; I really haven't had enough time to prepare."*

*"The boss wants me to explain the new accounting procedures at the board meeting today. How does she expect me to do that in only ten minutes? It's going to take at least a half-hour."*

*"I really couldn't care less about Jim's campaign for mayor. I'm not very interested in politics. But he's a nice guy and I'm flattered that he asked me to speak on his behalf."*

*"I sure wish I'd known that people would have to leave by noon. I only finished about half of what I was prepared to say."*

*"I thought you knew I'd need a movie projector and screen. The film I brought is the basic part of my presentation."*

*"Four p.m. really isn't the best time for me to talk about all this technical information. They'll be worn out after a full day's work and won't be in any mood to listen."*

### Audience Members

*"I wonder why she didn't leave any time for us to ask questions? Didn't she realize that we always have a Q-and-A session at the end of every meeting?"*

*"Well, that was a waste of time! I knew more about first-aid techniques than he did."*

*"I thought he was going to talk to us about investment management programs. If I had known he was going to try to sell us life insurance policies, I wouldn't have come."*

*"I couldn't hear a word she said. What's so difficult about using a PA system?"*

*"He just tried to cover too much in thirty minutes. I couldn't keep track of everything, much less remember it. Some of that stuff wasn't important, anyway."*

*"Why does he always lecture at us? Why can't a supervisor talk to us on a one-to-one basis?*

All of the above statements refer to conditions that bothered either the speaker or the listener, or both. But these are problems that cannot be solved simply by improving one's presentation or delivery skills. Rather, they develop because not enough care is given to *pre-speech* decisions about the eventual communication event. Such problems can be solved if three important steps are taken. First, one should decide whether or not to speak publicly, using objective criteria. Second, the speaker should engage in meaningful negotiations with members of the potential audience. Third, the speaker should carefully narrow the topic and identify the specific speech purpose. These three steps will be discussed in this chapter.

## DECIDING TO GIVE A SPEECH

In Chapter 1 we claimed that public speaking is an increasingly common and useful form of communication today. People who do poorly as public speakers or who carefully avoid speaking situations may be severely handicapped in their business and professional lives. Indeed, we assume that our readers recognize the life fact that they will occasionally have to speak to audiences and that they need to improve their communication skills.

However, we must remember an equally important assumption: the one-to-many communication form may be inappropriate for many types of interpersonal transactions. That is, giving a speech may be a less effective way of achieving one's communication goals in certain contexts and with particular groups of receivers. *We hope this assumption will not become an excuse for people who are fearful of public speaking to avoid it as often as possible.* But it is only fair, since we are identifying the kinds of goals that good public speaking can achieve, that we should also candidly note some things that public speaking cannot do. We need to identify situations in which a person should not deliver a speech presentation.

There may be times in which we have little choice about whether to speak publicly. A politician in a hotly contested campaign, a student in a speech class, or an employee whose job description demands public speaking may feel that a decision has been made for them; they must either participate or face unpleasant consequences. But most of the time we can exercise our judgment and identify situations that may or may not call for a speaker-audience transaction. The guidelines below will help in making that decision.

## Guidelines

1. *The potential public speaker should be well informed about the proposed topic and competent to speak on it.* This does not necessarily mean that the speaker needs to know more about a topic than the listeners. For example, a political candidate might not know as much about agriculture as the group of farmers he is addressing, but he should be well informed enough about farm issues to give his listeners confidence in his ability to represent their interests. But, as this example illustrates, a person who decides to speak publicly should do so in part because of some particular competence, background, knowledge, or perspective.

The author has occasionally been asked to speak on a topic about which he was relatively uninformed. The person making the request probably thought, "This person is an experienced speaker who teaches public speaking to others; I'll bet he could talk to our group about such-and-so." I have refused (I hope tactfully) on the grounds that my knowledge of the topic area is limited and that there are others much better equipped to speak on it.

Of course, people should not continually refuse to speak on topics that are important to their well-being or to the good of their organizations or communities. Instead, they may have to *become* more knowledgeable on issues that affect their lives. (Note again the speakers in the opening examples of Chapter 1—all four had to increase their expertise in order to give effective presentations on topics that mattered to them.) But until we are certain that we have something to say and some reason to say it, we should not agree to speak publicly.

© Howard Harrison 1967

**2.** *The potential public speaker should be committed to communicating with an audience.* The speaker should want to achieve a communication goal, to develop shared meaning, to inform or persuade a group of receivers. That commitment is psychological; it must come from within the person. I cannot *make* you committed. You must *feel* it. I can provide various external stimuli—rewards or punishment—that may cause you to respond in a certain way that does not necessarily include your commitment, such as:

> *"If you don't give this speech to new employees, you're fired."*
>
> *"I'll pay you $100 if you will come to speak to my service club."*
>
> *"Hey, the scheduled speaker canceled out, so I'm really on the spot to find a speaker for our group meeting. Do me this favor as a friend."*
>
> *"There will be some important people at the meeting; you could make some lucrative business contacts."*
>
> *"I've heard so much about your ability as a speaker; the group is anxious to hear what you have to say."*
>
> *"Anyone who does not complete this speech assignment will get a lower grade for the semester."*
>
> *"I really want you to talk to these people. Besides, after all I've done for you, I think you owe me one."*

These external stimuli do not preclude a speaker's internal commitment to communicate, to share with an audience what he believes to be an important message. But these reinforcements do not *cause* the commitment (internal behavior), even if they do cause the speech to be given (external behavior).

This distinction is important. The internally motivated speaker will almost always do a better job in public communication than an equally skilled but uncommitted person, regardless of the external payoffs. For example, who would we prefer as a classroom instructor: someone who is enthusiastic about the subject matter and wants to help students share the excitement, or an equally knowledgeable person who is indifferent to the subject matter and views teaching simply as a convenient way to earn a living?

**3.** *The speech topic and purpose should be relevant to the needs and interests of the specific audience.* The speaker should be convinced that this particular group of people can benefit from the message, that it is worth their time to participate in the communication event. Many speakers have learned that they have expertise and communication skills that receivers appreciate. These speakers have gotten rewarding audience responses in the past and seek out more of these heady experiences. The danger is that what they have to say may be of little consequence to this particular group of receivers. The stereotype of the college professor, the politician, and the minister who are willing to "speak at the drop of a hat" illustrates this problem. While beginning speakers should not *underestimate* their abilities or avoid legitimate speech opportunities, more experienced speakers should not *over-estimate* the degree to which they can adapt their special knowledge and skills to any group in any situation.

**4.** *The potential public speaker should carefully consider whether a different type of communication transaction would be more appropriate.* Why give a one-to-many presentation? What is the rationale? The answer should be: "Because in this instance a presentation is an efficient way to achieve understanding, to enhance skills development, to convince, inspire, or move to action." Why should professional people lock-step into a public speech strategy without considering alternative methods? Probably one reason is custom or tradition. Our culture has identified many contexts in which a speech is expected; it is a situational norm. Thus the minister gives a sermon, the legislator gives a political speech, the teacher gives a lecture, the sales representative "makes a pitch." Another reason for reliance on presentational speaking is a person's own habits and preferences. Some of us get used to using the one-to-many format and never really consider alternative strategies. And, while some people fear the public speaking situation, others fear its alternative, the more spontaneous dialogue in which they lose the control and the neat definition of roles that the public speech provides. For example, a professor who relies totally on the lecture strategy might be doing so not only out of tradition and habit, but also out of fear that students might not remember their subordinate role, might challenge his ideas, threaten his status, and clutter a neat, well organized 45-minute presentation.

Whatever the cause of the overreliance on public speaking, the pattern should sometimes be broken. We should analyze other ways to achieve our communication goals. For example, teachers can supplant lectures with simulation exercises, student reports and discussions, field trips, and media aids. Political candidates sometimes spend more time in their public appearances listening to voters' problems than giving a prepared message. Supervisors see that sometimes a speech to employees is not as effective as one-to-one or small group discussions with the workers.

We do not always have to make an either/or decision about whether to give a speech or use alternative communication strategies. *We can frequently do both*, combining prepared comments with group participation, films, small group problem-solving, and the like. But the key question should not be: "In which communication format do I feel most comfortable?" Rather: "In which ways can the participants' time be most productively spent and our communication purposes best achieved?"

These guidelines, then—a knowledgeable and committed speaker; a topic and purpose relevant to the specific audience; and the choice of public speaking as the most efficient way to achieve shared meaning with receivers—are crucial to the decision to speak publicly. An example illustrates how these criteria can be met. A highway-patrol officer was invited to make a presentation to a high school assembly about traffic safety. He had experience in teaching driving skills and had taken frequent refresher courses on handling a car in emergency situations (*guideline 1*). He had also seen many tragedies of reckless driving and wanted to do anything he could to minimize the senseless slaughter on the highways (*guideline 2*). The officer knew that young drivers have proportionately more traffic accidents than any other age group and that, since their driving habits are just developing, they are the most teachable in terms of safe driving methods. Perhaps more than any other single group, the high school students needed to hear what he had to say (*guideline 3*). Finally, he knew that it was impossible to try to work individually with students to improve their skills; that task would have to be handled by a driver education course. Instead, his purpose was to build awareness of the serious problem, to jolt the listeners into realizing that their driving could have serious consequences, and to make a few simple suggestions that could save their lives. With that communication purpose, and with the several hundred students and the time limit of one hour, the officer knew that a speech presentation with supporting visual materials was the best possible communication strategy (*guideline 4*).

## NEGOTIATING A SPEECH

One of the most frequent pre-speech errors is a speaker's failure to interact closely enough with representatives or agents of the potential audience. The term *negotiating a speech* refers to *the process in which a sender (speaker) and one or more potential receivers (audience member or designated agent) discuss in advance the arrangements, options, and constraints of the coming communication event.* The audience representative might be a club president or program director, a member of the news media, an organizational manager, a training officer, or any other person responsible for arranging an appropriate presentation. The negotiation process is a time for both parties to decide *whether* a speech should be given to a particular audience at a particular time, and what the topic and purpose of that speech should be.

Speech negotiations are important from both the sender's and receiver's perspectives. The speaker can obtain more good information about the prospective event so that the speech preparation process is more efficient and purposeful. More important, she can identify for the audience representative her special background and expertise, to assure that the eventual message will be one that she is especially equipped to deliver. In the absence of such careful discussion, a speaker might become virutally trapped in a public communication situation that does not optimize her own objectives or knowledge.

Conversely—remembering our receiver-centered orientation in this book—the speech negotiation process can assure that audience members will spend their listening time productively. Receivers make an investment when they participate in the public communication process, an investment of time, physical and emotional energy, and often money. We have all experienced instances when we felt that the investment was not worthwhile. But is the speaker solely to blame for a poorly adapted speech? Perhaps the audience representative who helped to determine speaker, topic, purpose, time, and place should be a key person to blame if the communication event is unproductive.

## Potential Problems

Before examining some of the specific factors that can be negotiated, let us first identify potential problems in the speech negotiation process. One problem is the "I'm-doing-you-a-favor" trap. Either the speaker or the audience agent implies that the other owes greater accommodation and should thus adapt more closely to the "givens" of the speech event. This issue is frequently addressed in the classroom. The teacher says, "I have the background and I know what is important; you students must adapt to the readings and projects I assign and remember what I say." And the students reply, "We are the consumers of education who are helping to pay your salary; we will tell you what is important for us to learn and will feel free to abandon your class if you do not adapt to our needs and interests." A better middle ground is being explored by instructors who introduce negotiation into the classroom. They seek open feedback from students and ask them to participate in the selection of learning goals, methods, projects, and evaluation techniques. At the same time, these instructors are assuring that their own input to the learning process is based on their knowledge of the subject matter and their classroom experience and skill.

If the speaker thinks he has the upper hand—as, say, a guest speaker for a service club that is desperate for a weekly program—he may make demands simply to assure minimum exertion of energy in preparing and delivering the speech. If the audience representative thinks that the receivers are doing the speaker a favor, like permitting a political candidate or a sales agent to sell themselves or their wares, the restrictions on time, place, and topic could neutralize the speaker's effort. Instead of falling into the "I'm-doing-you-a-favor" trap, both speaker and agent need to consider the best interests of the receivers. How can we best assure that the listeners' time will be well spent?

Will unreasonable time restraints keep the listeners from benefiting from the speaker's special knowledge? Will a change in date to give the speaker more preparation time unduly inconvenience the receivers? Will the absence of a question-and-answer session minimize the receivers' learning opportunity? The best speech negotiations consider these and other receiver-centered questions.

A second problem is the difficulty in distinguishing between negotiable and nonnegotiable factors, between the givens of a particular speech situation (parameters, constants) and those factors that can be altered. Why must the speech end by 1 p.m.? Because the club members have to return to their jobs. Why should the training session be held on Friday? Because that is the only time most of the employees can conveniently leave their regular duties. Why should the urban planning expert focus his speech on traffic problems? Because the audience is a homeowners' association that is fighting a proposed freeway. Why should the speech last no longer than thirty minutes and include some audience participation? Because the listeners are grade school children with a short attention span. Why should the speaker include simulation exercises in the workshop? Because the audience is seeking not just new information, but also skills improvement. Why will the company have to pay the speaker at least $200? Because that is how much her travel costs will be, and she cannot afford to participate at her own expense.

Of course, the potential speaker and audience representative might disagree about just how constant or changeable certain factors are. Theoretically, any human behavior can be changed; we can choose to do things differently if we want. But some elements cannot reasonably be negotiated, either because of the habits and expectations we have formed or because of the sheer impracticality of certain choices. We hope that neither party will stubbornly refuse to compromise or end negotiations with a flippant, "There's no reason for it; it's just our policy." But the speaker should be especially concerned about finding the "why's" of audience expectations, along with candidly assessing his own requirements for the potential speech. In some cases, neither speaker nor audience has ever seriously considered changes in the typical public speaking event to which they are accustomed. Thus an open, nondefensive pre-speech dialog might well lead to innovations that improve the speaker's effectiveness and the value of the message to the audience. The new awareness that some speech arrangements and speaker behaviors are not unalterable "givens," after all, may be one of the most useful outcomes of negotiating a speech.

A third problem is a speaker's willingness to do too much for a particular presentation. Where earlier we cautioned against one's unwillingness to accommodate the best interests of the receivers, here we note the opposite—that some people will bend over backwards to please an audience. As speakers, we need to be honest with ourselves and with a potential audience about what we realistically think we can achieve in terms of the givens for that speech situation—the speech topic, purpose, size and composition of the audience, the time factor, and so forth. It is better to achieve *limited goals* in a manageable communication event than to promise or agree to something that may cause negative responses when the speaker does not deliver. For example, a political candidate would be wise to select carefully the kinds of public speaking engagements to be made during a campaign. Exhaustion, overexposure, incomplete information, and inadequate preparation time are but some of the consequences of a heavy speaking schedule.

## Potential Variables

We have already implied some of the factors that need to be negotiated. The potential variables are many, but listed below are some of the more common ones.

1. *What is the speech topic and purpose?* This issue will be developed in the next section. Here we note that occasionally it can be a negotiable item. For instance, the speaker may want to give a persuasive speech to gain support for an energy conservation program, while the audience wants to hear an informative speech about new solar heating devices. Disagreement about topic and purpose can sabotage a public communication event before it begins.

**2.** *What is the date and time of day for the presentation?* A speaker may sometimes suggest a different date than the one requested, giving more time for preparation. The date may also conflict with other important events that limit audience attendance—a holiday or weekend, the beginning of a vacation period, income tax deadlines, or even Monday night football! Time of day can affect listener receptivity, as with a speech involving complex information after a heavy lunch, or a briefing at the end of a long, stressful day.

**3.** *What are the limitations on speech length?* We might think that the enthusiastic, knowledgeable speaker would want to negotiate for as much time as possible. Indeed, some do. But it is often more effective to suggest a shorter speaking time. It is probably better to conclude a short speech, with the audience wishing it had lasted longer, than to speak at length while losing audience attention and comprehension. Besides, a shorter speech provides more time for audience participation.

**4.** *What will be the location of the public speaking event?* If, for example, films or videotaping are involved, the negotiators may want to find a room with appropriate electrical outlets, lighting, and seating arrangement. If the speech calls for active demonstration, a room with movable furniture and some open space may be selected.

**5.** *Who will be in the audience?* Frequently treated as a "given," audience composition can sometimes be altered. People who are not usually a part of a particular communication setting might be invited to attend a speech on a topic of special interest to them. Or the speaker might want to discourage participation: the speech may involve privileged or classified information. It may be inappropriate for small children. It may involve instruction for beginners, and people with more advanced skills may think it a waste of time. Or it might assume special audience knowledge or skills, and people who do not possess them would become confused and frustrated.

**6.** *Will the audience participate actively?* In Chapter 1 we noted that the audience, though relatively passive, will nevertheless be behaving

in ways that communicate. In negotiating a speech, we may want to
plan for more active audience response. For example, we might seek
specific listener questions and comments, or include various group
activities in the speech event (especially useful in training sessions).
Sometimes it may be appropriate to limit participation, as with an
exceptionally large audience, or when it is important for listeners to
receive the complete, uninterrupted speech before asking questions. A
few speakers believe their speech content is crucially important and
should not be cluttered with bothersome or irrelevant questions; others
are defensive about their point of view and consider audience feedback
a threat. In such cases, attempts to restrict participation are usually
misguided. But an audience representative may try to negotiate for
audience participation, and the speaker should be willing to develop a
means to provide it.

**7.** *Will someone introduce the speaker and topic?*    Occasionally a
speaker will be embarrassed, or a speech objective damaged, by an ill-
conceived introduction. We ought to provide a program chairperson or
master of ceremonies with relevant information about ourselves, but
not our life histories. We might suggest that the introduction be brief,
that it refer only to certain key facts about our background, or perhaps
that it not mention the speech topic and purpose. Some may think it in
poor taste to become involved in one's own introduction. However,
since we have suggested that the "communication event" probably
commences *before* the speech begins, and since the audience certainly
will begin to assign meaning when they hear a third party outline a
speaker's background, it is legitimate for the speaker to provide some
input about that important portion of the communication process.

**8.** *Will the speaker be paid or receive other specific benefits?*    A handful of speakers make their living on the lecture or banquet circuit. But
most of us will do our public speaking either in the context of our
regular employment or as volunteers in political or social activities.
There may be times when an honorarium is available, but if an organization relies on volunteer speakers, probably no amount of negotiation
will yield a monetary benefit. Some groups offer to provide travel
expenses and a free meal (service clubs are examples), though the

"opportunity" to spend hours on the road and then eat rubbery chicken and cold green peas is a dubious payoff. But there may be times in which one's willingness to speak demands important tradeoffs—missing work, long hours of preparation, pre-speech expenses, loss of leisure time—and one must therefore consider asking for compensation during the speech negotiation process.

**9.** *Will the audience or organization provide technical or audiovisual support?*   Or will the speaker have to arrange for a slide projector and person to operate it, a loudspeaker system, photocopied materials, room setup, and the like? Political candidates, sales representatives, or speakers receiving large honorariums usually assume or share responsibility for these arrangements. The rest of us need to seek cooperation from the person requesting a speech.

In summary, the questions above are sometimes factors over which we have no control. They may be nonnegotiable. If so, the questions still provide a convenient checklist that we can at least use to get important information that will assist in speech preparation. We will at least *know* the time constraints, the audience composition, the location characteristics, and available support equipment. Thus, the pre-speech transaction with an agent of the potential audience can help us not only *modify the variables* of the event, but also *adapt to the givens*.

## NARROWING TOPIC AND PURPOSE

When we have decided to speak publicly, and when we have negotiated with audience members about the conditions of that communication event, our next step is to confirm the topic and purpose.

### Selecting the Topic

A speech *topic* (used interchangeably with *subject*) refers to the content area on which the speech will be based. This content area may refer to objects ("The new home videotape recorder"). It may include ideas, issues, and policies ("Who should go to college?" "Capitalism vs. Social-ism" "Affirmative action: Is it working?"). It may focus on people ("Vote for Grimes for Senator"). In training programs, a speech topic often involves processes ("Developing interviewing skills").

This text will not provide an elaborate discussion about selecting a topic. Rather, it is based on an important premise: *In the real world, topics are rarely "selected," but are thrust upon us by the life facts of our personal backgrounds, the natural movement of events, and the communication context.* We give speeches on particular topics because of what we know, what we want to achieve, and what people want from us. We would rarely expect to hear: "We've heard you are a good speaker; we hope you will come talk to our group on any topic you wish." Most of us will never receive such an invitation. A more typical request is: "We've heard so much about your work with retarded children. Would you be willing to talk to us about your therapy pro-gram?" Or if the speaker initiates the event, he might decide, "I think I'll ask the Jaycees if I can talk to them about the United Way cam-paign that I'm directing." In other words, except in isolated cases, the subject matter of a speech is dependent on the communication par-ticipants and situation. Speakers do not have to wonder "What in the world shall I talk about?"

One exception to this premise may be some students in a begin-ning speech course. Sometimes finding a subject for classroom projects is difficult. Fortunately, most instructors will suggest general topic areas or assign projects with a particular theme; for example, "Prepare a seven-minute demonstration speech on a sport or hobby you enjoy," or "Develop a persuasive speech that takes a stand on a controversial public issue currently in the news." But even with this guidance, the beginning speaker may feel inadequate. Common complaints are:

> *"I just don't know enough about that topic to discuss it intelligently for 7 minutes."*

> *"How will I ever get enough good information on that topic in the week we have to prepare?"*

> *"I like that topic, but I don't think the other students will be in-terested."*

*"I'm afraid that some people in the class will know more about the topic than I do and challenge me on it afterward."*

*"That's such a common topic; I'm sure other people will be using the same one."*

*"I suppose I could talk on that topic, but it bores me."*

If these or other concerns make topic selection for your speech projects difficult, some suggestions may help. First, remember that the classroom is a laboratory, a place to try out new activities and to get helpful feedback. Therefore, if other students have selected the same topic, or have more information on it than you do, or are less interested than some audiences might be, the learning experience of giving a speech on that topic may still justify its selection. Second, if your tentative topic is something about which you know little and that you will have little time to research carefully, junk it and find an alternative. Third, if the topic appears to be uninteresting to a typical student audience, work to make it interesting and relevant. This problem is so common in actual public speaking events that it is good practice to use classroom assignments to develop skills in stimulating interest. (See, for example, the section in Chapter 9 on "Maintaining Interest and Attention.")

Finally, take some time to do a more thorough inventory of your own *background*, *experience*, and *interests*. Write down as many conceivable speech topics as you can. Do not evaluate the topics at this point; just write them down. Glance through magazines and newspapers to help expand your list. Ask family and friends to suggest additional items. Then, after the list is fairly lengthy, perhaps with several dozen items, select the four or five most promising. Gradually, the best topic for a classroom assignment will emerge in your mind. At that point, you will have selected a general topic and are ready to narrow it for the actual speech.

### Narrowing the Topic

Our concern in this text is thus not so much in selecting a topic but rather in *narrowing* it. If we know our own abilities and goals, if we know the audience and the situation, if we want to conform to the inevitable time limits, then our major task is moving from a general subject to a specific one. For example, suppose that a specialist in energy conservation (general topic area) knows that the audience will be composed of city officials. The specific topic might be "burning waste materials to heat public buildings." If the audience is to be a homeowner's association, the specific topic might become "lowering home energy bills." Or suppose the important constraint is time. An expert in first-aid training might decide, "In today's meeting I'll help the receivers develop skills in mouth-to-mouth resuscitation. That will take up most of my allotted time. Next week, I'll cover cardiopulmonary resuscitation." Some examples of general subject areas that have been limited for a specific communication event are listed below.

| General topic | Specific topic |
|---|---|
| Microwave cooking | Imaginative casseroles |
| New-employee orientation | Selecting a retirement program |
| Controlling growth | Commercial zoning restrictions |
| Union contract negotiation | The cost-of-living provisions |
| Cross-country skiing | Ski maintenance |
| Acme Furniture products | The new dining room line |
| Anderson for U.S. Senator | Anderson's tax-reform proposals |
| Affirmative-action programs | College recruiting practices |

Topic narrowing may appear to be a simple, common-sense process. But it is frequently ignored. A speaker may overestimate the amount of information that a particular audience can absorb in a particular time period. Or he may be so interested in his topic, so emotionally committed to it, that he cannot condense such "exciting" and "important" information. The result is that while narrowing a topic appears to be an obviously good idea, we may either forget or be unwilling to do it.

## The Speech Purpose

By far the most important part of a decision to speak publicly, an essential pre-speech function, is the selection of a speech purpose. In general, this is a statement of what a speaker wants to achieve in a public communication event. Four principles important in developing a speech purpose are listed below.

**1.** *The statement of purpose should be clear and specific.* The following examples are inappropriate because they give little specific guidance during the preparation process:

> *"The purpose of this speech is to talk about advertising."*
>
> *". . . to discuss the candidate's qualifications."*
>
> *". . . to sell my company's product."*
>
> *". . . to improve public awareness of the pollution problem."*

**2.** *The clear statement of purpose should precede gathering and organization of material.* An obvious point? We might all be surprised by the number of speakers who, if they develop a purpose sentence at all, do so *at the end of the preparation process.* That is, the purpose becomes an after-the-fact description of how the speech actually developed! This phenomenon is not unique to public speaking. Ask some organization members, "What are your goals? What are you trying to achieve in your work?" They will often reply by describing what they have, in fact, been doing, instead of providing any prior objective that guided their work. Or the novice writer, perhaps using ideas and words like a child with building blocks, begins putting them together until they create an essay. But in answering the question "What were you trying to say?" the writer simply describes what happened to turn out. Similarly, the speaker who has selected and even narrowed a topic may plunge into speech preparation without having considered, thoughtfully and strategically, what is an achievable objective for the particular situation and audience. When this happens, it is no wonder that a presentation appears to receivers to be badly adapted to their interests.

**3.** *The purpose should include the desired effect on or response of the audience.* It should thus be *receiver-centered.* A speech is given to affect the thoughts or behaviors of the audience. Carefully identifying the specific topic says nothing about what the receivers are supposed to

do with that topic. Are they supposed to understand it better? Believe
the speaker's claims? Change their points of view? Buy something?
Vote for someone? Appreciate something more? Achieve aesthetic satisfaction or happiness? Become angry? Be able to remember something
or write it down? Be able to exhibit new skills? Like the speaker better
as a person? What is supposed to happen, what condition should exist,
as a result of the speech? Whatever it is, it belongs in the statement of
purpose.

Examples of speech purpose sentences that are not only specific
but also identify potential effects on or responses of receivers are given
below:

> *"The purpose of this speech is to convince the Board of Directors
> that our current product line should be maintained."*

> *". . . to get at least 25 signatures on a petition opposing construction
> of the new freeway."*

> *". . . to develop audience understanding of the most important
> considerations in buying a new house."*

> *". . . to demonstrate and explain techniques of the tennis serve that
> will help listeners improve their tennis skills."*

> *". . . to improve employee understanding of the new profit-sharing
> program in the company."*

> *". . . to win audience support in the form of money contributions and
> volunteer work for candidate Jones."*

> *". . . to build enthusiasm and confidence among the listeners, who
> have all volunteered to seek funds for the United Way campaign."*

> *". . . to provide receivers with the information they will need to pass
> the job certification test."*

> *". . . to entertain the banquet audience with a humorous message
> about the new club president."*

Notice that in each purpose sentence, we identify not only a topic but
also what we want to happen as a result of the message—contribu-

tions, expressions of enthusiasm or laughter, increased comprehension, skills improvement, and many other potential responses.

It can be argued that selection of a speech purpose is too restrictive. While it guides speech preparation, it may also stifle creativity and spontaneity. Too often this argument is a convenient excuse for laziness. It is easier to jot down random ideas and see what develops; or perhaps to make a vague mental note of one's purpose, but never really specify it in writing. But we believe that a speaker can still be very creative in the way he chooses to fulfull the purpose. In the examples above, two speakers could tackle the same purpose and come up with quite different but equally effective messages.

Furthermore, the purpose is not written in stone. If in the process of speech preparation we find that the original purpose is less reasonable or less appropriate for a particular situation, it can easily be altered. The speech purpose should be viewed as a helpful guide to selecting materials, developing ideas, saving preparation time, enhancing organization, and adapting closely to the audience.

A speech purpose can usually be written in one concise sentence. However, some speakers identify indirect or secondary purposes that can aid preparation. For example, if a professor's primary purpose in a lecture is to develop improved student understanding of Van Gogh's painting, she might also seek to develop enthusiasm and appreciation for the great artist's genius. That indirect purpose may then prompt her to go beyond simple explanation and to provide interesting anecdotes, displays of especially popular Van Gogh works, and testimony from art critics. A problem with multipurpose speeches, however, is that we may forget our priorities and get sidetracked on less important information. Thus, for most speeches it is a good idea to identify the central purpose and develop our speech to achieve it.

**4.** *The purpose should be adapted to listeners' needs and interests.* Sometimes the formulation of speech purpose is troublesome because while we know what it should be, we wish it were something else. That is, we would prefer to aim at one objective, but know that the situation clearly calls for another.

Schoolteachers and trainers often find themselves in this dilemma. They like a particular subject and enjoy talking about it. They wish

© Howard Harrison 1972

their purpose could be "to help the listeners *understand* such-and-such." But they know that their purpose should be to *improve learner skills, to change behavior*. Or the clergy may enjoy discussing theological issues, but they know that their congregations want specific application of religious principles to their daily lives. Thus if we are honest with ourselves, and if we truly adopt a receiver-centered perspective, we will develop speech purposes not in terms of what we enjoy talking about, but rather in terms of what the receivers need or want to hear, to learn, to believe, to do.

## SUMMARY

Though public speaking is an increasingly useful communication tool, we should not assume that it is appropriate for any audience situation. Good public speakers do not decide to make a presentation unless they are well informed on the speech topic, committed to achieving a communication goal, convinced of the relevance of the speech topic and purpose to the specific audience, and certain that a one-to-many transaction is the best type of communication process in the particular situation.

A speaker often has an opportunity to negotiate a speech, to discuss in advance with potential receivers the arrangements, options, and constraints of the eventual communication event. During the negotiation process, the speaker should avoid demanding too much from the audience or, conversely, agreeing to do too much. The speaker should consider any factor that can be altered. Depending on the particular speech, these include topic and purpose; date and time; length; type of audience involvement; compensation; and many other negotiable factors.

After deciding to speak publicly, a speaker may already have a general topic area. However, the topic should be narrowed and a specific purpose developed. The purpose is the most important aspect of pre-speech activity; it is a statement of what a speaker wants to achieve in the communication event. This statement should be worded in a single, concise sentence; precede the gathering of materials; clearly identify the desired response of the receivers; and adapt closely to the needs and interests of the receivers.

## QUESTIONS FOR STUDY

1. In the section on "Deciding to Give a Speech," what factors are relevant to the student in a public speaking course, even though the instructor has already "decided" that speeches will be given?

2. Think of an actual situation outside the classroom in which you might be presenting a speech. What variables of that communication event might you negotiate ahead of time?

3. For the following general topics, what are possible specific speech topics that might be developed?
The U.S. space program
American films, 1979

Child abuse
Modern marriage
The 1980 presidential campaign
Careers in law enforcement

4. In the examples above, what are some potential speech purposes?

5. How might problems that develop during the actual speech presentation be linked back to poor negotiation or poor selection of
topic and purpose? Draw several of these cause–effect links.

# chapter 3

# GATHERING AND ORGANIZING MATERIALS

**LEARNING OBJECTIVES**

After reading this chapter, you should be able to:
1. Identify sources that are available and problems that may arise in gathering information for classroom speech projects.
2. Make a convincing argument for good organization in public speaking.
3. Develop a variety of organizational plans for a particular speech topic and then select the best plan for the particular audience situation and purpose.
4. List suggestions for gathering and organizing speech materials.

3

In the past few decades, our culture has experienced an information explosion. So much new information has been generated so quickly that we might consider modern society to be a part of the "age of information." That is, the fundamental problems today may be the need to seek, discover, record, recall, and utilize information as we make decisions that affect our lives. One of the most important contributions of computer technology, for example, is the development of information storage and retrieval systems, of data banks that at the flick of a button can print out the relevant information needed for particular decisions. Other information systems, such as libraries and organizational files, are struggling to find space for the flood of printed information that increases each year.

An important implication of the information explosion is the problem that each one of us faces whenever we have to make a decision or to communicate with others—we can know only a smaller and smaller fraction of all the relevant information available in any particular area. A hundred years ago, a medical doctor might have been able to learn nearly all the relevant information about abdominal surgery. Today a good surgeon must not only specialize but must struggle to keep up with the research literature in a narrower professional area. Even then, the surgeon may have to seek the opinions of colleagues with equally narrow expertise.

In an age of information, why is public speaking especially important? Because one person with special knowledge can often provide more reliable information more quickly to a group of receivers who, by themselves, might be unable to find and evaluate the necessary information. For instance, if an employees' association is attempting to develop a new retirement plan, one method might be to form a committee to gather information and develop recommendations. But that difficult and time-consuming process could be eliminated simply by asking an expert in retirement programs to present a speech to the association. Hundreds of people-hours will be saved and, if the speaker has been chosen carefully, the information obtained will probably be more reliable than what group members could have learned on their own. Thus public speaking is a good way of getting the best information to a particular group at the appropriate time. Speakers who have specialized information are in great demand as communicators—much more so than a hundred years ago, when the breadth of available

information was smaller and more people shared that information. Public speaking is one of the chief methods by which modern society deals with the information explosion.

The purpose of this chapter is to help the speaker gather and organize information. To many people, this may be the least interesting, least rewarding aspect of the public communication process. They like the excitement of the actual speech delivery and interaction with the audience, but hate the drudgery of message preparation. As listeners, however, we have all heard politicians, teachers, club presidents, professional colleagues, and others whom we wish had given more attention to careful selection and structuring of information. This chapter will discuss this crucial process.

## GATHERING INFORMATION

In Chapter 2, we noted that selection of a topic and purpose may not be particularly important problems in real-world (nonclassroom) speaking, because this decision is made for us by the people and events we encounter in everyday living. We speak on a particular subject because we are knowledgeable in this area, or because that is what needs to be done at the moment. A similar point may be made about gathering information. In preparing a speech for a classroom project, the student may need to become informed on a brand new topic. But in real-life public speaking, we do not usually have the opportunity to speak on a subject *unless we already have some information and interest in that area*. Thus, most public speakers today do not start from scratch to research a topic. They already have much information well in mind, or they know where to find whatever else they need. But even well informed, experienced speakers need to know some of the problems and techniques for efficient information-gathering. That is the purpose of this section.

### Typical Problems

Gathering information may appear to be a simple, straightforward procedure that any intelligent person can do. However, several problems can arise; a few of these appear in the following list.

© Howard Harrison 1975

**1.** *The speaker seeks only those materials that confirm personal biases or support the main thesis.*  Such a person enters the research process knowing in advance precisely what he wants to find. For example, suppose a club member who has traveled extensively and is familiar with group charter programs is asked to prepare a presentation on possibilities for an organized club tour. She has traveled to Europe, Mexico, Hawaii, and the Far East—and prefers the latter. So she begins collecting information about the very best tour packages to the Orient. Perhaps she is not knowingly deceiving the group, but the fact is that her research into similar packages to other parts of the world has been halfhearted and incomplete. Her discovery of exciting possibilities in the Far East is a *self-fulfilling prophesy*—she has found precisely what she expected to find. This is not only unfair to the audience, but can be devastating to a speaker's objectives, especially if some of the receivers can supply information that contradicts the speaker's point of view.

**2.** *The speaker obtains incomplete, irrelevant, or outdated information.* In a rapidly changing world, this problem is becoming an increasingly frequent hazard for the public speaker. Especially vulnerable are people who give the same type of speech over and over again—the teacher who lectures on a particular topic each semester, the politician who has a "standard" speech on particular issues, the supervisor who provides an orientation message to each group of new employees, the sales agent with a similar presentation for each group of potential customers. We may become comfortable with a particular body of information and resist change. Or we may become so caught up in our hectic lives that we do not devote new energy to something we have done before. But even the expert needs to supplement his background, to seek more depth and currency of information. As in the problem discussed above, incomplete or otherwise inadequate information not only detracts from the speaker's effectiveness but can contribute to *bad decisions*, especially if the speaker is considered authoritative and his advice is followed.

**3.** *The speaker selects materials that are not adapted to specific audience backgrounds and abilities.* The academic/scientific community is especially guilty of this fault. Its members may not appreciate (empathize with) the minimal background that outsiders have in their subject area; the content is just too sophisticated. But the reverse can also be true. The speaker may not truly appreciate the depth of information listeners already have. For example, a public health officer who spoke to a high school class about drug abuse spent much of her time outlining the various drug types and their effects. The snickers from the audience should have told her very quickly that her receivers already knew a great deal about this topic. But she continued, oblivious to the fact that many students not only knew as much as she did but also had actually *experienced* the effects of various drugs. If we cannot give our listeners something new, why give a speech? Why not suggest a different type of communication event, like a group discussion, in which information can more easily be shared?

**4.** *The speaker becomes preoccupied with the raw message rather than with the total process of communication.* By this we mean that the emphasis is on gathering information in isolation from the eventual speech event. The information (message) becomes important in itself rather than as a means for developing shared meaning with listeners. Thus a speaker may become so excited about the topic and about the new information he is finding that he forgets about audience interests and backgrounds, time limits, question-and-answer periods, other speakers, and even the purpose of the speech. Such a person becomes a perfect model of the *message-centered speaker*, one who believes that the message is an object, a body of information—rather than the *receiver-centered* view that the message is what the audience says it is, what its members interpret from the speaker's information.

## Obtaining Materials

The theme of the previous section was: Get good information that is current, complete, and adapted to audience interests and to the unique communication transaction. How do we achieve this general objective? In this section we shall discuss the usual sources of information.

1. *The speaker's background.*   Probably the most common source of information when preparing a speech is one's own background. Assuming that we should not agree to present a speech on a topic about which we know nothing, we should always have some base level of information that can at least be the starting point. And in some cases no additional source of information is necessary. For example, a young lawyer who had just passed the bar exam was asked by a professor to talk with a group of pre-law majors about his law school experience— how he prepared for law school and what he found when he got there. The receivers did not need the lawyer to provide explanations or statistics about admission criteria or a survey of various curricula; that information was readily available in brochures. Instead, they wanted him to talk about his personal experience, and no supplementary information was needed.

The danger, of course, is that some speakers come to rely on their personal backgrounds to the exclusion of new and broader sources. Experience, common sense, the "school of hard knocks"—these can fool us into believing that nothing else is necessary beyond what we already think we know. Nevertheless, though personal experience can be overemphasized, it should usually be the starting point for obtaining information.

**2.** *The Library.* We shall not discuss techniques for finding materials in the library, but rather focus on various types of information that can be found there. What are some of the general resource categories in the library? How can they be useful, especially to the beginning public speaker?

*Periodicals* include both popular magazines (*Time, Psychology Today, Harper's*) and scholarly journals (*Harvard Business Review, American Historical Quarterly, Journal of Communication*). They are probably the most commonly used library resources for public speaking, because they are both current and varied; periodicals focus on nearly every conceivable topic. Many government publications are also included under the periodical category; larger libraries may have separate departments and staff to handle the huge volume of government materials. Indexes such as the *Readers' Guide to Periodical Literature* and the *Monthly Catalog of United States Government Publications* provide ready access to periodical subject matter.

*Newspapers* are another important source of information for speakers, especially those who discuss contemporary public issues. For example, in a recent political debate the challenger won some points by quoting the incumbent's statement to a newspaper reporter and then citing contradictions in more recent statements. Though some listeners are skeptical of the accuracy of the press, straight news reports (as distinguished from special features or editorials) are usually accepted as a valid account of what has occurred. We have become a visual culture and more people today rely on televised news than printed news. However, these televised reports are difficult to obtain after they have been broadcast, and the print medium remains the primary authority on "what really happened" at a particular time and place. Most libraries have a microfilm collection of newspapers that are more than a few months old. The microfilm projection instruments are easy to use and permit rapid scanning of hundreds of newspaper pages.

*Reference books* include dictionaries, encyclopedias, almanacs, biographical directories, atlases, indexes, books of famout quotations, statistical summaries, and bibliographies. These volumes are usually located in a central, easily accessible area of the library. They can be the starting point for research, or a speaker may already have the basic materials for a presentation but needs some final bits of information, such as an accurate map to use in drawing up a visual aid; the credentials (biography) of one of the experts being quoted in the speech; a dictionary or legal definition of key terms; additional citations for a bibliography; names, dates, and events for historical background of contemporary problems or issues being discussed. Those unfamiliar with this resource should browse through the reference section and notice the great variety of volumes. Once we know they exist, we may think of new ways to provide support for and expand on our ideas.

*Film collections* provide yet another valuable source of information found on many college campuses, though not always in the library. Some are available for preview; others must be ordered and may also involve a rental fee. A speaker seeking an appropriate film for his presentation should plan for a lead time of several weeks. As a general rule, speakers should avoid showing films without first previewing them, and last-minute rentals may not provide ample opportunity for this. Many film collections include film strip and slide collections, some of them with accompanying cassette tape soundtracks.

*Nonfiction books* are indexed by title, author, and topic in the card catalog. Surprisingly, this is the least utilized type of library material for most speakers. There are at least two reasons for this. Modern public speaking situations, especially those in the normal context of business and professional activity, simply do not provide for enough time during speech preparation, and relevant material can usually be found in shorter magazine articles. And since most public speakers already have substantial information on their topic, they tend to use library resources as *supplemental* and not as their central preparation strategy. Nonfiction books are of value not so much in preparing a particular speech as in keeping up with one's field of interest. Thus, a speaker who regularly gives speeches about public education will want to be well read in the latest books, but is not likely to say: "I have to talk to the Lion's Club; I think I'll go read some books on my topic."

**3.** *Professional and organizational documents.* One of the major sources of printed materials available for public speaking today is not in the library at all, but in the files and data storage systems of corporations, government offices, and nonprofit organizations. In-house publications, committee reports, professional newsletters, and the like are typical of this group. Suppose a manager in XYZ Corporation is preparing a presentation for the annual stockholders' meeting. Where would she find the best materials about the corporation's past performance and forecasts for the coming year? From the organizational files and computers and from industry newsletters. Most of these materials could be obtained without ever leaving the corporate offices. Her challenge in this situation is to find the relevant information quickly, and sometimes this is difficult. While some organizations have developed very efficient information storage and retrieval systems, perhaps the crucial document is a letter in someone's desk or rough notes taken at a committee meeting.

**4.** *Information-gathering interviews.* These can be especially useful for the speaker who wants to be well prepared. Interviews can provide information that may not be in print and cannot be found in any other source. They offer a chance for feedback and elaboration. And they are current; the interviewee may supply information that is not yet public knowledge. Interviews may take more time and energy, and the results are not always verifiable; unless tape-recorded, they may yield information that the interviewee may later deny and that cannot be checked.

Two special uses of interviews can be very helpful. First, they can help the speaker seek information more efficiently. For example, a member of an organization could tell a speaker precisely where to find key sources, saving time and legwork. Second, interviewees can provide a final verification or check of planned speech content. The speaker might say, "In my first point, I'll be claiming that departmental reorganization is necessary. Do you have any thoughts on that issue?" The interviewee's opinion, and reasons, can help in a final revision.

In arranging an interview, the speaker should let the interviewee know what kinds of information he will be seeking. During the interview, four basic types of questions can be helpful.

a.  *The open-ended question* permits the interviewee to respond in depth and along lines that appear appropriate to him. For example: "What is your viewpoint on this issue?" or "Tell me about your background in this area." The open-ended question can be useful at the beginning of an interview as a way of encouraging the free flow of ideas and of avoiding any prejudicing of the interviewee's answers that more directive questions might cause.

b.  *The closed-ended question* calls for a very specific response, especially yes or no. It is often useful in follow-up questions to the open-ended response. Examples are: "How many of your employees are enrolled in the hospitalization plan?" or "How long have you worked with this company?"

c.  *The probing question* attempts to obtain more in-depth responses to determine reasons or feelings behind the respondent's feelings or arguments. For example: "Is that what you hoped would happen?" or "Why do you say that?"

d.  *The paraphrase* is a statement that rephrases what the interviewer thinks he has just heard. It helps to verify accuracy or shared meaning and often causes the interviewee to respond in more depth. An example is: "So you feel that unless we solve this problem soon, it will be too late?"

In selecting interviewees, we need to assure that they have good information and are in a position to know; that they are open and candid, willing to express their ideas without being secretive or deceptive; and that they are willing to let the speaker *use* the information they provide, in some cases to be quoted directly.

5.  *Observation.*  Speakers often use what they have seen or heard as the basis for their opinions and explanations. We are suggesting here that observation should become a systematic, regular method of gathering materials. For example, a citizen was arguing for a traffic signal at a busy intersection near his home. He spent some time counting vehicles during rush-hour periods and took photographs of traffic jams

at the intersection. The data he collected by this method became the primary supporting material for his argument.

The speaker should ask the following questions when considering the observation strategy.

a. Am I observing the right things, the phenomena that will give me the information I need, that will support my arguments, or that will be acceptable to my listeners?
b. Am I recording the event accurately? (Good note-taking, film, tape recorder, etc.)
c. Am I observing enough phenomena to be able to generalize from them, or will my conclusions be based on unrepresentative or limited information?
d. Does my observation intervene in a way that actually changes the event from what it would normally be? Do people behave differently, simply because they know that I am watching?
e. Am I guilty of selective filtering, of looking for and receiving only those phenomena that I want to find or that I expect to find, thus missing other important features or events?

As speakers, we like to think that we are "in touch with reality," that our receivers are confident that we know what we are talking about. Careful observation can be one of the best information-gathering strategies if it assures us and our listeners that the speech is based on real behavior and events.

6. *Creating ideas and perspectives.* This method is often forgotten. It does *not* mean that we should fabricate data or "create a reality" that is a figment of our imagination. Rather, this strategy means that the speaker thinks about the topic, tries to analyze it in a variety of ways, and generates perspectives that perhaps others have not thought of before. For example, suppose an instructor suggests to her listeners techniques that she herself learned from others. After gaining more experience, however, she develops some of her own methods to help her students learn better. Those methods are *new information* that she has created. Or suppose that a speaker has obtained much factual data to support his arguments, but needs some specific ways to phrase his

conclusions that will be especially persuasive to this audience. His creativity in the wording of arguments becomes his own contribution to speech content, to the materials of the speech. This method of information-gathering should probably be a part of every speech presentation.

### Suggestions

In addition to the recommendations above, the following suggestions serve as a final check on the information-gathering process.

**1.** *Rely on others to assist in the process.* Speech preparation need not be lonely. Other people can not only supply content materials (as in the interview technique noted above), but can also provide feedback as hypothetical audience members. Ask others to help play with ideas and strategies in selecting the best approaches—it will demonstrate one's commitment to receiver-centered communication. This suggestion is essential when the speaker is representing others in the speech. If, for instance, the chairperson of a committee must make a public statement to the media on a problem that the group has been considering, it is crucial that others help in the development of that statement.

**2.** *Consider speech purposes, audience, and available preparation time.* There is no "right way" to obtain materials; the process is always contingent on the unique communication context. Some speakers have a staff of assistants to help collect information; most of us do not, and must sandwich speech preparation between other tasks in our busy lives. And in some cases we must react spontaneously, with no time at all to get materials. The audience, too, has various expectations about the depth and quality of information. A local service club would not expect a civil engineer to be as precise or sophisticated in his presentation as would a professional engineering society.

**3.** *Remember that the collected information is not the speech.* It is only one component of a much larger communication process. Too many speakers, especially those who are "message-centered," view gathering information as their major task—everything else is polish,

the cosmetics necessary to make a good impression. But this should not be the case. The collected information is *not* communication; the *transaction* between speaker and listener is communication. The information might just as well be back in the book or the file or the speaker's memory unless it is transmitted, received, and acted upon. People with an information orientation may quickly discover that having accurate data and well-supported ideas in no way assures effective speechmaking.

**4.** *Do not view gathering information as a separate, specific phase of speech preparation.* Rather, it is an ongoing process. The good speaker begins thinking about materials before and during speech negotiation. He may begin to play with ideas and an organizational plan. He gets a new idea and goes back to find new information. He tests out his presentation with a friend who suggests changes and additional information. Just before speaking, he hears a comment from a previous speaker or audience member and decides to add or change the content. During the speech, he notices confusion on one of the points and quickly develops an alternate explanation. After the speech, he gets feedback from the listeners, new information that he may try to use the next time he makes a similar presentation. The speaker who thinks that information-gathering is a distinct phase forgets that a good speech *evolves*; as a result, he may stop collecting materials when he begins to develop an organizational plan and may not adapt further to the specific and spontaneous communication event.

## SPEECH ORGANIZATION

Linda Martinsen had been a deputy district attorney for three years, assisting in the prosecution of felony cases, when she got her first chance to be chief prosecutor in a particularly complicated second-degree murder case that would involve dozens of witnesses, conflicting testimony, several applicable laws, and a detailed factual situation. After the jury had been selected and the trial began, Linda's first major task was an opening statement, to help jurors understand the case from the prosecution's point of view. It would be her first opportunity in the trial to persuade the jury, to get them to think about the alleged crime in a way favorable to the prosecution. The defense attorney would make a corresponding statement from the defense viewpoint.

But how to achieve this purpose? Of the hundreds of bits of information that the many witnesses would discuss, which should be mentioned? And how long should the opening be? At what point would the jury lose interest, stop listening as carefully, or be unable to distinguish the crucial points from the less important ones? Linda's problem was not just strategic; it was *organizational*. Somehow, she had to "make sense" of this mass of information such that twelve very different people would understand, believe, and remember essentially the same things. So she asked the advice of a crusty old attorney who had prosecuted hundreds of similar cases. How should she organize all this material into a concise, persuasive ten- to fifteen-minute statement? His advice was simple. "Tell the story," he said. "Tell the story!"

And so she did, using those details that eventual testimony would support, and presenting them in a narrative or chronological form. Her speech began, "On March 18, 1977, the defendant, Henry Martin, was returning from work and stopped at a bar for a drink . . ." About 10 minutes later, she concluded, ". . . the gun went off, and she fell to the floor. The defendant rushed to his car and sped away. Two hours later, at the hospital, Francine Martin died of the gunshot wound inflicted by her ex-husband, the defendant, Henry Martin." End of story. End of speech. The jury understood an event from the attorney's perspective and would remember that scenario throughout the trial.

This example is typical of what many public speakers today face— relatively large amounts of complex information that must be presented in a relatively short period of time to receivers with limited prior background in the subject matter. It is obvious that the *structure* of the message, the ordering of selected information into a particular sequence, is crucial. In this section, we shall discuss speech organization, noting some of the options that speakers may consider.

## Purposes of Good Organization

Why should a speech be consciously organized? Why shouldn't speakers who are knowledgeable and who have gathered an impressive

© Howard Harrison 1978

amount of information simply "let it flow," developing the ideas spontaneously as they come to mind during the speech? The reason is
obvious. The free, unstructured approach just doesn't work very well.
In contrast, good organization can achieve at least three purposes.
First, it can help the speaker; a general plan of key points can help in
sifting through the important information and "fitting" the key ideas
and data where they belong. The plan will let the speaker view the
logical structure of ideas in skeletal form, before it gets cluttered with
detailed information. And most important, that general plan—if prepared carefully and perhaps jotted down in brief notes—will help the
speaker remember important information as he delivers the speech.
Well organized speakers are less likely to "lose their train of thought"
or leave out important information.

A second purpose is to help the listeners better receive the message. Since each of us is unique, an audience of, say, 50 people can
think about a particular subject or idea in 50 individual ways. Using
an organizational plan that receivers can recognize and understand

will better assure that they will think about (interpret, assign meaning to) the message in essentially similar ways. Good organization enhances shared meaning.

A third purpose of organization is to create positive audience responses toward the speaker as a credible person. It might be comforting if audiences would just listen carefully to my message, do their best to follow my line of thinking, and not think badly of me if my progression of ideas is jumbled and confusing. But audiences do not respond that way. They are usually intolerant of poor organization, as they probably should be. And too often their perception that "This speaker is poorly *organized*" becomes "This speaker is poorly *prepared*." Or, worse yet, "This speaker doesn't know what he is talking about."

## Types of Speech Organization

In this section we shall provide a brief inventory of speech organization plans. It is not an exclusive list, however. The creative speaker, like the creative writer, can develop a variety of alternatives.

It is important to view the organizing process as a natural human trait. Every person, in perceiving the world, tends to organize those perceptions in various ways. It could be argued that man is the "organizing animal." We structure our lives, our families, our activities, and our thoughts. Even people who claim to live more spontaneously, who reject the "traditional" structures that they think are too rigid and confining—even these people develop a framework for looking at and interacting with the world, accepting some things and rejecting others. If this tendency to organize is true, what are the implications for the public speaker? It means that he will tend to think about his message, either consciously or subconsciously, in some organized way. This does not mean that it will necessarily be good or systematic organization, nor that the eventual spoken message will be perceived as being structured. But the capacity and the motivation to organize information are inherent in our thinking processes. Our goal in this section is to bring that human tendency to the conscious, strategic level. Thus, speech organization should not be thought of as a tedious, artificial ritual, but rather as something that *we will do*, and that with even minimal conscious effort can significantly improve communication.

*Time order.* Perhaps the oldest form of speech organization is chronological, or time order. The earliest human beings probably communicated to their tribal groups using rituals that involved narratives of legends passed down orally to each generation—they told stories. Today, time order is useful not only to support ideas with extended illustrations or narration, but also to enhance instruction in a "how-to-do-it" or step-by-step process. For example, suppose a golf instructor is attempting to explain the mechanics of the golf swing to some beginners who will soon try it on their own. He decides on the time sequence below:

1. Gripping the club
2. Addressing the ball—the stance
3. The backswing
4. The downswing
5. The follow-through

Notice that this plan is not the instructor's only choice. He might have talked about various parts of the body throughout the swing—arms, legs, head, etc. Or he might have structured the speech in terms of typical problems—bending the left arm, raising the head, improper swing tempo, and so forth. But the time order appeared to be the most systematic for this particular audience and speech purpose.

*Space order.* Sometimes it is convenient to structure a message in terms of space, or proximity. We think of some topics according to how they are arranged in relation to each other. Again, the instructional message strategy relies heavily on space order. For example, a teacher of interior design might divide her message, or a series of lectures, into:

1. The kitchen
2. Dining areas
3. Family and living rooms
4. Bedrooms
5. Bathrooms

Persuasive speakers can also use space order. For example, a legislator urging a new policy in natural gas distribution and regulation might discuss the program in terms of its impact on the industrial Northeast, the agricultural Midwest, the Sunbelt states, the Mountain states, and the Pacific Northwest.

*Topical (nominal) pattern.* It sometimes makes sense to organize a speech according to key topic areas. These areas usually have a name that is quickly recognizable, even though there may be no logical link or progression from one term to another. A common topical plan is to label things according to their function:

Topic: Reorganization plan for Corporation X

1. Administration and accounting
2. Production
3. Marketing, advertising, public relations
4. Sales
5. Research and development

Topics can also be categories of people, as with a political scientist who might label political philosophies as reactionary, conservative, moderate, liberal, and radical. A good topical structure should avoid overlap to be clear to the listener and to help the speaker filter out non-topical information.

*Analytical pattern.* *Analysis* may be thought of as *a detailed examination of a topic or problem area from many different perspectives*. It is similar to the topical approach, though usually less specific or concrete. For example, suppose that a speaker wanted to inform an audience about drug abuse. An analytical approach might be:

1. Drug abuse can be viewed as a medical problem
2. It affects families
3. It is also an educational problem
4. Drug abuse is related to law-enforcement problems
5. Most important, it is a problem for people who use drugs

By contrast, a *topical* plan might discuss drug abuse in terms of, say, various drug categories:

1. Marijuana abuse
2. Cocaine abuse

3. Amphetamine abuse
4. Heroin abuse
5. Etc.

Notice that the analytical pattern can be based on several *definitions* of the same term. For example, if a psychologist were discussing the concept of love in human interaction, she might structure the speech according to the various definitions of "love": as a feeling of attraction, as sexual desire, as affectionate behavior, as devotion and trust, and so forth. The author has lectured about communication theory by using a series of definitions of "communication" as the key points in the speech, each point looking at the process from a different perspective.

*Comparison and contrast.*   Certainly every college student is familiar with comparison and contrast, an organizational plan that is divided according to specific similarities and differences between two or more things. Those dreaded essay exam questions ("Compare and contrast Melville's *Moby Dick* with Cooper's *The Deerslayer*") may have been intimidating, but they did require that we think deeply and analytically about the subject. In informative speaking, the comparison and contrast is a good way of revealing important distinctions between ideas, objects, or behavior. A sales manager, for example, might instruct new sales agents about the company's product in comparison to competing lines so that the agents can make the same subtle distinctions with potential customers. In persuasive speaking, one might compare a favored and an opposing policy, using similarities to show how the favored policy is no worse, and differences to show how it is better:

1. *Similarities*
   a. Both will provide the needed service
   b. Both use a procedure that has been tested and found effective
2. *Differences*
   a. My plan will save money
   b. My plan will be easier to staff
   c. My plan will help more people in a shorter time

*Problem–solution patterns.* One of the most common types of persuasive speech structures is the problem–solution plan, in which the
speaker first describes a problem, a felt need, and then develops a
solution. Nearly all speeches that advocate policy changes—in business conferences, legislative speaking, and any other area in which
receivers will be asked to act on the basis of the speaker's message—
can utilize this pattern. The example below is typical:

1. *Problem:* Profits are declining on product X
   *a.* Labor costs are rising
   *b.* Raw material costs are rising
   *c.* Consumer preferences are changing (demand is falling)
2. *Solution:* We should develop a new product line, Y
   *a.* Production costs will be less
   *b.* Public demand will be greater
   *c.* The plan can be implemented without significant detriment to
   the company

Notice that the *substructure* under the problem and solution points can
embody a different type of organization, in this case the analytical
pattern.

An important variation of the problem–solution format is the
*method of residues.* In this scheme, the problem is developed as usual.
Then the speaker lists several potential solutions and, on the basis of
advantages and disadvantages of each one, discards all except the one
he is advocating, the best solution.

Another variation, which some people might consider a separate
category of organization, is the *comparative advantage* method. This
approach is especially useful when the receivers generally agree on the
problem phase, but disagree on the optimal solution. Suppose a teachers' association is agreed that current educational programs need improvement. One faction argues for greater enforcement of discipline
and a return to more traditional curricula; others believe that a more
open, innovative approach is necessary. A speaker for the traditional
position might argue:
*Problem (agreed by all factions)*: Student aptitudes and performance
levels are declining
*Solution*: Return to more traditional learning methods

Comparative Advantages
  a.  Will be less expensive
  b.  Will not require new expertise from teachers
  c.  Will have greater support from the community, especially parents
  d.  Will achieve better results in terms of student performance

The comparative advantage approach does not require its advocates to argue that the alternative solution(s) will fail, but rather that the solution they advocate will be *better*.

The problem–solution format is one of the least imaginative, yet easiest plans to develop and understand. It is likely that anyone involved in policy-making will use the format regularly.

*Causality patterns.*   In Chapter 10 we shall identify causal arguments as one of the important logical techniques for supporting one's conclusions. Here causality is offered as a general organizational plan. One approach involves cause–effect, including long sequences of causal relationships. Speeches on ecology and environmental problems often rely on this approach:

1.  Demand for beef increases pressure on ranchers to produce more
2.  This may result in overgrazing in areas that cannot naturally sustain the increased number of cattle
3.  Overgrazing leads to decreased soil capacity for holding moisture, resulting in erosion
4.  This decline in natural vegetation destroys wildlife habitats and future grazing potential of the land

Sometimes the speaker can begin the organizational plan with the effect and move backward to discuss the causes:

1.  Effect: Achievement scores for graduating high school seniors have significantly declined
2.  Causes: There are several possible reasons for this
  a.  Too much television
  b.  Not enough teachers
  c.  Inappropriate teaching methods
  d.  Poor parental support and motivation

Again, the causality pattern is often used as the substructure of a larger point in the speech. Notice that causal relationships occur in a time sequence. Thus the speaker who uses the *time-order* approach may discover, in moving chronologically through the information, that many points will be cause–effect in nature.

*Proposition–support pattern.* Though usually a part of a larger organizational plan, the proposition–support approach can be the essential feature of speech structure. This is simply stating an argument or conclusion, and then providing supporting evidence to back it up:

*Proposition:* The property tax laws are detrimental
*Support:*
    1. Examples of people who have been hurt
    2. Statistics showing that tax increases are far out of proportion to other economic factors
    3. Experts who conclude that property tax laws are causing severe problems

Of course, this pattern can be reversed. The speaker can present the specific evidence *before* actually stating the conclusion. The pattern might then be called "support–proposition." Strategically, it is sometimes better, in a speech on a controversial topic, to wait until the end to suggest the proposition (after the evidence has been carefully laid out). In that way, the audience will not be as likely to have an immediate negative response before adequate supporting materials have been provided.

*The refutation pattern.* When a speaker is participating in a formal debate, or when the speech is a response to an opposing point of view with which listeners are familiar, the refutation pattern can be useful. It requires simply that the speaker adapt directly to his opponent's specific points and refute them. This speech structure is thus essentially dependent on a previous speech, though the speaker can rearrange his rebuttal in ways that may seem more logical and easy to follow. The speech thus becomes a series of "They said–we say" arguments. The plan can be especially useful when the speaker has little time for advance preparation, as in speaking spontaneously in a group discussion after another person has developed a contrary argument. Below is an example of this technique.

1. They argue that the proposed housing development will not overburden the schools in the area; however, the schools are already filled to capacity.
2. They claim that traffic access is adequate; however, current streets are now crowded and must soon accommodate 2000 more vehicles per day.
3. They conclude that demand for these middle-priced homes is high; however, the real need is for low-priced housing.

*The motivated sequence.* One of the common organizational plans that has been taught in public speaking courses for many years was developed by Monroe, who termed his structure the *motivated sequence* (Monroe, 1939, pp. 340–345). Technically, this plan is a kind of problem–solution pattern that attempts to adapt to a systematic thought process, moving the listeners step-by-step according to ways in which they allegedly think about the problems. It has five steps:

1. The *attention* step—prompts listeners to focus on the speech topic
2. The *need* step—identifies the essential problem that demands a solution
3. The *satisfaction* step—provides a solution that will meet the need
4. The *visualization* step—creates a "picture" of the plan in action, of the needs being met with the proposal
5. The *action* step—identifies things that the audience can do to help initiate the proposal

Whether people actually think in this systematic way is open to considerable dispute. But as a general structure, the motivated sequence may be a convenient pattern for organizing materials according to the *response* the speaker seeks from the audience.

The several organizational plans discussed above are by no means a complete list. Further, several different types may be used within the same speech. In the next section, we shall suggest some ways to implement these structures in the most effective ways.

### Suggestions for Organizing Speeches

How do we know, either as senders or receivers, when a message is well organized? Howell and Bormann provide some convenient criteria (Howell and Bormann, 1971, pp. 111–113):

*Unity*: Each element is logically related to the central thesis; the pieces seem to fit neatly under that heading

*Coherence:* Each element is related closely to adjacent points, as a "brick is cemented to its neighbors"; effective linkages in moving from point to point

*Relevance:* Ideas should not only flow logically (unity) from the central thesis, but should also be related directly in terms of importance or relevance; logical but insignificant or incidental ideas (in terms of desired audience response) should be avoided

*Conciseness:* The points in the outline are not repetitious; speaker does not continually return to points already covered, except in transitions or summaries

*Comprehensiveness:* As a function of the audience and the context, a comprehensive outline deals with all of the important ideas relating to speech purpose; no gaps remain.

Additionally, we offer several suggestions.

**1.** *Be tentative in developing speech structure.* Do not rush into a structure during the first stages of preparation; do not finalize it too early. Play with ideas; consider alternative patterns. Let speech organization evolve. Both writers and speakers often report that as they develop the content of their message, a structure seems to emerge naturally. Perhaps the subconscious mind has been working on the problem and a solution suddenly becomes part of conscious thought. Almost without warning, the communicator "sees" an obvious, logical structure to his ideas. Give the ideas a chance to generate a structure. Since the best organizational plans are contingent upon the speech purpose and the kinds of information to be presented, preparing a final plan too early may yield a mismatch between content and structure.

**2.** *Consider audience receptiveness and ease of comprehension.* A plan that is logical or convenient for the speaker may not be appropriate for the receivers. For example, developing complex information for other professionals in the same field may permit a tight topical or analytical pattern, because the listeners already understand background materials and implied assumptions for the ideas. But an outsider or novice audience might need a time-order scheme (chronological) as the speaker takes them step-by-step through the complicated process being developed. Or, as mentioned earlier, if the audience may not be receptive to a bold generalization on a controversial issue, it may be advisable to develop supporting materials first and then lead up to the central thesis.

**3.** *In most cases, make organizational strategy apparent to the listeners.* The speaker needs to make "process comments," to tell the receivers where he has been and where he is going. This may help to keep them from getting lost and may suggest that the speaker is well prepared. For example, "I'm going to develop my ideas along four main points— the classroom areas, the lounge areas, the administrative offices, and the recreational areas." The use of numbers in developing the key points, and announcing those numbers as each point is discussed, can also reveal the organizational plan. The author once had a professor of Russian history who, recognizing that most historical data in this area were new and unfamiliar to the students, actually wrote a skeleton outline of his lecture on the board before every class, thus improving comprehension and accurate note-taking. An exception to this general suggestion might be some persuasive speeches; prior discussion of the structure might prompt some people to begin disagreeing before the speaker had developed the persuasive materials. But assuming that the speaker's objective is not to deceive or unfairly manipulate the audience, it is usually wise to make the organizational plan very clear.

**4.** *Prepare and practice transitions.* Even experienced speakers who have confidence in their ability to develop their main points sometimes give too little attention to how they will move smoothly and clearly from point to point. The result is that while the receivers may understand point A and point B, they don't understand how they relate, how the speaker got from A to B. It is most unfortunate when the speaker simply avoids transitions altogether, except perhaps for a terse "The next point is . . ." or "Number three, . . ." Remember that if we must get, say, 25 divergent minds thinking as a group about point A, we may have to exert a similar effort to get those same minds to think as a group about point B. For example, "What I've tried to do in this first point is show you that we have a serious problem. But perhaps the more important question is: What can we do about it? If it has been with us for so many years, is it perhaps insoluble? In the second part of my speech, I'm going to argue that there are some things we can do about it. I have three suggestions."

**5.** *Avoid digressions or overelaborations.* One of the indicators of poor organization is a rambling speaker who seems to be continually "getting off the track." Avoid unplanned meandering; stick to the intended structure. (The exception, of course, is when receivers indicate that they do not understand a particular point and the speaker goes into more depth or answers their questions.)

**6.** *Make sure the speech structure follows good outlining form.* That is, outline a speech just as you would outline any other information. It should be mechanically correct. Coordinate points are of essentially equal weight; they should all have the same numbering scheme (1, 2, 3, or a, b, c, etc.). Subordinate points modify main points (a, b, and c under point 1, for example, should modify point 1). Avoid errors like the following:

    **1.** There are several types of alternative energy sources to fossil fuels
       *a.* Solar energy
       *b.* Geothermal energy
       *c.* These sources becoming more practical economically
       *d.* Wind and tidal energy
    **2.** Nuclear energy is a good alternative to fossil fuels

Avoid dividing a main point into only one subpoint; we cannot divide a thing into just one subordinate part. While good outlining form may appear overly rigid, it can actually help the speaker think more clearly during the preparation process. A good outline can often reveal glaring holes in speech content that the receivers are likely to notice.

## SUMMARY

In an "Age of Information," gathering and organizing materials for a public speech has become an especially challenging process. Most speakers who know their topic well face a problem not of insufficient information, but rather one of speech resources that are too extensive, varied, and complex. Careful selection and structuring of this information is essential.

The good speaker recognizes that information should be objective and unbiased, that it should be complete and current, that it should be related to audience background and abilities, and that the resulting "message" is only one ongoing part of the total communication process.

Information-gathering should always start with one's own knowledge and experience; in many public speaking situations no further information is necessary. When this must be supplemented, the library, professional or organizational literature, interviews, personal observation, and even the creation of new ideas can provide material.

The organizational options for a public speaker are varied, and the process of structuring the speech is continual and evolving as the speaker thinks through the available materials, the speech purpose, and the nature of the audience. Common organizational patterns include chronological or time order, space order, organization by key topics or by different levels of analysis, comparison and contrast, problem–solution techniques, cause-and-effect patterns, proposition–support and refutation patterns, and a special method called the "motivated sequence." However, most speeches contain several different types of organization in the substructure of main points.

To be especially receiver-centered in organizing a speech, we should apply the criteria of unity, coherence, relevance, conciseness, and comprehensiveness. We should also be tentative in developing structure, consider listeners' ease of comprehension, make our structure apparent to them, use transitions and summaries, avoid unplanned digressions from the intended structure, and follow good outline form.

## QUESTIONS FOR STUDY

1. What are some problems that may arise in the information-gathering process?

2. What are some of the key sources of information that are over-looked when a speaker relies totally on the library in gathering speech materials?

3. How might the use of a particular type of question during an information-gathering interview (open-ended rather than closed-ended, for example) lead to radically different interview results?

4. What might be useful types of organization for the following topics?
New ideas in home design
The dockworkers' strike
Improving your tennis game
Reelect Senator Hill
Marriage in the 1980's: A forecast
Rising gasoline prices
Job skills for sales personnel

5. How do the suggestions for good outlining reinforce a receiver-centered view of public speaking?

# chapter 4

# DEVELOPING
# AN INTRODUCTION
# AND A CONCLUSION

**OUTLINE**

**LEARNING OBJECTIVES**

After reading this chapter, you should be able to:

1. List three or four reasons why effective introductions and conclusions help both speakers and their listeners.
2. Develop several alternative introductions and conclusions for a single speech topic and purpose.
3. Offer suggestions for improving introductions and conclusions for classroom projects in the basic public speaking course.

# 4

The high school teacher was well prepared to talk about the internship program he had developed for the students in his classes. His purpose was to generate support from the local PTA so that they would encourage the school board to fund similar programs. The teacher's first words were, "I'm going to talk about the internship program I developed. Its three basic features are, first, . . ."

A champion swimmer on the college team had been asked to discuss the women's intercollegiate athletic program with high school girls who were planning to attend college. She had planned to discuss briefly each sport in which women competed, to hand out pamphlets that described the program, and to answer questions at the end. This was her introduction: "Uh, my name is, um, Gwen Morrissey and, uh, I guess I'm supposed to talk to you about, uh, the women's athletic program at the University. I don't know why they picked me—I'm, uh, not very good at talking to groups. Oh, well, here goes. . . ."

A businesswoman was a guest lecturer in an accounting class at the local community college. She had just finished the third of four main points. She glanced at her watch and noticed that the bell would ring in another couple of minutes. So she concluded by saying, "Well, I was planning to tell you some other things, but I see the time is about gone, so I guess I'll just end here." And she gathered up her notes and sat down.

The chairperson of the United Way campaign was speaking to a service club about the benefits that accrued to the community from the programs supported by the annual fund drive. He spoke for about twenty minutes. His final words were: "And so the YMCA is also the beneficiary of United Way funds." He paused, looked up at the listeners, gave an embarrassed smile, gestured awkwardly, and said "That's it." The audience, finally realizing that the speech was over, began to applaud dutifully.

The senator was speaking to officials of a labor union at a national convention. His topic was recent legislative proposals that would affect the union membership. After about half an hour he said, "And, in conclusion, just let me say that. . . ." Twenty minutes later he was still talking.

All of the above examples are hypothetical. But events like them occur so frequently that they are recognizable to nearly everyone who

regularly listens to public communication. They all demonstrate critical flaws in introductions and conclusions, the subject of this chapter.

We could have discussed the process of beginning and ending a speech in a few paragraphs in Chapter 3. But such brief coverage might have implied that this topic is of secondary importance, the "icing on the cake" after speech preparation is essentially complete. We believe that introductions and conclusions are not only crucial components of the total communication process, but can be key determinants in achieving the speech purpose and meeting one's communication objectives. Therefore we are devoting an entire chapter to the subject.

Beginning and ending a speech is a special problem for students in an introductory course. The author has heard students begin speech after speech with such words as: "My speech is about . . ."; "Mine's on . . ."; "Today I'm gonna talk about . . ."; My topic is . . ."—and similar repetitious, unimaginative openings. Likewise, the speech simply ended abruptly when the final point was completed, or included such words as "That's all I have to say"; "Are there any questions?"; or "That's it." Certainly, moving comfortably and fluently into your classroom speeches and wrapping them up efficiently is one of the most important skills objectives in the basic course.

As the opening examples show, effective introductions and conclusions are not just a problem for the beginning speaker. Indeed, gaining significant experience as a public speaker does not necessarily assure good introductions and conclusions.

In many cases, the more speaking a person has done, the more relaxed and routine the speaking situation becomes, the greater the chance that careful preparation of a beginning and ending will appear unnecessary. For example, the teacher who has never had any problems with presenting lectures, the politician who can "talk at the drop of a hat," or the supervisor who has given hundreds of briefings to employees without major error are all tempted to avoid the additional work of developing these "extra" or "nonessential" elements. Furthermore, the more message-centered the speaker—the more he views the body of the speech as the key to effective communication—the more he ignores the total transaction between speaker and listeners, and the greater the chance that he will give only marginal attention to effective introductions and conclusions.

In this chapter, we shall make suggestions for all speakers regardless of their proficiency. We urge all public communicators to remember that speech preparation is not only a practical, strategic process but also an artistic, creative process. That artistry can help make the communication event not only meaningful but also pleasant for the receivers. The opening and closing of any speech are key indicators about the care with which a speaker has approached the creative enterprise of communication, about the thought and imagination that went into speech preparation.

## INTRODUCTIONS
### Purposes

What are the purposes of introductions? There are several, although some are more important than others, depending on the communication context.

**1.** *Introductions should stimulate audience attention.* In most speeches, the sender will probably have early attention from listeners simply due to curiosity and custom. Receivers are usually willing to give initial attention to any speaker. But this is usually very short-lived unless the speaker is able to sustain it with speech content. Thus, the introduction can be the earliest suggestion that what is about to be presented is or is not worth listening to. It can establish a basis for maintaining interest throughout the speech.

**2.** *An introduction can help channel the divergent minds of the listeners toward a particular topic and purpose.* It can get all of them ready to listen to the message in about the same way. In many speech situations, listeners may be thinking in generally similar ways about the message they expect to hear, but the good opening can focus their thinking in very specific ways, assuring that the important points occurring early in the message are not lost simply because the receivers were not properly oriented to the sender's line of thinking.

**3.** *The good introduction helps establish a mood.* Is this going to be a grimly serious message, a casual or friendly one, or a practical, informative transaction? What kind of attitude does the speaker expect from the listeners? The introduction can reveal that intent very quickly. If, for example, we are prepared early for receiving some very shocking or at least sobering information that the speaker hopes will heighten our concern, we may be more receptive to that information when it is suggested in the introduction. The opening should put us in the right frame of mind to hear the intended message.

**4.** *The introduction can be used as a vehicle for formalities or procedural information that do not fit neatly elsewhere in the organizational plan.* This may involve thanking people, recognizing specific audience members, acknowledging previous speakers or events, or providing supplemental information about one's own background and interests. It might even explain how this particular communication event came to be, or how one was selected to be the speaker. But this purpose can be abused if the speaker lets these procedural formalities *substitute for* other introductory comments that help listeners get into the topic. The speaker still must prepare the listeners for a particular topic, purpose, or theme.

**5.** *The introduction can help make the speaker more at ease.* Regardless of its content, the opening helps the speaker establish a rapport with the listeners and get used to the unique one-to-many transaction. It can be thought of as a brief "warm-up" period, like limbering-up exercises before strenuous physical exertion. Many speakers report that, after initial nervousness during the introduction, they have calmed down and can develop ideas with more confidence and control by the time they get into the main points of the speech.

The importance of these five purposes differs, depending on the situation. For example, in a crisis situation a speaker might not have to worry much about stimulating attention, but might need to set a mood of calm, rational discussion. Or with a group of very different people, such as a random public audience attending a political speech, perhaps the crucial purpose is to channel divergent minds toward one

topic. But taken together, the objectives noted above reaffirm the importance of the introduction for any public speech.

## Typical Introductions

In this section we shall identify several different ways of developing an introduction. The list is not exclusive, however; the creative speaker may find other useful ways of beginning the speech.

**1.** *A quotation.* A common technique is to quote the words of a person whom the listeners will quickly recognize and respect, or who has the credentials to comment on the speech topic. For example, "The noted anthropologist, Margaret Mead, has written. . . ." Or, "These words by President Carter's chief economic advisor suggest the problem that I shall be discussing today." An interesting variation of this technique is to select a person who has a negative reputation with the receivers. That person's name will likely prompt immediate attention, and his ideas that are antagonistic to the receivers' attitudes can then be contrasted with the speaker's central thesis.

Four guidelines are important in using an opening quotation. First, it should be selected with the specific audience in mind. Second, it should be highly relevant to the central point of the speech. Third, it should be brief, usually no more than a few sentences. Fourth, the speaker should practice reading it aloud so that it can be delivered fluently and in the speaker's own conversational style. Unless all four of these guidelines are followed carefully, the quotation can have a negative impact on audience responses.

**2.** *A startling statement, fact, or statistic.* Some speakers like to get attention and focus on a key problem by shocking the listeners in the introduction. For example, one speaker began: "I have, on several occasions, tried to kill myself. Yes, you heard me correctly: I've tried to kill myself several times. I did not use poison, sleeping pills, a razor-blade, or a gun. I did not jump off the Golden Gate Bridge. No, I used two common ingredients—alcohol and an automobile. Thus, perhaps without really intending it, I have tried to kill myself by driving while intoxicated. And on one occasion, I very nearly succeeded." Another speaker, arguing for population control, began: "Twenty-five percent of all the human beings who have ever lived are alive today."

If selected carefully, the shocking statement can be a highly persuasive device. But if the remainder of the speech is bland and uncompelling, it becomes a kind of anticlimax to the memorable introduction. Therefore, the speaker should consider carefully whether the body of the speech can sustain the high emotional level of the opening.

3. *A story.* The narrative or story will be referred to frequently throughout this book as a useful technique for many purposes, such as holding attention, providing supporting materials, or clarifying complex information. It can also be one of the best ways to introduce a speech. A story can include suspense and emotional content. For instance, a speaker on child abuse told of a particularly poignant case of mistreatment and of the legal system's inability to deal with the problem. A story with an ironic twist or surprise ending can also prepare the audience to think seriously about the topic.

Like the shocking statement or statistic, the opening story must be sustained by equally meaningful and interesting information in the speech body. And it must also be representative of similar instances. An atypical or isolated case in the introduction, especially with a skeptical audience, can actually destroy a speaker's intended objectives. Finally, the opening narrative should not be too lengthy in relation to the rest of the message.

4. *Statement of thesis and review of main points.* By far the least imaginative, yet most commonly used introduction in public speaking today is a straightforward statement of thesis and listing of main ideas. For example, "In the next twenty minutes I shall attempt to describe and demonstrate the correct procedure for taking orders from customers. My presentation will have three parts. First, I shall outline the objectives that our company wants to achieve in dealing with the public. Next, I shall explain the step-by-step process that we'd like you to follow. Finally, I shall implement some of these suggestions by describing a typical employee–customer transaction." Many speakers think that this type of introduction is the most efficient and business-

like, and they rely on it to the exclusion of every other type. But notice that it also requires little preparation or consideration of the unique speech situation and audience. Thus, at times it is simply the lazy way out of the artistic development of good introductions. It also assumes that the audience is already focused and of one mind on the topic, and that they are highly attentive. While these conditions may frequently exist with the "insider audiences" of the business and professional world, they are rarely found with more varied, heterogeneous audiences.

We suggest that this type of introduction be included as a *portion* of a larger introduction and not as the exclusive method of getting the receivers into the speech.

**5.** *A question to the audience.* There are two ways in which an opening question can be used in an introduction. Actually seeking a physical or vocal response from the receivers is the first way. For example: "I'd like to see a show of hands from those of you who own your own homes. (Pause.) Fine. Now let me see the hands of those whose property taxes have risen significantly in the past five years. (Pause.) Thank you. I notice that most of you raised your hands twice, suggesting that you are having to deal with a growing tax burden." Or: "When I use the term 'police brutality,' what do you think of? Would anyone care to describe what comes to mind?"

The second type of query is called the *rhetorical question*. This is actually *an argumentative statement phrased in the form of a question*. It does not call for an active physical response, but rather prompts a mental response; listeners answer the question in their heads. For example, if the speaker is attempting to persuade the listeners about the alleged unfairness of property taxes, she might ask, "Is it fair to ask 40 percent of our citizens to pay over 80 percent of our taxes? Is it reasonable to expect retired people on fixed incomes to pay increasingly higher property taxes each year? Is it fair for governments, whenever they want more revenue, to automatically raise property taxes without considering other types of revenue?" She hopes that her listeners will answer "No" to each of these questions and will thus be in the proper mood to accept her central thesis.

Many speakers like questions in the introduction because it tends to induce active receiver involvement in the topic. It is obviously more effective with favorable or passive audiences than with hostile listeners who are ready to disagree and to answer the questions in ways contrary to the speaker's intention. Some speakers are reluctant to use this technique because they fear not only the hostile response, but also the lack of any response at all. What happens, for example, when the speaker asks for a show of hands, has based his later comments on the assumption that many people will do so, and then discovers that no one does respond? In some cases it is advisable to prepare the receivers for the eventual question. For instance, "In just a moment I'm going to ask you some questions. If you will answer them as openly and frankly as you can, it will help us all understand the problem of careless driving much better. All right, now, here's the first question." Using this technique assures that the question will not jump out unexpectedly, catching the audience by surprise. It also tells them that it is legitimate for them to speak up, that the sender expects them to do so.

Another word of caution: Once the speaker prompts audience response, it is sometimes difficult to get back to the prepared remarks. Many people introduce the speech with some questions, start a long and involved audience discussion which may or may not be directly related to the central purpose, and then have difficulty cutting off participation and getting back to the planned remarks. Therefore, the speaker who uses this opening strategy should keep an eye on the time and consider appropriate ways of returning tactfully to the speech outline.

**6.** *An audiovisual aid or demonstration.* This topic will be discussed later in Chapter 6 as an overall speech strategy. Some speakers, however, like to begin the message with a short display, exhibit, or demonstration of a process. For example, some speeches begin with a brief slide presentation or five- or ten-minute film that leads into the speaker's comments. One speaker said, "Please watch as I attach some equipment to my arm." [Demonstration.] "What I have just demonstrated is how easily you can take your own blood pressure readings and thus better protect yourself from a heart attack."

These introductions are frequently vivid, but if the later content is relatively lackluster it may again appear anticlimactic. Therefore we recommend that this type of introduction be used primarily when the remainder of the speech also has auditory or visual support. But certainly in terms of creating initial interest, focusing on the key ideas, and putting the speaker at ease, this type of opening can be very effective.

**7.** *The use of humor.* A traditional stereotype of a speech introduction is that the speaker will tell two or three amusing anecdotes with some vague relationship to the audience, topic, or situation, and then move quickly on to the main points. Indeed, according to the extent to which humor puts the speaker and audience at ease, meets audience expectations, gets their attention, and identifies the key topics, it can be a good strategy.

Humor should not be used as an introduction if any of the following conditions exist: if the speaker has rarely been successful in "being funny" by telling jokes; if the reference or story is plainly unfunny (feedback from others before the speech might be a good check on whether the listeners are likely to be amused); if the speech purpose and topic are grimly serious; if the speech context is one in which business and professional people usually do not engage in humorous exchanges, like a weekly board meeting or briefing; if the story might offend some people in the audience; and if the humorous comments have little or no relationship to the speech content or situation. Speakers should assure that there is a practical point to their use of humor so that, if it does "bomb," they can still make a relevant application of the story to the topic or idea.

## CONCLUSIONS

If an introduction is an important factor in determining how the audience will listen to a message, then certainly the conclusion will affect the ways in which they remember the message. Many mediocre speeches have achieved their purpose to a large extent because the conclusion prompted precisely the response the speaker hoped it would. Unfortunately, some very good speeches in terms of content and delivery have not achieved noticeable effect because the last messages the audience heard were either bland, awkward, disorganized, or poorly delivered. Think back to a recent film or stage play you have seen. Do you remember the opening scene? Perhaps, but probably not very vividly. But what about the conclusion, that last poignant scene that left you with a final significant idea or that prompted a strong emotional response? You probably remember that fairly well. Good speakers, like creative writers, know that the conclusion is what people remember and what is likely to have major impact on how we think and behave.

## Purposes

The major objective of a conclusion is *to enhance, by whatever means, the achievement of the speech purpose.* All other goals are secondary. Is the purpose to assure that listeners understand and remember a message? Then the conclusion should reiterate the main points. Is the purpose to inspire the receivers? Then the conclusion should have some inspirational or emotional impact. Is the purpose to elicit audience belief, to convince them of a point of view? Then the conclusion should provide the final, most compelling reason for believing a particular way. Is the purpose to instruct, so that the receivers now have the ability to behave in a particular way, to exhibit certain skills? Then the conclusion should assure that the receivers know precisely what behaviors are expected of them. The conclusion must always complement the primary purpose of the speech—which, as we know from Chapter 2, is the audience response that the speaker hopes to achieve.

Secondary purposes of a conclusion are varied and depend on the situation. One purpose is to provide a *final affirmation of the speaker–audience transaction*, of the relationship between communicators. This may involve thanking the receivers for their attentiveness and participation and for the opportunity to speak to them. It may also reassert the value of the communication event in which they have just participated; the conclusion says, in effect, "We have achieved something important here today."

Another secondary purpose is *to build positive audience regard for*

© Howard Harrison 1972

*the speaker*, for his motives, his ability, his good will. Ideally, this process of developing a positive image will have begun long before, perhaps from the beginning of the speech negotiation process and continuing throughout the speech. But the conclusion is one of the times during which an audience is likely to assess how well they like the speaker as a person and respect him as someone who has something important to say.

Another possible secondary purpose of the conclusion is *to provide a transition between the prepared speech and the next phase of the communication process*. Perhaps the speech precedes a question-and-answer session, or small-group activities, or a general legislative session, or an adjournment for several hours or days until the next meeting. Some reference in the conclusion to "what happens next" may frequently be appropriate. In other words, it not only provides closure for what has just been achieved, but may also open a new communication event.

## Typical Conclusions

As with introductions, there is no one best conclusion. Developing an ending is both an artistic and a pragmatic (strategic) process. Below are several options.

1. *Restatement and review.* A very functional, though unimaginative, type of conclusion is a restatement of the central thesis and review of main points. It is heavily utilized in informative speaking like instructional messages in the business and professional context. The review may be especially useful when the audience is taking notes, as in a lecture or briefing. However, there is no reason why a review must be the total conclusion. It can be supplemented by one of the techniques listed below. Thus, the speaker might summarize key points and then develop a more imaginative closing that is interesting, memorable, or even inspirational.

2. *An example or illustration.* A final story may have just the illustrative or emotional effect that the speaker needs to leave the receivers with a vivid reminder of the central thesis. The example should not be too lengthy, but rather should be in proportion to total speech length. It is also important not to dull the impact of the example with follow-up explanations or summaries; when the concluding example is finished, *stop talking and sit down!* We once heard a student argue convincingly for volunteers to assist in educational activities for mentally retarded children. She concluded with a moving story of an old and unhappy woman who had reluctantly volunteered and whose life had been given new purpose by the love and appreciation she had received from the children. But then the speaker destroyed the impact of the story by presenting a three- or four-minute explanation of how people could sign up, information that could have been presented earlier or perhaps written on a flyer for distribution after the speech.

3. *A provocative statement or question.* Perhaps all that is needed to conclude some speeches is a brief sentence or two that, by dramatic or catchy wording, captures the essence of the message and leaves the receivers with something they can remember long after the speech has

ended. A classic example of this technique is Patrick Henry's ringing conclusion to his speech before the Virginia legislature: "I know not what course others may take—but as for me, give me liberty or give me death!" Another example is Lincoln's conclusion to the speech at Gettysburg: ". . . that government of the people, by the people, and for the people shall not perish from the earth."

Our public speaking is not likely to occur in such momentous situations as these. Nor will our conclusions be as dramatic. But we can nevertheless try to develop creative concluding statements that our listeners will remember. For example, a speaker attempting to build the awareness of high school students to the problem of drinking drivers had earlier referred, by name, to three high school girls. Shortly before graduation exercises, they had been killed when their new car, a graduation present for one of the girls, ran head-on into a bridge abutment. The speech concluded, "Some of you will heed my warning; others will ignore it. But for Debby, Linda, and Susan, it is too late."

If phrased as a question, the final sentence can prompt receivers to think deeply and personally about their own relationship to the speech topic. One speaker concluded, "When the victim was raped and beaten on the New York City street, 36 people looked the other way. If you had been there, what would you have done?" Finally, the concluding question can be *rhetorical*, as was discussed in the section above on introductions. The question is actually an argumentative statement calling for a mental response in the audience that is favorable to the speaker's persuasive purpose.

4. *A quotation.*   As in an introduction, a quotation can be an effective way to conclude the message. The same guidelines noted earlier apply to the conclusion as well. The quotation should be selected with a specific audience in mind; it should be relevant to the central thesis; it should be brief; and the speaker should practice reading it fluently and naturally. In a persuasive speech on a controversial issue, the quotation should be drawn from a source that the receivers are likely to accept as credible and whose words directly support one or more of the speaker's arguments. In an inspirational message, like a speech to a graduating class or in a religious service, the quotation might be more literary, perhaps a passage from poetry. The speaker who is knowl-

edgeable on the topic and who has assembled speech materials carefully should have no trouble selecting a statement that provides both
logical and emotional support.

**5.** *A challenge or request.* When the speech purpose is to elicit specific audience behavior, such as contributing time or money, the best
conclusion may be a direct request. Some speakers prefer to be fairly
nondirective; they outline a problem, show why help is needed, and let
the receivers supply the next logical point—"We should help." But
often that message should be explicitly stated, with specific behaviors
identified. For example, a high school teacher speaking to a group of
parents was opposing a school board proposal to save money by eliminating the "extracurricular programs" of art, music, and debate. She
concluded this way: "I ask you to help us save these important programs. First, you can write or call school board members and tell them
about your support of these programs. Second, you can contribute your
money to the Student Activities Fund that has been started. Finally,
you can talk to your children and to other parents about the importance of these activities for a well-rounded educational program. If you
will help us, together we can assure quality education for our children."

**6.** *Use of a visual aid.* Perhaps the final message that the audience
receives can be visual rather than oral. Or a visual message can be
combined with a spoken one.

Thus, what the audience remembers about the speech may be
especially vivid because it involves two media or channels of communication—sight as well as hearing. An effective use of photographs, for
example, occurred when a social worker in a large city appealed to the
city council for funding for park and recreation areas in a slum district.
She concluded by showing before-and-after pictures of a restored tene-
ment area in a neighboring city. The striking contrast between the two
left the council with a persuasive image of how, with a minimum of
money and effort, an ugly environment could be transformed into a
beautiful one. Had they forgotten any of the specific data in the speech,
they could still have recalled the photographs.

**7.** *A link with the introduction.* Sometimes a conclusion can refer

back to information presented in the introduction, providing a sense of completion, unity, or wholeness for the communication event. One technique is to begin a story in the introduction, but not reveal the outcome of that story until the conclusion. For example, the speaker might describe a situation that involves a serious problem—real people in a real event. She then develops the body of the speech, identifying the magnitude of the problem, outlining potential solutions, and then supporting what she considers to be the best solution. She concludes by saying: "And remember the problem that I raised in the introduction. How did these people solve their dilemma? They did exactly what I am suggesting here. This is what happened. . . ." Perhaps the conclusion provides a surprise ending to the story, an ironic twist that will remain with the audience long after the speech has ended. We once heard a speaker introduce his speech with an example of a man who had an outstanding educational background and some remarkable professional achievements. In the conclusion he revealed one more detail about the man—he had been blind from birth.

Another way of linking the introduction with the conclusion is through repetition of key ideas or phrases. Suppose a speaker had begun with the story of Robert F. Kennedy's campaign to revitalize the Bedford-Stuyvesant district in New York City, and quoted his words, "Some people see things as they are and ask 'Why?' I dream dreams that never were and ask, 'Why not?' " Then, the conclusion might be, "And Robert Kennedy's words should remain with us as we embark on this campaign: 'Some people see things as they are. . . .' " The key statement has thus been heard twice, at the beginning and at the end, and may become the reminder of the speaker's central idea.

**8.** *A combination of approaches.* The categories above, and additional closings that the imaginative speaker might create, can often be combined in a single conclusion. It might begin with a summary of key points and then a provocative statement or illustration. The speaker might display a chart (visual aid) on which are listed the suggestions for action or the proposed solutions. A quotation might be followed by a single-sentence restatement of the central thesis. Whatever the combination, the conclusion should *support the speech purpose*; it should be developed primarily to achieve the intended audience response.

## Suggestions for Beginning and Ending the Speech

A rereading of the opening examples in this chapter can provide important insights on how not to develop introductions and conclusions. The high school teacher was too abrupt and did not give the audience a chance to focus their different perspectives on the single topic. The swimmer destroyed her credibility with an awkward, apologetic opening. The businesswoman concluded too abruptly, without providing any closure for what she had covered. The United Way chairperson had not planned any conclusion at all, and sheepishly had to tell the listeners that he was finished. And the senator prepared the audience for an ending, but then kept talking. Some additional suggestions may be useful.

1. *Develop the introduction and conclusion as the last step in the speech preparation process.* Speech development is a process in which the message evolves gradually as the speaker plays with ideas, rearranges materials, adds and deletes information. Rarely does the final product perfectly resemble the speaker's original intentions. It is important to "see how it comes out" before trying to make the speech body fit with particular opening and closing comments.

2. *Avoid unplanned digressions or overelaboration.* Do not belabor introductions or conclusions. If the opening is too long, the audience may think, "C'mon, get on with it!" If the closing rambles on and on, they may think, "When is this going to end?" It is probably better to be too brief than too lengthy. We have noted that public speaking today usually has fairly specific time constraints. In the business and professional world, "time is money," a valuable resource that the speaker should not waste in an involved introduction that severely limits his development of key ideas. Incidentally, one reason why conclusions are often too lengthy is that they have not been planned carefully. The speaker senses that he should end by saying something very dramatic or striking—but since he did not plan anything, he continues to summarize and rehash, hoping that sooner or later just the right phrase will burst out spontaneously as the fitting conclusion. Many speakers stumble and grope for several minutes in the conclusion, almost as if

they were waiting for an act of God to provide them with the ringing words that will prompt the audience to burst into applause. It just doesn't happen that way, so speakers must plan for a tight, concise conclusion.

**3.** *Consider writing out verbatim—and rehearsing orally—the first and last sentences of the speech.* In Chapter 5 we shall argue against the use of the manuscript for most public speaking situations. However, in order to get off to a good start and to end with a fluent, cogent statement, many speakers try to minimize the chances for a misstatement. In rehearsing the speech, they assure themselves that they can begin and end smoothly and conversationally with these well-worded statements.

**4.** *Be prepared to abandon the planned introduction and conclusion and to adapt to the unexpected.* Some speakers hold rigidly to their planned remarks even though the actual speech situation has not developed as intended. Perhaps there has been a last-minute change in the meeting format, in the composition of the audience, or in the time limits for the message. Maybe a previous speaker has preempted some of the materials or the speaker has learned, in pre-speech conversation, that the listeners have particular attitudes that make some intended remarks inappropriate. Perhaps the speaker gets a better idea just before beginning the speech. Yet it is surprising how often speakers get so ego-involved in the materials they have prepared that they seem to have the attitude, "If I went to the trouble to prepare this, so help me, you people are going to hear it!" This rigidity can only impede speech effectiveness—as with the professor of English literature who had planned to conclude his lecture with a stirring but lengthy quotation from Tennyson. The bell rang before he could begin the poem— but he hurried into it anyway. Students noisily put away notebooks, chatted with neighbors, and even hurried out to get to their next class. But the professor was determined to read from Tennyson, so he did it to a half-empty room of inattentive people!

**5.** *Listen to the introductions and conclusions of other speakers.* Note strong and weak points. Evaluating and borrowing from the techniques of others is one of the best ways to improve.

## SUMMARY

Though introductions and conclusions are crucially important in achieving a speech purpose, many speakers, even good ones, give little or no attention to them. Yet the quality of the opening and closing is often a relevant indicator of the thought and artistry that went into speech development.

Introductions should stimulate audience attention, channel divergent receiver thoughts, establish a mood, cover the formalities, and help relax the speaker. Some of the more popular options include: a quotation, startling information, a story, a thesis statement and a review of main points, a question to the audience, a demonstration, and humor.

The conclusion should enhance the speech purpose, but it can also achieve secondary objectives. A good conclusion can affirm the positive relationship between speaker and listeners and provide a transition to a new phase of the communication event, such as a question-and-answer session. Typical conclusions include restatement and review (the least imaginative), an example, a provocative statement or question, a quotation, a challenge or request, visual aids, a link with the introduction, and many combinations of these.

The good speaker will develop openings and closings at the end of the speech preparation process; avoid unplanned remarks, except to adapt to unexpected developments; and will even write out and practice the first and last sentences in the speech, so as to get off to a good start and to end smoothly and forcefully. Openings and closings should be altered to adapt to the unexpected; those that others use should be studied.

## QUESTIONS FOR STUDY

1. Why is the use of the story a good introductory technique? The startling fact or statistic? The audiovisual aid?

2. What are some of the potential problems with using the question to the audience as an introduction? A quotation? Humor?

3. In some public communication events, why can the conclusion also be thought of as a transition?

4. When can a quotation be a good conclusion? An example or illustration? A restatement or review?

5. Why should the development of introductions and conclusions be the final step in the speech preparation process? Why might well-prepared introductions and conclusions have to be changed as the speech presentation begins or while it is in progress? Give some examples of such situations.

# part two

# THE SPEECH PRESENTATION

# chapter 5

# DELIVERY STRATEGIES

**LEARNING OBJECTIVES**

After reading this chapter, you should be able to:
1. Explain the advantages and disadvantages of each presentational form, especially in terms of speech projects in the classroom.
2. Assess your own strengths and weaknesses in terms of audible or vocal factors.
3. Identify the four categories of communication disorders, noting typical problem areas in each.
4. List reasons why an extemporaneous, conversational (natural) delivery style is a useful strategy for most public speaking situations.

# 5

One of the most common audience complaints after a speech presentation is, "You know, it's really a shame. I think that speaker had some really important ideas, but he just couldn't communicate them very well." We have all suffered through long, agonizing speeches in which the speaker's lack of fluency, vocal characteristics, or physical mannerisms have neutralized any benefit we might have gotten from the intended message. The example below is typical.

A group of more than one thousand college students and faculty had assembled to hear a Pulitzer Prize-winning novelist discuss his work. His visit to the campus had been advertised for weeks; expectations were high. His fee was $2000 plus expenses. A professor of English provided a glowing introduction, and the novelist was greeted with enthusiastic applause. But the speech that followed was vivid evidence that the man should have been satisfied with writing as his medium of communication. A speaker he was not. In the first place, his message was actually an essay that was meant to be read, not heard. Secondly, he read the essay badly, using almost no inflection or emphasis, speaking too slowly and softly, losing his place in the manuscript, and making frequent pauses in awkward places that distorted the intended meaning of his sentences. Third, his visual style was unappealing. He avoided eye contact with the audience, keeping his head and eyes down. He fidgeted and shuffled with his hands and feet. His glasses continually slid down his nose and he pushed them back up every few seconds.

The novelist continued this way for almost an hour. He did not appear to notice the many people who began leaving after about thirty minutes. When he finished, the considerably smaller audience gave him polite applause. The moderator asked for audience questions. The speaker answered two or three in the same monotonous style, and people continued to filter out of the room. Finally—mercifully—the moderator thanked the novelist and adjourned the meeting. The speaker took his $2000 and flew back home to his writing, perhaps totally unaware of the shambles he had made of the communication event.

The newspapers reported the event by quoting passages from the prepared manuscript that had been given to reporters in advance.

They provided a brief biography of the speaker's past achievements and mentioned that about one thousand people attended the speech. They avoided, of course, any mention of the ineffective presentation or the disappointed audience. That is a typical response. The press, and perhaps the general culture as well, are much too tolerant of the speaker who has good ideas but bad presentational style or poor delivery.

This chapter is based on the premise that listeners who give of their time and energy to participate in a public speaking event have a right to expect more than good ideas or information. They should not have to endure speakers who give little attention to delivery, who assume that audible and visual factors are merely incidental to the communication of ideas. Indeed, we argued earlier that meanings are in people, that the message has no content except what the listeners interpret. And the message is not only the speaker's notes or spoken words, but also the total set of visible and audible events that the audience perceives. *Delivery is just as much a part of speech content as the information the speaker intends to present.* The *message* is the total communication event. Thus we should not view delivery—the actual presentation of the message—as merely a cosmetic feature that may or may not enhance our speech objectives. Rather, it is an intrinsic and crucial component to which every public speaker should give careful attention.

Of course, there is always the danger that someone with an excellent delivery will have nothing important to say—or, worse, that impressive, engaging delivery will influence others without good reasons or reliable information. Some politicians and salespeople, friends, even teachers and parents, can persuade us to believe or act in certain ways by "talking a good line," but they may perhaps give little thought to how it may affect our lives. In the concluding chapter of this book, on "responsible public communication," we will discuss this problem in more depth. But for most of us, delivery is our most important concern as speakers. We are never quite as fluent, never quite as confident as we'd like to be about the way we look and sound to an audience. It is for good reason, then, that we spend some time studying and practicing speech delivery.

## THE PRESENTATIONAL FORM

Every public speaker must decide how the prepared message should be presented to the audience, the ways in which the *spoken* message will conform to a speech plan and prepared notes. Presentations take four general forms: *manuscript*, *memorization*, *impromptu*, and *extemporaneous*.

### The Manuscript Speech

Manuscript speaking involves word-for-word reading of a prepared text. A speaker reads a carefully written essay, with little or no deviation from the planned wording.

Manuscript speaking is tempting to use for several reasons. First, a speaker can be reasonably confident that the planned remarks will be delivered accurately if the manuscript is adhered to. For example, public officials like the President or Secretary of State, who are speaking not just for themselves but for entire nations, want to assure that their words are delivered as intended without deviation. During delicate international negotiations, officials spend long hours preparing carefully worded documents for public presentation. Political campaigners have also come to rely on the manuscript. Heavy coverage by the news media has meant that an unintended comment could devastate a campaign. For example, in the 1976 Presidential primaries, Jimmy Carter suggested the legitimacy of neighborhoods' retaining "ethnic purity." That term suggested to some that Carter was justifying racism, and the resulting outcry forced him to apologize and probably cost him some valuable political support from minority groups. He called the phrase "an unfortunate use of words," and certainly a carefully written manuscript would not have included it. Politicians today are rarely "off the record," and from bitter experience many have learned to read a speech whenever their remarks on controversial issues might be quoted.

Likewise, business and professional people, recognizing that their comments might become part of the permanent record, sometimes use a manuscript delivery. Since their speeches often reflect organizational policy, a carefully written message can be reviewed and modified by colleagues before it is delivered. In most courtrooms, judges do not deviate from a previously approved set of jury instructions; even a

© Howard Harrison 1972

slight variation in wording may bring complaints from the attorneys or a reversal of verdict by an appeals court. Thus, some speakers believe that a manuscript protects them and the people they represent.

A second reason why many speakers use a manuscript is to calm their fears about making mistakes in front of an audience. The manuscript becomes a crutch, a security blanket to assure that one will not seriously misstate the prepared comments.

Third, a manuscript is used to assure proper speech timing. Radio and television broadcasters measure air time in seconds and must know precisely how long certain messages will last. A speaker at a noon meeting of a service club knows that the audience must return to their jobs at 1 p.m., and a classroom lecturer knows that when the bell rings, students will get up and leave. The speaker who has practiced the manuscript speech will know its reading time fairly accurately.

Though there are legitimate uses for the manuscript delivery, most public speakers today should use the method rarely and with caution. First, manuscript preparation is usually an enormously time-consuming task. For even a short speech of fifteen minutes or so, seven or eight typed, double-spaced pages are required. People who speak frequently simply cannot devote the necessary time to manuscript preparation. While corporate executives or United States senators may be able to afford the luxury of a speech writer, most of us cannot and therefore should avoid manuscripts, simply because they take too much time and effort. They are impractical.

A second reason to avoid the manuscript strategy is the difficulty of maintaining a natural speaking style. In normal conversation we use emphasis and pauses without conscious thought in a spontaneous expression of *complete thought units*. But when reading a manuscript, we tend to "read words accurately" rather than "express ideas meaningfully." We may pause at awkward places—for example, at the end of a printed line rather than the end of a thought unit. A monotone often develops. Eye contact with the audience becomes more difficult. Some speakers become too formal and appear rigid and aloof. The written style may include long, complex sentences and less common wording, and the speaker then sounds even more awkward and unnatural. A natural reading style develops only after long experience (as with newscasters and actors), and most of us will have great difficulty achieving it in our less frequent speech presentations.

The most important problem with the manuscript speech is that it is not conducive to spontaneous audience adaptation. This book is based on a receiver-centered approach to public speaking. Some adaptation to the audience is usually warranted in *any* public speaking situation. It might involve referring to the remarks of a previous speaker, adding more detailed explanation when receivers appear to be confused, cutting out prepared material to conform to new time limits, pausing to respond to audience comments or questions, or actually changing speech information to be consistent with new developments or previous speakers. Whatever the reason, a prepared text can hamper the inevitable need to modify a presentation in a particular speech context.

*Suggestions.* If, despite the problems, it appears that a manuscript delivery is justified, a speaker should at least consider the following suggestions.

1. *Write the speech with simple sentence structure and wording.* Remember that the audience will hear it only once and cannot reread it as they would a written essay.
2. *Practice reading the speech aloud.* Frequently, sentence wording will not sound natural and should be modified before presentation. Practice reading in complete thought units as they might be uttered in normal conversation.
3. *Work on eye contact.* Try "gulping in" a whole line of print and speaking that line while looking up at the audience.
4. *Make reminder notes in the margins* like "slow down," "louder," or "eye contact." Underline key passages that need vocal emphasis, and use parentheses to assure good phrasing.
5. *Be willing to deviate from prepared comments* if the audience clearly needs elaboration.
6. *Use a typed, double- or triple-spaced manuscript* with clear divisions or notations at main points.
7. *Number the pages, but do not staple.*
8. *Always end the typewritten page with a complete sentence.* Never divide a word or sentence to put on the next page. Avoid hyphens at the end of any line of type.

Figure 1 illustrates a sample page from a typical manuscript speech. It incorporates many of the suggestions noted above.

### The Memorized Speech

One of the ancient canons or fundamental norms of good speechmaking was *memoria*, or memory. In the Greek and Roman schools, students memorized long passages from literature and public oratory, and these materials became part of their fund of knowledge to bring with them to varied public speaking situations. To be able to quote passages from memory and apply them to a wide variety of subjects was a desirable trait. And in the public forum, the good speaker did not rely on notes, but rather recited a prepared speech from memory. Not surprisingly, when read today these speeches appear flowery and poetic, as much literary as rhetorical.

The use of memory as a delivery strategy continued throughout the early history of America. In the schools, students presented *decla-*

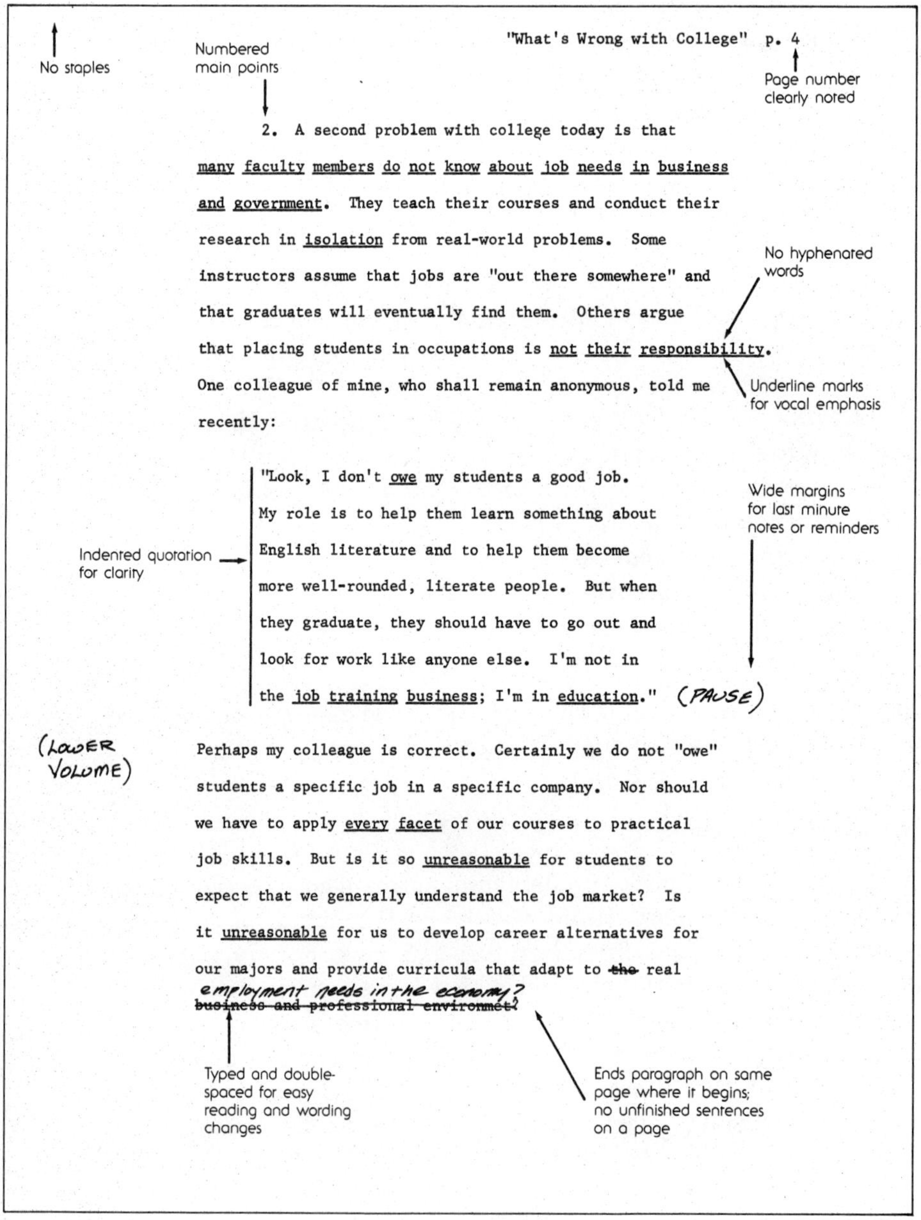

No staples

Numbered
main points

"What's Wrong with College"   p. 4

Page number
clearly noted

2. A second problem with college today is that
many faculty members do not know about job needs in business
and government. They teach their courses and conduct their
research in isolation from real-world problems. Some
instructors assume that jobs are "out there somewhere" and
that graduates will eventually find them. Others argue
that placing students in occupations is not their responsibility.
One colleague of mine, who shall remain anonymous, told me
recently:

No hyphenated
words

Underline marks
for vocal emphasis

Indented quotation
for clarity

"Look, I don't owe my students a good job.
My role is to help them learn something about
English literature and to help them become
more well-rounded, literate people. But when
they graduate, they should have to go out and
look for work like anyone else. I'm not in
the job training business; I'm in education." (PAUSE)

Wide margins
for last minute
notes or reminders

(LOWER
VOLUME)

Perhaps my colleague is correct. Certainly we do not "owe"
students a specific job in a specific company. Nor should
we have to apply every facet of our courses to practical
job skills. But is it so unreasonable for students to
expect that we generally understand the job market? Is
it unreasonable for us to develop career alternatives for
our majors and provide curricula that adapt to ~~the~~ real
*employment needs in the economy?*
~~business and professional environment?~~

Typed and double-
spaced for easy
reading and wording
changes

Ends paragraph on same
page where it begins;
no unfinished sentences
on a page

**FIGURE 1**

*mations*, or memorized recitations of great speeches. And in both political and ceremonial settings, public speakers often prided themselves on their ability to recall long passages from great literature for their appreciative audiences.

Today, the memorized speech, or even long sequences of memorized material within a speech, is virtually obsolete. Perhaps it is partly due to the decline of the oral tradition in our schools; students are rarely asked to present memorized recitations. Perhaps increased leisure activities, along with the huge impact of television, have eliminated long hours that a hundred years ago might have been used to polish and memorize a speech. But clearly the most important reason is that the memorized speech is an inefficient form of public communication for busy people in their everyday lives.

The same disadvantages noted above for manuscript speaking apply here, only more so. Preparation time is great, the delivery style is usually unnatural, and close adaptation to a unique speech situation and spontaneous events nearly impossible. And the speaker might also forget the intended words; almost all of us can remember with horror a time when we "blew our lines" in a play, ceremony, or contest. Most important—in an audience-centered approach to public speaking, the crucial rationale for delivering a message a particular way is to enhance the likelihood of shared meaning between sender and receiver. The speaker is not a performer in a one-way communication setting, but rather a participant in a two-way process. Memorized delivery may be appropriate in a play or formal ritual, but destructive in a speech context. Most people who give occasional speech presentations throughout their lives will probably *never* encounter a situation in which a memorized delivery is the most effective form of communication.

In summary, the speaker who depends nearly exclusively on either manuscript or memorized delivery strategies will become virtually crippled in terms of the typical demands for presentational speaking today.

## The Impromptu Speech

An impromptu delivery strategy is essentially spontaneous communication without notes or careful planning. Impromptu speeches are often termed *ad lib* or *off-the-cuff*. In the business and professional world, speakers with significant background and expertise in a particular area sometimes forego extensive speech preparation. From past experience they know that they can discuss their topic intelligently and fluently regardless of time limits or audience. Most speakers, however, have difficulty with impromptu delivery.

One problem we face is organization. Though we may have a general plan of three or four key points, substructure may be confusing and digression common. Recall, for example, someone telling a story or describing an event, continually expanding on irrelevant information while the listener is thinking, "Get to the point!"

Another problem might be called the *paradox of information*. The more knowledgeable a speaker is in a particular field, the more difficult it may be for him to sift through a huge body of data and ideas to come up with a meaningful message for a specific time limit and audience. In general, the more information a speaker has, the more care he should take in sorting, condensing, and arranging it.

A final argument against the impromptu strategy is audience reaction. Most receivers can quickly tell when a speaker has not prepared the speech. He has no notes, his comments lack fluency and organization, he is repetitious, and he often appears to be confused and groping for ideas. The audience might imply that the speaker is saying indirectly, "I did not consider you people or this occasion important enough to waste my time in extensive preparation."

Despite these problems, sometimes spontaneous public communication is necessary. Public officials may be called on to answer detailed questions at a press conference or public meeting. A teacher may need to respond in depth to a student's question. An executive in a conference may be asked to discuss policy alternatives. A job applicant may have to outline his career objectives for an interview committee. A legislator may have to answer new or unexpected arguments against a proposed bill. A law school student may be asked to analyze an assigned case for the class. The possibilities seem endless, and suggest that most speakers will eventually have to use the impromptu strategy for at least portions of their presentations.

People in the public eye should try to predict the kinds of information others might request. Public officials should have briefing sessions with advisors to go over potential questions and answers. People who represent organizations should bone up on statistics and examples that can be used to support their points of view. To some extent we can *prepare* for impromptu speaking situations, even though the specific communication requirements cannot be known in advance.

In a situation that obviously calls for extensive impromptu comments, a speaker should first be sure that he understands listener expectations. Is an audience question clear? (We have all experienced the frustration of having a speaker respond in lengthy detail, only to finish and have the inquirer say, "That wasn't my question.") The clarification process may also "buy time," giving a few extra moments to consider a reply or to develop a quick, general organizational plan. The eventual message might lack fluency and continuity, but at least it can be thoughtful and relevant. We should recognize, too, that an audience does not expect these spontaneous replies to be polished prose, and will excuse minor deficiencies in presentation.

### The Extemporaneous Speech

In discussing the extemporaneous strategy, we do *not* mean "impromptu, off the top of the head, ad lib, makeshift, or spur of the moment." Rather, we shall define the term as it has come to be used in modern speech communication training. An extemporaneous speech is one in which a speaker assembles information and materials, carefully structures an outline, and even rehearses the delivery. However, the speech is not written verbatim; it is not a manuscript. The speaker instead lets the *specific language* of the presentation develop naturally as he delivers the speech from the outline. That is the key: careful preparation and practice, but spontaneous language development.

One disadvantage of the extemporaneous strategy is that exact speech length is difficult to predict and thus more difficult to adapt to situations like radio or television presentations. Another disadvantage is its lack of formality (most of us do not naturally speak in highly styled, formal prose), making it an unlikely strategy for such events as inauguration addresses or formal ceremonies. Perhaps the greatest problem is that extemporaneous delivery may intimidate the beginning speaker. Novices may fear that the right words won't come to them when needed, that they may stammer or grope for proper phrasing, that they may be unable to explain a point in the outline. Hence they succumb to temptation; they write out more and more of the speech until soon it is virtually a manuscript with its attendant shortcomings.

Nevertheless, speakers should use the extemporaneous mode as much as possible. It is the optimal strategy for most speaking situations, even for the beginning speaker. The main advantage is that it combines the best elements of the manuscript speech (careful preparation of ideas and organizational plan) with the best elements of natural delivery (simple and spontaneous word choices and normal, unaffected vocal inflection).

Another advantage of the extemporaneous mode is that the speaker makes the best use of preparation time. Since an extensive manuscript and tedious memorization are unnecessary, the speaker can spend more time collecting and arranging materials (see Chapters 3 and 4) and rehearsing the presentation.

A third advantage is ease of adaptation. With little trouble, the extemporaneous speaker can make last-minute changes, insert new information, delete sections to shorten the speech, or alter the wording of main points. After the speech has begun, the speaker can spontaneously elaborate on ideas the audience does not appear to understand, or eliminate portions if time runs short. The speaker can even pause throughout the speech and answer audience questions.

Again, the extemporaneous strategy demands that the speaker not become preoccupied with precise language or perfect fluency. If key ideas demand precise phrasing, a sentence outline will assure that such careful wording can be used for main points. Portions of the introduction or conclusion might also be written out—and, of course, all quotations of outside sources must be delivered verbatim.

In conclusion, a good extemporaneous speech might combine elements of the three other forms. For example, suppose a business manager is presenting a marketing proposal to a group of colleagues. She has a carefully prepared outline and well-researched supporting materials. She has practiced the speech, and though the precise language varied with each rehearsal, she knows that it can be presented in about ten to twelve minutes. To assure that she can deliver her

main points flawlessly, she commits the thesis sentence and three key
subpoints to memory, along with the concluding sentence (memorized
strategy). She practices reading two paragraphs from a published
marketing report and a quotation from a public official that will be
used as supporting evidence (manuscript strategy). She considers
likely questions that the listeners will ask and mentally prepares
possible responses (impromptu strategy). But the bulk of the speech is
extemporaneous—spontaneous language from outline notes.

## AUDIBLE FACTORS

In addition to deciding on the form of presentation of a speech, we must
decide what vocal style to use. How loudly should we speak? How
rapidly? How precisely should sounds be enunciated? How varied
should the inflection be? How planned or calculated? Are there oral
mannerisms that should be avoided? These questions are among those
that need to be asked when considering *audible style*—vocal characteristics that the audience hears.

### Style: Formal or Casual?

The speaker has two major options: the *formal* style and the *casual*
style. The formal style has a long history. Many famous public speakers have used a stately, oratorical style with carefully planned inflection, dramatic pauses, increased volume, overly precise enunciation,
and other vocal traits that give the speech a formal, ceremonial tone.
We can all remember speakers who, when they got behind the podium
and began to speak, seemed almost to become different people because
their oral style changed so radically. Many people have come to expect
this formal style simply because it has been used so often. When we
give a speech, we may find ourselves changing our customary delivery
style to fit what we assume to be norms of a "good speaking performance."

But public speaking today should not be viewed as a performance
(sender-oriented), but rather as an attempt to develop shared meaning
of a message with an audience (receiver-oriented). Our goal should not

© Howard Harrison 1969

be to impress people with a beautifully modulated voice; rather, it
should be to maximize the chances that the audience will attend to and
understand our message. We therefore suggest for most public communication the second option—a natural, casual style. Our term for
this style is *conversationality*. With this strategy, a speaker uses
language and vocal inflection much as in normal, face-to-face conversation. *The emphasis given to words and phrases, the speed and loudness of the delivery, the word choices—indeed, all audible characteristics of the presentation—are similar to the speaker's oral style in
everyday interaction.*

Of course, some changes from a purely conversational delivery
may be necessary. A speaker may have to talk more loudly or articulate more carefully because of poor acoustics. More precise language
may be required to assure message accuracy as, for example, with a
technical engineering report. In addition, key points sometimes need
special vocal emphasis. In general, however, the most effective public
speakers today use a casual, spontaneous oral style.

The conversational strategy fits nicely with the extemporaneous
delivery mode. The speaker appears more relaxed and warmer; he may
actually *be* more relaxed, simply because he is exerting much less
effort in presenting the message. Still, a speaker's habits and stereo-
types may make it difficult to escape from a more formal style, and he
may want to remind himself not to lapse into an unnatural delivery, by
inserting reminders in the outline notes to "relax!" or "be conversational."

For most people, a conversational style is easy to develop and
causes few problems. As in normal conversation, the speaker can
expect some imperfections in fluency—an audible pause like "uh," a
minor pronunciation error, a grammatical slip, or a slurred phrase.
Fortunately, while the speaker may notice these minor errors, the
people in the audience rarely do. As in more casual interaction, the
listeners filter out these flaws and focus on content. For a very few
speakers, however, the vocal characteristics and gaps in fluency may
be serious enough to call attention to themselves. In the remainder of
this section we will examine some of the problems that, if uncorrected,
may impede a conversational delivery.

Voice scientists often refer to four categories of communication disorders: articulation, language, voice, and rhythm. The following discussion may be a kind of checklist for readers to assess their own delivery problems.

## Articulation

Articulation problems are essentially the improper formation of speech sounds by the articulatory mechanism—the teeth, tongue, lips, and hard and soft palates. Sometimes the problem is substitution of sounds. The cartoon character Elmer Fudd substitutes *w* for *r*—"I'll twap that awnwy wabbit!" Another example is Tweety Bird's classic line, "I tawt I taw a puddy tat!" Some substitution is due to different cultural backgrounds. In speaking English, people of German background may substitute *v* for *w* ("I vant it"); a native-born Japanese may mix-up *r* and *l* ("flied rice" for "fried rice"). Some people on the East Coast substitute *er* for the final *uh*, as in "Ameriker" or "Afriker." And, of course, we are aware of substitutions in a Southern accent, where "farmer" becomes "fahmuh" and "oil" becomes "awl." But audiences are not necessarily distracted by articulation errors that stem from cultural differences. The problem instead is in improper articulation that is not tied to language or culture, errors that stand out from the rest of a speaker's generally correct speech.

A common substitution is the lisp, using *th* for *s*. American culture has regrettably come to associate a lisp in an adult male with effeminacy and in a female with childishness. It is almost always distracting.

Another articulation problem is distortion. Some speakers simply do not enunciate carefully enough, and sounds become slurred and partially omitted. Others are hampered by organic problems, as in the case of a person with a cleft palate. Still others have dental devices like bridges or orthodontic retainers that impede clear articulation. Whatever the cause, distorted or mumbled speech may call attention to itself, thus distracting the audience from the speaker's message.

## Language

Language is a symbol system used for communication. *Language disorders* is a broad term referring to limited ability to use this symbol system in oral communication. Common language problems faced by public communicators are errors in *vocabulary*, *pronunciation*, and *grammar*. A speaker may distract or confuse an audience if his natural speaking style includes, *from the audience's point of view*, an improper use of language. The key factor is the audience perspective. Some usage is not improper, though the listeners may think it is. For example, for many years speakers who used so-called Black English were considered "substandard" in their use of language. They pronounced words differently, appeared to err in grammar and syntax, and used a vocabulary that was unfamiliar or confusing to non-black audiences. Black English is a legitimate and systematic variation from the general American dialect, yet even today some black speakers have difficulty gaining acceptance from audiences due to their language usage.

Many language problems are linked not to culture but to individual characteristics. Educational background may limit language development. The home, school, and community environments of children sometimes preclude varied and accurate language learning. Problems may be caused by emotional or neurological deficits during childhood. Sensory deprivation like a hearing loss also causes language deficiencies. Anyone who has observed language training for deaf children knows what an enormously handicapping problem deafness can be. Fortunately, most public speakers are not bothered by serious language handicaps, but people who make errors in normal conversation are likely to transfer those flaws to the public arena.

*Vocabulary* limitations—continuous use of the same descriptive terms throughout a speech—can adversely affect the receivers. For example, a contractor was presenting a proposal to the county commission for a new subdivision. In making his case, he noted that the sewage capacity was "good," the architectural style of the homes was "real pretty" and "real nice," fire and police protection were "real good," access roads were in "real good condition," and the area schools were "real good" and had "plenty of room." The contractor's limited vocabulary resulted in many probing questions from the skeptical commissioners. Another common language problem is the repeated, tedious, and often incorrect use of "like," or such phrases as "I mean" or "ya know," usually as substitutes for more varied descriptive language.

*Pronunciation* errors are deviations from a culturally accepted or dictionary prescription of the sounds of words. Standards of pronunciation are based on conversational utterance of educated or literate speakers. It varies with region, of course, and is subject to gradual change. Most audiences have a general awareness and expectation of "good" pronunciation. Glaring errors distract us from a speaker's generally fluent delivery, especially when committed by experienced communicators like newscasters, politicians, the clergy, or teachers.

Pronunciation errors include the use of the *wrong sound* (*theatre*: THE-uh-ter, not the-AY-ter); an *omitted sound* (*police*: po-LEECE, not PLEECE); an *extra sound* (*drowned*: DROWND, not DROWN-ded); or a *misplaced accent* (*cement*: suh-MENT, not SEE-ment). Pronunciation flaws often involve proper names. For example:

| | |
|---|---|
| Des Moines | Duh MOIN, not Dez MOINZ |
| Illinois | Ill-uh-NOY, not Ill-uh-NOYZ |
| Oregon | OR-ih-gun, not OR-ee-GON |
| Arab | AIR-ub, not AY-rab |

Surnames pose occasional problems for English-speaking people, especially if those names are non-European. But common English words are also frequently mispronounced. In the following list are some familiar examples:

| | |
|---|---|
| genuine | JEN-yu-wun, not JEN-yu-wine |
| chassis | CHASS-ee, not CHASS-iss |
| rapport | ruh-PORE, not ra-PORT |
| subtle | SUH-tul, not SUB-tul |
| err | UR, not AIR |
| toward | TORD, not tuh-WARD |
| nuclear | NEW-klee-ur, not NEWK-yuh-lur |
| realtor | REEL-tur, not RE-luh-tur |
| adult | uh-DULT, not ADD-ult |
| larynx | LAIR-inks, not LAR-nix |
| cavalry | CAV-ul-ree, not CAL-vuh-ree |
| jewelry | JEW-ul-ree, not JEW-ler-ee |
| candidate | CAN-duh-date, not CAN-uh-date |
| library | LI-bruh-ree, not LI-bair-ee |

| picture | PICK-chur, not PIH-chur |
| relevant | RELL-uh-vant, not REV-uh-lunt |

A public communicator who reads or quotes from manuscript should try to anticipate pronunciation errors and even write the difficult words phonetically so that they will not cause a glaring distraction.

*Grammar* can be broadly defined as the choice, forms, and placement of words in a sentence. Fortunately, most speakers exhibit reasonably correct grammar in normal speech. But occasionally speech habits or colloquialisms divert audience attention from the message. The double negative is common, as in "I won't never do it." "This here" and "them there" are substandard. So are improper verb forms ("I've been woken up" or "I drunk it all down"). Hundreds of examples of such grammatical errors can be found in any basic composition text. In general, when we consider a sentence like "My daddy he done it real good" (rather than "My daddy did it well"), we can understand why some ungrammatical speakers have difficulty. People sometimes equate poor grammar with low intelligence or poor ideas or other negative qualities. The irrepressible Dizzy Dean never suffered because of poor grammar ("He slud into second base but got throwed out anyways"), and some speakers purposely use an uneducated language style as a ploy to emphasize colloquialism or to win favor of a specific audience. But for most of us, failure to detect and remedy common grammatical errors will usually be a serious handicap in many different communication situations.

## Voice

The human voice consists of three primary variables: *pitch*, or the vibration frequencies that determine the highs and lows; *loudness*, the force or volume of the sound; and *quality*, or overall characteristics of the vibration and resonance of the sound waves. Usually the conversational style naturally integrates these three variables with little conscious effort, but voice problems can become public speaking problems for some people.

The *pitch* of some male speakers' voices is too high, and some females too low, for audience expectations, suggesting effeminacy in men and masculinity in women. Both sexes can develop a *monotone* delivery, an absence of regular pitch variation or inflection. The monotone is especially common among speakers who choose the manuscript delivery strategy. Embarrassing breaks in pitch may affect adolescent boys whose voices are changing. Older speakers suffering a gradual hearing loss may have trouble monitoring and controlling the pitch levels.

*Loudness* can be a problem for the public speaker, especially some women, who must strain or shout to be heard in a large room. While such speakers may be advised, "Project your voice outward," the fact is that for many low-volume voices an attempt to increase loudness could seriously strain or damage the vocal mechanism. We notice, for example, how a person who must speak loudly for extended periods (like a chairperson at a political convention) often experiences hoarseness or loss of voice. What has happened is that the vocal cords have become aggravated and swollen from the continued high volume, and will not vibrate normally. A person with a low-volume voice should use an efficient loudspeaker system for any speech to a large audience. Some speakers try to speak too loudly, perhaps due to habit or to personality factors, sometimes because of a hearing loss, and sometimes because our culture has perpetuated the notion that vocal intensity indicates a dynamic, fluent, forceful speaker. Also, many speakers develop a monotone, with no variation between loud and soft.

*Vocal quality* is much more difficult to define and identify than pitch or loudness. We often use vague adjectives like *gravelly*, *strident*, *hoarse*, *piercing*, *mellow*, or *harsh* to describe vocal quality. *Hypernasality*, a more precise term, refers to the occasional problem in which too many of the resonating sound waves pass through the nasal cavities instead of through the oral passages. In the English language, only the *m*, *n*, and *ng* sounds are formed with air passing through the nose. When other sounds, especially vowels, are uttered with most of the air going through the nasal passages, a speaker is hypernasal, and the vocal quality is unpleasant. In contrast, *hyponasality* (also called *denasality*) results when the air that should be resonating in the nasal passage passes through and resonates in the mouth instead. We experience this problem when we have a severe cold, as do a few people who have permanent sinus or bone-structure problems that can only be corrected by surgery. The reader can experience denasality simply by holding the nose and saying "Spending money is nice." The *m*, *n*, and *ng* sounds become more like *b*, *d*, and *k*, and the sentence becomes "Spedik buddy is dice."

A *hoarse*, *gravelly*, or *raspy* voice may be caused by swollen vocal cords or mucus on the vibrating mechanism. We notice how distracting a speaker can be when he sounds as if he needs to clear his throat; audiences squirm helplessly, totally unaware of the message and preoccupied with the unpleasant vocal quality. Still another problem is *breathiness*, in which too much air escapes through the vocal cords, giving the voice a whispery quality. Although the Hollywood starlet may consider breathiness sexy, for the public speaker—especially one using a loudspeaker or recording equipment—this vocal flaw is highly detrimental.

Many voice problems can be corrected. Since they may be the result of physiological and psychological problems, a speech pathologist is probably the best source for advice and therapy. Speakers should become aware of their vocal characteristics, and one way is to listen to a tape recording of one's delivery. At first it may be an unpleasant experience. "That doesn't sound like me" or "That's terrible" are common responses. (Actually, the way we hear our own voice is determined not only by sound waves through the air but also by bone conduction, the sound vibration throughout the skull. The tape recorder "hears" our voice the way other people do, through air conduction only. Thus the playback is a fairly accurate indicator of the way other people hear us.) Listening to the tape and getting feedback from others can either confirm effective vocal traits or identify distracting problems.

## Rhythm

Every language has an oral dimension called *rhythm*—the speed of utterance, and recurring patterns and intervals between speech sounds. In learning a second language, we usually develop vocabulary and grammatical competence before we gain rhythmic competence. Hence, it is usually easy to tell that a person is just learning our language simply by noting the different rhythm patterns.

Delivery speed and intervals between sounds develop naturally in most children, and these patterns continue through adulthood. Our culture ascribes meaning to rhythmic variation, and it becomes an important component in the total process of oral communication. Because rhythm is both natural and communicatively meaningful, we have earlier advocated a conversational public speaking style. The problem is that too many speakers become inhibited, overly formal, or frightened in front of an audience and have trouble maintaining the conversational style. Rhythmic patterns become awkward and hard to listen to, and the natural process of vocal inflection is altered.

One rhythm problem is a delivery that is *too rapid*. Though some people speak rapidly in normal conversation, the speed may increase in the public situation. The cause may simply be anxiety, a desire to make the unpleasant speech situation as brief as possible. Another cause is the tendency to try to cover more information than can be presented in a limited time. We have all heard the rapid-fire disc jockey reading a commercial; presumably the sponsors want to say as much as they possibly can in a thirty- to sixty-second time slot. We have heard professors who, anticipating the bell, rush through the last portions of a lecture. There is evidence that increasing words per minute cuts down the time available to comprehend each verbal symbol and, beyond a certain speed, leads to a decrease in understanding (Foulke, 1968; Sticht and Glasnapp, 1972).

The obvious corollary of a rapid delivery is one that is *too slow* — that is, the regular intervals between words and phrases is too long. Even at the normal English speech speed of about 100 to 125 words per minute, the audience can think much more quickly, somewhere between 400 and 500 words per minute (thought speed). This means that listeners can anticipate what might come next and even think about other unrelated ideas. When the speaker's delivery sinks below normal rates, the audience may become nervous and impatient, anticipating words that are too slow in coming. Or the audience will discover that it can attend to other things and still listen enough to understand the message. The most important flaw of a too-slow rhythm is that it more closely resembles a monotone style, as the longer pauses between each sound make the pattern of naturally varied inflection more difficult to hear.

A third rhythm problem is the *unnatural pause*. Speakers who read from manuscript too often pause at the ends of printed lines, after all punctuation marks, or after a predictable grouping of five or six words. An example of unnatural pauses is the novice actor trying to read Shakespeare. Although the great playwright utilized a poetic form called *iambic pentameter* (ten-syllable lines with a two-syllable rhythm pattern), he did not intend the lines to be read in predictable one-line patterns like those of a children's poem. If our novice actor pauses at the end of each line rather than at the end of a complete thought unit, the meaning may be lost. Another example might be an inexperienced broadcaster who has not yet learned to read conversationally; his awkward rhythm patterns are distracting. In sum, the pause is a meaningful rhythm characteristic that we use every day without thinking. But when poorly timed or omitted, it can retard an otherwise effective delivery.

A final rhythm problem is especially serious—*stuttering*. Though stuttering is a complicated disorder and difficult to define, for our purposes we can simply think of it as an obvious and distracting interruption in the flow of speech, one that is likely to recur. It can include repetitions of single sounds or "blocking" on particular syllables or words (inability to utter the sound at all). Severe stuttering may be accompanied by facial distortions or other unnatural bodily movement. Most stutterers are well aware of their speech problem, and many tend to avoid public communication situations. Those who do speak publicly have learned to manage their stuttering. While severe stuttering is rare, *all normal speakers have some occasion to repeat or hesitate on speech sounds*. When these situations arise, the speaker should not preoccupy himself with the problem. Since it occurs in normal conversation, there is no reason to try to eliminate it from public speaking. As a speaker gains experience, he will learn to disregard occasional stutters and focus on his message.

## Suggestions for Improvement

We have urged beginning speakers to utilize a conversational vocal style. However, if that natural delivery contains audibility factors that impede a speaker's effectiveness, some conscious changes may be necessary. The following suggestions may help.

1. *Use the preceding analysis of articulation, language, voice, and rhythm as a checklist for analyzing your own audible style.*

2. *Avoid overreacting to minor flaws* that are a part of your normal conversational delivery. Audiences do not try to listen for errors; they tend to listen for what they think is the speaker's intended content. Many audibility factors are barely noticeable and do not detract from the speaker's delivery.

3. *Listen to a tape recording of your own voice;* it will be a reasonably accurate representation of how receivers hear you. Become better acquainted with your vocal strengths and weaknesses.

4. *Dialects are legitimate characteristics* of ethnic and geographical groups. If you speak a different English dialect than your listeners, or if English is a second language and you have a "foreign accent," it may not be wise—or necessary—to attempt any changes. In many situations, audiences will quickly adapt their listening to a unique vocal style. However, try to assess the requirements of your chosen career or of particular speech events to decide whether your dialect may cause problems. Speech professionals can help you change dialectal patterns if you think it is necessary.

## VISUAL FACTORS

What the audience sees in a speech presentation is another nonverbal dimension of public communication. Receivers notice the speaker's physical features and clothing and the speaker's physical behavior. Both factors combine to affect the meanings that an audience creates.

A speaker's dress and grooming have sometimes been labeled "stage presence." That term is inappropriate, however, because it implies a *performance orientation* with both costume and role for playing a part in a theatrical production. We believe that such a performance model is now obsolete. Today we tend to think of physical appearance more as an *identifying link* between speaker and listener. Instead of emphasizing speaker-audience differences and separation with special dress and grooming, a speaker needs to narrow the sender–receiver gap by assuring that these nonverbal factors are not a distraction, but rather enhance audience receptivity.

A primary requirement of a speaker's clothing is that it be comfortable. Some high-heeled shoes, tight-fitting pants or dresses, and heavy, hot fabrics may distract the speaker through physical discomfort. Dress and grooming habits can also affect a speaker *psychologically*. A new hairstyle, new glasses, or trendy clothing might be a source of apprehension if the speaker fears audience disapproval, or they could be a source of confidence.

Even more important than speaker comfort is message effectiveness; listeners may be easily distracted by a speaker's physical characteristics. But what is *appropriate* physical appearance? It can be argued that suitable dress and grooming criteria can only be determined by the individual, in this case the speaker. Some people use a self-reference criterion, applying purely personal needs and tastes as to what is acceptable appearance, with little regard for audience expectations. A speaker who adopts the "do-your-own-thing" standard has every right to do so, but he should not be surprised at negative responses from some audiences.

## Accommodation to Receiver Expectations

As first suggested in Chapter 1, a more meaningful point of view is *accommodation*: a move away from a speaker-centered orientation ("I'll do what makes me happy") toward a more audience-centered basis for communication behavior. For example, if a speaker is more comfortable in jeans and sweater in a relatively formal situation like an awards banquet or church service, the meaning that the audience interprets may be: "I do not consider you or this occasion to be important enough for me to make any special accommodations." If the message the speaker wishes to communicate is truly important, if receiver understanding and acceptance are sincerely sought, the speaker must be willing to adjust to audience standards of acceptable physical appearance. Accommodation means neither deception nor abandonment of personal convictions. Rather, it is simply the willingness to make minor adjustments in normal preferences so as to increase the chances of communicative effectiveness. By considering the relative formality of the speaking occasion and dressing appropriately, or by avoiding clothing or accessories that are distracting, the speaker can enhance speech effectiveness with attention to appearance.

An audience is also acutely aware of the way a speaker moves; eye movement, facial expression, gestures, and postural changes are all important. We often hear students criticizing a professor's lecture style in terms of bothersome physical mannerisms. "He's always pacing back and forth; it drives me crazy!" "She keeps tapping her pencil on the podium." "He buries his head in his notes and never comes up for air." "Those glasses—on and off, on and off!" Certainly professors are not unique. Many public communicators have physical behaviors that may become distracting. While listeners do not necessarily focus on these behaviors and may receive the intended message accurately regardless of the speaker's physical actions, one should never assume that such movement is irrelevant to the communication process.

## Eye Contact

What strategies should the public communicator use? In terms of eye movement, we suggest that the speaker gain as much freedom from notes as possible and try to make direct person-to-person *eye contact* with many people in the audience. One outmoded suggestion for eye contact is: "Look just above the last row in the audience, perhaps at the back wall." We categorically reject this suggestion. To utilize the conversational delivery style, a speaker needs to establish the kind of eye contact that is appropriate for face-to-face dialog.

The importance of eye contact can be demonstrated with a simple experiment. In a casual conversation with a friend, try closing your eyes while that person is talking. Your friend will probably stop abruptly and ask what's wrong. You then reply, with eyes still closed, "Nothing is wrong. I'm hearing you. Go right ahead with what you were saying." Your friend will probably be unwilling to continue the conversation until you respond to his message with "normal" eye contact. This little test suggests the effect of eye contact on our willingness to communicate, our wish that the public speaker acknowledge our presence and importance with direct eye contact.

A byproduct of good eye contact is an increased ability to hold attention. If a speaker looks directly at a person in the audience, the eye contact has a "grabbing" effect. (Most teachers know that the easiest way to get a daydreaming student to listen to the lecture is to look directly at him.) Conversely, looking away from a person is a kind of psychological "release" that permits the listener to attend to other things. While eye contact cannot guarantee complete audience attention, especially if the message is inherently uninteresting, it is an important factor in audience receptivity.

For several reasons, speakers may avoid regular eye contact with the audience. One common explanation is that they simply have not practiced it in a public communication context. Perhaps they have relied too heavily on a manuscript. Or, a speaker may simply be frightened. The audience may seem threatening, and the speaker learns that if he never looks up at them he will not receive negative nonverbal feedback. Sometimes a speaker will maintain eye contact with only those people who appear to be giving positive responses to his message, avoiding those who appear passive or hostile. Sometimes the speaker becomes so engrossed in his speech content that he simply forgets that the audience is out there. Whatever the reason, eye contact in general American culture is among the most potent communication tools, but is also the most common problem with a speaker's delivery.

## Facial Expression

Another visual factor is *facial expression*. The facial muscles are capable of enormous variation in movement and positioning. As we know from actors and pantomimists, facial communication can not only be highly meaningful (certainly the focal point of bodily posture), but can also be developed through practice. In other words, facial expression can be a *conscious* strategy for the communication of feelings and ideas.

The problem with *planned* facial expression is that it too often appears contrived and insincere. The painted smiles in automobile showrooms, beauty contests, and political campaigns are good examples. But the opposite extreme—passive, expressionless facial features—is equally unacceptable. When the speaker is discussing happy themes, the face should look happy. Grave or unhappy messages should be accompanied by more serious looks of concern and even sadness.

How can the speaker make facial expression congruent with the mood of the message without appearing artificial? If the speaker uses the conversational speaking style, facial expression is likely to develop naturally. If the speaker selects topics of real personal concern, enthusiasm, or commitment, natural expression will be more likely than if the speaker selects a topic of only casual interest. Viewing one's speech on videotape is a good way of becoming aware of one's nonverbal facial behavior in a public situation. A speaker may discover, "I'm really coming across too seriously; I'm too grim. Next time I'll try to smile more." Or "I really do look bored. No wonder the audience seemed restless. I'll try to show my enthusiasm." In general, however, we caution against becoming too concerned with facial strategy. The normal expressions that people exhibit in everyday conversation will develop, in most cases, as a speaker grows increasingly familiar with the public speaking situation.

## Gesture and Posture

Another factor in the speaker's movement is *gesture and bodily action*. Though facial expression can be included in this category, for the moment we shall consider primarily hand and arm movements, bodily stances or postures (including postural changes), and footwork, or shifting positions in front of the audience. Obviously, the number of different kinds of gestures and combinations of movement are practically infinite; the speaker has an enormous range of options. And almost any movement, positioning, or posturing carries symbolic content or meaning when the audience perceives it.

To what extent should gestures be a conscious strategy, carefully planned to help achieve specific objectives? One school of thought with a long history in speech education has held that bodily action should be as carefully prepared as verbal content. Students trained in this tradition often planned animation for a public speech as carefully as they would have rehearsed for a starring role in a dramatic production. Some teachers developed elaborate notational systems and training

© Howard Harrison 1968

methods to help students practice specific movements in appropriate
places. The practice of cultivating stagelike gestural emphasis continues to some extent. Students in speech contests sometimes display
movement that appears precise and studied. We once observed a "communication consultant" in an executive-training program attempting
to teach business executives how to use "strong, authoritative" gestures at particular times during their public presentations. The result
was almost comical, since the gestures did not fit naturally with the
specific ideas or the speakers' personal styles.

    Most contemporary public speakers avoid planned gestures and
facial expression for several good reasons. As with other nonverbal
factors, a planned movement may appear unnatural and thus distract
or confuse the audience. A planned gesture may be mis-timed, appear-

ing out of proper sequence with the idea being expressed. It may be overdone or appear stiff or awkward. Like facial expression, the planned gesture may also lack congruence with the spoken idea. Natural gestures accompanying normal conversation, in contrast, are nearly always properly timed and generally appropriate to the idea being expressed. The reader may recall a heated argument, a conversation at a party, a child describing a new toy, or a salesperson closing a deal—all proofs that bodily action need not be planned to be meaningful. We all gesture fluently every day, and usually without conscious thought.

A careful gesture strategy may be appropriate for a manuscript or memorized delivery mode, the speaking style we discourage as impractical for most speaking situations. In the extemporaneous mode, on the other hand, a speaker lets the specific wording develop naturally as she moves through her outline. Planning gestures to enhance particular phrasing is thus futile.

Some speakers discover that, despite their interest in natural, spontaneous bodily action, their movement in public communication is infrequent, inhibited, and awkward. They make comments like "I don't know what to do with my hands," or "I can't find a comfortable posture," or "I just freeze up and no movement seems appropriate." These comments are typical of beginning speakers. We have found that with increased exposure to the speaking situation, a person tends to become more involved in the message and less preoccupied with physical behavior. The result is usually the gradual development of natural gestures.

Bodily action may require serious attention, however, if particular mannerisms become distracting. A common problem is random pacing back and forth, often as a subconscious release of tension. Another problem is repetitious hand and arm gestures. A typical movement is the "apple-picker gesture," in which the speaker moves his hand out and back, out and back (like a person picking apples), almost as if he were reaching out to grab the words that come next in the speech. Another overused gesture is a perpetual chopping motion with one hand. A postural distraction is the constant shifting of weight from one foot to the other, with possible shuffling of whichever foot is not supporting body weight. And of course, facial mannerisms like a nervous tic can also bother the listeners.

## Suggestions for Improvement

A conversational delivery style is visual as well as audible. Developing fluent, natural animation is often merely a function of getting used to the public speaking situation. The suggestions below summarize our advice for improving visual factors.

**1.** *Use the preceding discussion of eye contact, facial expression, and gestures or bodily action as a checklist for self-analysis.*

**2.** *Remember the receiver-centered perspective.* There is no inherently "good or bad" visual style, except so far as receivers become distracted or take unintended or unproductive meanings from a speaker's behavior. Therefore, get feedback from those receivers, especially other students and instructors. Ask them to discuss any negative meanings they took from your animation, noting especially any distracting mannerisms. When viewing a videotape replay of your speeches, ask another person to sit in and provide a receiver's perspective.

**3.** *Avoid planning or rehearsing specific gestures at specific points in the speech.* However, in rehearsing your extemporaneous presentations, experiment with different types of animation that seem to be typical of what you would use in normal conversation. In practicing speeches, get used to moving while you talk. Use facial expressions, postural changes, gestures so that these movements can become a natural part of your eventual presentations.

## SUMMARY

Regardless of how carefully the speech content has been prepared, it is meaningless until delivered to an audience. The speaker must first select a presentational form—manuscript, memory, impromptu, or extemporaneous. This last form is usually best, because of ease of preparation, adaptability, and potential for combining the best elements of the other three delivery styles.

In terms of audibility factors, the natural or conversational style should be used for most speeches. However, when using this style a speaker may distract through articulation, language, voice, or rhythm habits that may require some conscious attempts at improvement. Visually, speakers should be willing to accommodate audience expectations concerning physical appearance, and should attempt to utilize natural movement. Comfortable and appropriate clothing, eye contact, facial expression, gestures, bodily action, and posture are all factors that can affect audience receptivity. While the speaker should become aware of distracting mannerisms, the main speech goal should be to adapt one's natural physical characteristics to the public communication event.

## QUESTIONS FOR STUDY

1. For the following situations, what might be effective delivery forms? Why?
   Religious service
   Political convention
   Classroom presentation
   Business conference
   Orientation for new employees
   Televised speech

2. Despite the usefulness of the extemporaneous form, in what situations might other delivery strategies be useful?

3. What is the difference between articulation and pronunciation? What are some examples of each?

4. What are some of the implications of a receiver-centered (as opposed to speaker-centered) approach to speech delivery?

5. What are some common traits that you have observed in other students' visual style—their eye contact, facial expression, or gestures and bodily movement—that impeded their speech effectiveness?

# chapter 6

# AUDIOVISUAL AIDS

**LEARNING OBJECTIVES**

After reading this chapter, you should be able to:
1. List some reasons why audiovisual aids can improve public speaking outcomes.
2. **Describe several different types of audiovisual aids that can be used in speech projects in the basic course, giving advantages and disadvantages of each type.**
3. Apply the suggestions for preparing and using audiovisual aids in the classroom setting.
4. Identify special problems in presenting demonstrations.

# 6

A state governor was finalizing plans to run for reelection. He and his staff decided to invite three advertising agencies to make presentations on the kinds of promotional materials and messages they could provide. The campaign would be large and expensive, and the advertising contract would be very lucrative. Hence, the agencies gave high priority to the preparation of their proposals. Each selected its best speaker to make the presentation to the governor's staff.

Two of the agencies relied essentially on their speakers' persuasive skill and on extensive written handouts that identified in depth the kinds of campaign strategies that would be used. The documents also contained statistical analyses of costs, voting behavior, demographic characteristics, and results of public-opinion polls. Overall, the presentations were thorough, professional, and persuasive.

The third agency also prepared detailed written materials and assigned an excellent speaker to make the presentation. However, their strategy was to let the potential client *see and hear* samples of the kind of campaign they would direct. Their graphics department had prepared a variety of sample posters, bumper stickers, and billboard mockups, including possible campaign themes and slogans. Borrowing old videotapes of the governor from a local television station, the agency had prepared thirty- and sixty-second commercials complete with background narration. They also had a videotape of "testimonials," excerpts from taped interviews of people on the street who were asked to comment on the governor's record. Finally, a series of black-and-white photographs of the governor during his first four-year term—shaking hands with people, speaking to a group of farmers, walking with National Guardsmen to inspect flood damage, hiking with his wife and children—were displayed to demonstrate possible television and newspaper images. As the speaker finished her presentation, she handed out the written materials and briefly reviewed what the governor's staff would find in them, thus avoiding a tedious repetition of what they could read on their own. One week later, this third agency signed a contract to handle the advertising in the governor's reelection campaign.

Perhaps the outcome of this story is not surprising. Isn't it common sense that permitting the audience to visualize the campaign would enhance the impact of the presentation? So why didn't the other two

agencies use this approach? Perhaps because for them it was too expensive and too risky. It was expensive in terms of time, money, and energy. The third agency had to obtain many more materials and allocate significantly more of its staff to the project. And the speaker for that agency had to prepare her message more carefully, planning the display of materials and the use of the videotape deck and monitor. The approach was also risky. More technical problems could have developed during the presentation. Even more crucial was the chance that the staff might not have approved of the sample materials the speaker presented. She was more explicit in demonstrating how the campaign would actually look, unlike the other two speakers who merely described possible strategies. This vagueness might have been less likely to alienate the listeners, and thus less risky.

## USES AND TYPES

In this chapter we shall discuss the use of audiovisual materials in presentational speaking and explore some of the problems and potential of the various types. We suspect that speakers sometimes avoid these materials because of the effort, expense, and risk involved. It is simply much easier to give a speech without having to trouble oneself with anything except the prepared verbal message. But if one approaches public speaking from the receiver-centered perspective, the use of audiovisual aids becomes more important as a means of assuring that receivers will understand and appreciate the intended message.

### Why Use Audiovisual Aids?

If a speaker must usually devote more effort to message preparation when audiovisual aids are used, what are the benefits? Why should we go to the trouble, when good speakers for over two thousand years have tended to rely on the verbal message to achieve their communication goals? There are several reasons.

1. *Some topics, especially those involving physical objects or processes, simply cannot be explained well—shared meaning is less likely to*

© Michael Alexander 1970

*occur—with the oral message alone.* For instance, a sales agent explaining a new product to a group of potential buyers would of course want to display it during the presentation. Or an instructor discussing a new technique of cardiopulmonary resuscitation (CPR) would probably demonstrate that procedure as well as explain it. Not to use visual aids with some topics would increase the speaker's burden; hence, the extra effort to prepare these aids may frequently save energy in delivering the verbal message. The speech can be briefer and less precise because the visual support clarifies the explanation.

2. *Multi-channel communication is usually more effective than single-channel in promoting the perception, comprehension, and retention of*

*messages*. That is, we can receive, understand, and remember speeches better if they are reinforced by other means in addition to the speaker's oral delivery. We use multimedia communication to teach children, but sometimes assume that adults cannot benefit as much from the same methods. The fact is that if receivers of any age can watch a demonstration, see pictures, hear a tape recording, view a film, feel an object, or even *do* an activity along with the speaker, the presentation will have both more immediate and long-term impact.

**3.** *Audiovisual aids tend to increase receivers' attention spans.* The longer the verbal message, the greater the likelihood that attention will decrease. Audiovisual materials break up the tedium of lengthy speeches with new and interesting message forms. The more abstract the speech ideas, the more a concrete demonstration, object, picture, or recording can maintain acceptable levels of attention.

**4.** *The use of audiovisual materials can enhance our self-confidence as speakers.* We know that we do not have to depend solely on our own spoken words, on our verbal fluency, but that we have help—material that the audience can see or hear that will help us be effective. This does not suggest that speakers should rely on these aids as a security blanket; rather, it simply means that an added benefit to some speakers is that they will not be as bothered by anxiety or lack of confidence.

**5.** *The use of audiovisual aids often facilitates favorable audience response.* In addition to the speaker's intended message, the receivers may assign additional meanings to the presentation. For example, the receivers' conscious or unconscious responses might be:

> *"This speaker has devoted some real preparation time and effort to this presentation; I appreciate that."*

> *"This speaker is certainly creative."*

> *"This speaker is using visual aids because he wants me to understand; he is adapting to me, rather than forcing me to adapt to him."*

> *"That was an interesting presentation; she certainly is a good speaker."*

*"Taking the time and effort to prepare the visual aids shows a real commitment to the topic; the speaker obviously cares about it and believes in what she is saying."*

*"The audiovisual aids support the speaker's ideas; they make him more believable."*

**6.** *We are part of an increasingly visual culture.* People under 30 are members of the world's first television generation, and people of all ages have come to rely on *seeing* messages in addition to simply reading or hearing them. We have perhaps become more passive as receivers in communication events. Reading and listening are inherently active processes, as the receiver uses mental or intellectual energy to attend to and comprehend a writer's or speaker's verbal message. But visual messages like films, television, pictorial displays, or physical demonstrations tend to pull us along. While we may decide to be active perceivers, these visual media do not always require that active commitment. Thus we have gotten used to being more like passive receptacles for information input—as receivers, whether in a classroom, a theatre, or in front of a television set, we seem to be saying "Okay, I'm waiting; fill me up." The receiver-centered public speaker should recognize the reality of a visual culture and be willing to adapt to it. The visual dimension of a speech presentation may be the key factor in achieving one's communication goals.

**7.** *Audiovisual materials have become an increasingly essential part of presentational speaking* in business, the professions, and public affairs. Political campaigns, interoffice communication, training programs, sales presentations, classroom instruction, and public service speeches are communication events in which audiences are increasingly *coming to expect* multimedia support for the verbal message. In addition to the obvious practical benefits, these aids are also used because they conform to business and professional norms. The speaker is "playing the game" by the rules that receivers accept.

To some people, this is a flimsy rationale for using multimedia materials. Indeed, many professors, ministers, public officials, and businesspeople still hold rigidly to the traditional public speaking model and resist more varied methods of presentation. But while not

all speeches need audiovisual aids, we suspect that successful communicators will use them more often. They will become a normal component of speech preparation and delivery which, if not included, will limit effectiveness and even prompt negative responses from the listeners.

## Types of Audiovisual Aids

In this section we will discuss various types of audiovisual aids and the advantages and disadvantages of each.

*The human body.* When a speaker personally exhibits a particular behavior (like swinging a tennis racquet, performing first aid techniques, or operating a machine), the body becomes a visual aid that provides information above and beyond normal animation. Along with personal demonstration, the speaker may select another person for assistance, as with a speech on self-defense maneuvers, lifesaving techniques, or current fashions. The main advantages of the body as visual aid are animation, adaptability, and realism. We can move around to appropriate positions and postures, change behavior to meet unexpected situations, and actually show how a particular activity should be performed.

One problem with the speaker's own demonstration is that there may be difficulty continuing effective speech delivery. For instance, in demonstrating an activity that requires strenuous physical effort (a common problem for instructors in athletics or the military), the effort may cause the speaker to become winded, and delivery will thus be strained and unnatural. Another problem is greater difficulty in using notes during the physical demonstration. On the other hand, if the visual aid is another person, the subject may perform awkwardly or with embarrassment, thus distracting the audience from the intended message.

*Physical objects.* Audiences appreciate seeing appropriate physical objects that have the advantages of realism and exactness. Sports equipment, arts and crafts products, and various mechanical devices are common visual aids in this category.

Objects are sometimes too big or too small to be practical for a particular speech environment (New Types of Single-Engine Aircraft, Techniques of Diamond Cutting). With some objects we are unable to show the inner workings (The Catalytic Converter in United States Automobiles). Some objects are unavailable for display (Primitive Artifacts), and others may have to be shown out of proper perspective or context because the larger objects of which they are a part cannot be exhibited (Radar Devices in United States Missiles). Nevertheless, the speaker will discover that objects, when appropriate, can attract attention and clarify a complicated verbal explanation. They are essential when the speech purpose is to develop audience skills in such activities as operating equipment or creating arts and crafts.

*Models.*  Models are replicas of the real thing. Their size can be varied to be practical (Aerodynamic Features of the SST, The DNA Molecule), and cutaway views in some models permit us to concentrate on important aspects. For example, medical instruction often utilizes plastic models of body parts, which can be further disassembled to show inner workings. Models can also prevent embarrassment, as with the life-size dummy used to demonstrate mouth-to-mouth resuscitation.

Unfortunately, appropriate models are often expensive and difficult to obtain. They are less than realistic, and precise dimensions and features are difficult to achieve. But for some types of instructional messages designed to train people for specific tasks, either real objects or their replicas are crucial.

*Electronic media.*  Except for the telegraph, the electronic media are Twentieth-Century phenomena. They now comprise a potent communication tool, and the public speaker today has many options for improving a presentation that the great speakers of the past never dreamed of.

Even a short speech of ten minutes or so can include dozens of *slides* or *filmstrip frames*. Films and slides are readily obtainable commercially, and many organizations create slide programs for their own use. The speaker may arrange slides in proper sequence well in advance, and move through the program at desired speed. Filmstrip and slide projectors, many with remote control, are lightweight, reliable, inexpensive, and adaptable to most speech settings. No special screen is necessary; a clean bare wall will usually suffice.

The use of *tapes* is also widespread. Audio tape recorders have become popular in business and professional speaking; tapes are easily prepared, and the machine can be turned on and off throughout a presentation. For example, a speech pathologist instructing teachers on recognizing student speech problems described various disorders and then played back real examples from her therapy experiences.

A popular new instruction and sales device combines the slide projector with the tape recorder; a taped verbal message plays along with the slide sequence, and an electronic impulse on the tape activates the advance of each slide at the appropriate place in the narration. These portable machines usually include a self-contained viewing screen for small audiences.

Thousands of *films* are available for rental or purchase. Most colleges have film libraries, and many organizations produce their own films for in-house or public use. The sequence of introductory remarks, film, concluding remarks, and question-and-answer has become very popular. Moving picture projectors are a staple of instructional programs, and the common reel-to-reel movie projector now has a more convenient counterpart—the cartridge film projector.

*Opaque and overhead projectors* are also easily obtainable and simple to set up and operate. They are used to project book pages or single-page documents onto a large screen or wall. The opaque projector is bulkier, but can project and enlarge any image that is printed or drawn on regular paper; the overhead variety can only project from transparencies (clear plastic pages). However, these transparencies can now be easily developed for only a few cents per copy by using transparency paper in a photocopying machine. Thus, most public speakers can, with little trouble, prepare their own visual materials for opaque or overhead projectors.

For large audiences or outdoor speeches, *voice amplification systems* are essential audio aids. In addition to the common microphone, new devices include: a speaker's podium with self-contained microphone, amplifier, and loudspeakers; a hand held bullhorn powered by battery; and a wireless lavalier microphone that transmits to an amplifier and loudspeakers on an FM-radio frequency, providing the speaker with great freedom of movement while maintaining consistent volume and quality. Newer hotels, convention centers, lecture classrooms, legislative hearing rooms, courtrooms, and other public facilities have built-in voice amplification systems that are very efficient and reliable.

The most complex, expensive, and potentially exciting audiovisual supports for contemporary presentational speaking are *videotape systems*. They can be used by the speaker not only for presenting supporting information but also as a substitute for the speaker's live appearance before the receivers. For example, an instructor, executive, or politician can reach several separate audiences at once or tape a speech for later replay. Lightweight, portable color systems are now available in cassette or reel-to-reel. The "television generation" may find a speaker's use of videotaped information especially appealing and persuasive. And the combination of speaker and videotape replay provides a dual advantage: the strategic impact of carefully planned audiovisual materials, and the spontaneous adaptation of the speaker to audience responses.

Though electronic media offer many advantages, they can also pose significant problems, especially for the one-time-only speech. These are just a few of the possible disadvantages:

Poor quality of sound, especially on small tape recorders, movie projectors, TV monitors, or faulty PA systems.

Inadequate amplification for large rooms or audiences.

Inexperience in using sound systems—the speaker's vocal volume and varying distance from microphone causing inaudibility or sound distortion.

Loss of electric power.

Film or tape breakage during presentation.

Malfunction of equipment, especially burnt-out tubes, light bulbs, and fuses.

Accidental erasure of video or audio tapes.

Inadequate preparation of quality tapes, films, or transparencies, or use of commercially made materials that do not relate closely enough to the specific speech purpose.

Equipment that is prohibitively expensive to buy, rent, or transport.

Too much time required to set up and take down equipment.

Inexperience in operating equipment, like threading movie film.

Improper projection angle, causing a distorted image.

Too much room light to see projection clearly.

Most important, these aids sometimes minimize the personal appeal of the speaker, especially when the lights are dimmed, sound is loud, and most of the audience attention is diverted to the electronic message. Admittedly, some inexperienced speakers with high anxiety might argue that this is exactly what they want to happen!

Because speakers such as training officers, teachers, and sales representatives need to use these aids regularly, they often develop ways of systematizing their use and have experience in coping with potential problems. For the rest of us, the use of electronic media requires practice. But most public speakers will eventually have to learn to use them.

*Pictures and diagrams.*   Almost any audience likes to look at pictures. Photographs, paintings, and drawings can often improve a presentation. They are usually easy to obtain, or we can develop them especially for a particular speech. Obviously, topics involving particular places, people, or artistic themes rely heavily on pictorial content. Diagrams or drawings of actual objects can depict three-dimensional views and concentrate on important features.

Some pictures, like large color photographs or original paintings, can be too expensive or inaccessible for a one-time-only presentation. Some drawings and diagrams are too complicated with irrelevant information, or too small to be seen by a large audience. And some speakers may be unable to prepare these visual aids themselves, because of the artistry or time necessary for effective results.

*Graphs and charts.*   Graphs and charts illustrate statistical and conceptual relationships. The pie, line, and bar graphs summarize bulky statistical information in relatively simple form, and the statistical chart shows interrelationships (for example, the amount of rainfall according to year and location). Organization charts demonstrate very well the links between various subgroups.

The problem with a graph or chart is that the viewer must spend time getting oriented to what it is designed to show and how it should be read. For example, in discussing economic trends over the past few years, a speaker might first have to explain carefully the terms, symbols, and lines on the graph. From reading some textbooks, we know how long a process that can be! Furthermore, since the speaker usually utilizes only a portion of the data, the excess information in the chart or graph may become distracting.

*Maps.*   Maps are often indispensable, because they show dimensions, distances, terrain, contrasts, and geographical relationships. Speeches on the weather, international politics, travel, transportation, military activities, historical topics, and various business and government issues all demand the effective display of maps.

Appropriate maps are often hard to obtain and can be expensive. Printed maps are usually too small and almost always show unnecessary details that either confuse or distract, as with a common automobile road map. Hand-drawn maps are rarely precise or neat, though they can be constructed to the appropriate size and without irrelevant data.

*The chalkboard or easel.*   By far the most popular visual aid, the chalkboard is readily accessible in almost any public speaking environment, often in the form of a movable panel. The speaker can adapt the writing or drawing for the size of the audience, and ease of erasure permits spontaneous modifications.

This aid sounds ideal, doesn't it? We take quite the opposite, and probably controversial, point of view that *except for everyday, informal communication situations, the chalkboard as a visual aid should be avoided.* We believe that speakers commonly use the chalkboard as a substitute for better visual alternatives because they lack energy and

© Howard Harrison 1978

creativity. They lose audience contact while they are writing or drawing. The materials are rarely neat, precise, or artistic. Previous
erasures show as messy smudges, and the new writing is sometimes
not dark enough to be seen clearly. Glare from lights or a window may
restrict the view of part of the audience.

The availability of a chalkboard also tempts unplanned use on the
spur of the moment. Suppose the speaker senses some confusion in the
audience. Instead of simply elaborating verbally, he says, "Well, uh,
perhaps I can show you what I mean here on the board." He searches
for chalk, draws an image that is inaccurate and too small, hunts up an
eraser, tries again, and perhaps eventually writes or sketches something that may or may not clarify his point. The audience watches him
struggle and becomes impatient. The haphazard attempt to use a quick
visual medium has actually detracted from the speech. Again, we urge
that the chalkboard be used sparingly; there are better ways.

A possible improvement over the chalkboard for spontaneous
sketching or writing is the large tablet on an easel, with colored felt-

tip markers. This aid is portable and less messy. And the speaker can prepare information beforehand, flipping over the tablet pages at the appropriate points in the speech.

## PREPARATION

The effective use of visual aids requires careful planning and preparation of materials, always with an eye to the purpose and main ideas of the speech and the audience for which it is intended. The following suggestions will help the speaker achieve maximum effectiveness of the visual dimension of his speech.

Prepare visual aids *well in advance* of the speaking situation. Last-minute attempts to find appropriate pictures, draw charts, or arrange for demonstration equipment are not only hectic, but also reflect negatively on the speech. The audience can usually sense the lack of careful preparation. If the visual aid is another person, it is crucial to discuss his role with him beforehand so that he will know *precisely* what is expected of him. Spontaneous volunteers rarely do an optimal job in a demonstration, and may even sabotage (usually unintentionally) the speaker's objectives.

Make the visual aid and all its components *relevant* to the speech topic. Too often, speakers toss in extra materials as an afterthought simply because the aid is available, looks good, and "might as well be shown." We once attended a slide-illustrated lecture about a trip through Aztec ruins in Mexico. The speaker could not resist spending about five minutes showing slides of his wife and children on a trip to Disneyland!

Earlier we noted that a possible audience interpretation of fluent audiovisual aids is that the speaker is knowledgeable and worked hard on the presentation. While that is a desirable response, it should not encourage a speaker to use these aids solely to impress an audience. The main purpose is to assure clarity and interest. Therefore the speaker should screen the visual materials carefully: Are these devices really necessary? What do I hope to achieve that cannot be gained without them? Will I insult my audience's intelligence by using an aid for so simple an idea?

Make certain the visual aids are *simple and clear*. If a speaker must make a lengthy explanation about what the visual materials are supposed to illustrate, the materials are no longer an "aid" and burden the speaker with new speech content. Visual aids must be large enough to be seen, and dark or contrasting colors can help. A *series* of simple charts, graphs, or pictures may be more comprehensible than one large complicated one.

If the visual aids involve writing or drawing, be *neat and artistic*. Speakers in business or professional settings often have artists or printers prepare their visual aids, because they know that sloppiness can cause a transfer of negative attitudes to the speaker's objectives and ideas. In Chapter 1 we noted that the verbal and nonverbal processes are interrelated and inseparable. Thus the speaker with verbal fluency can be betrayed by the nonverbal impact of a pencil-drawn chart on a torn piece of notebook paper, a graph on smudged posterboard, messy writing on a blackboard, and even an object or model in disrepair.

The speaker should *practice* using the visual aids beforehand. This step in speech preparation is frequently overlooked. The speaker practices the verbal message orally and occasionally *thinks* to himself, "At this point I will pick up the object and show how it is used." But he doesn't actually *do* the demonstration ahead of time; he just *imagines* himself doing it. As a result, many speakers have been surprised by unexpected problems. Perhaps the color slides were not in order, or a device would not work properly, or an important detail had been omitted from a diagram, or the aids were bulky to hold, clumsy to manipulate, or difficult to set up. Practicing will not guarantee that unexpected problems will not arise, but it can significantly reduce their likelihood and improve speaker confidence. We especially encourage the speaker to rehearse *in the presence of a listener*, asking that person to interrupt whenever he cannot see or understand.

## PRESENTATION

No matter how well prepared, visual aids that are ineptly presented can be at best useless and at worst a distraction. The following suggestions will help optimize a speaker's use of visual aids during the presentation.

## Using Visual Aids

Make certain that visual aids, during use, remain in *clear and constant view of the entire audience*. Do not let your hands or body, the podium, or other visual aids obstruct the vision of particular audience groups. If the speech includes videotaped playback, more than one viewing monitor may be necessary for everyone to see without effort or strain. Receivers who cannot see well may lose interest or become resentful that the speaker does not appear concerned with their well-being. Except for a few well planned lecture or conference rooms, most speaking environments are *not* ideally suited for visual presentations. Hence the speaker may have to spend some time moving around with the visual aid so everyone has an opportunity to benefit from it. Some speakers nervously play with demonstrated objects, bouncing them around as the audience struggles to focus on them. As a rule, speakers should touch the visual aids only when absolutely necessary in the context of the speech.

The speaker should maintain *eye contact* with the audience, even though we may find it more comforting to look at the visual aids because, unlike the audience, these *things* we have prepared do not glare back at us, do not threaten us. But just as with touching the materials, we should look at them only when absolutely necessary— when we must see where to point or when we must manipulate them in some way. The receivers may decide whether they want to look at us or at the materials. Since eye contact has such potency for maintaining audience attention, we cannot abandon this crucial tool.

Use or display visual aids at the *proper psychological point* in the speech. The use of visual materials usually leads either to improved audience understanding and interest or distracts the audience from the speaker's message. If visual aids are in view before or after the speaker actually applies them, the speaker cannot simply say, "Don't pay any attention to that; I'll get to it in a minute." The audience *does* notice, and is thus prepared psychologically to think about it. For

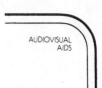

example, a park ranger was discussing poisonous snakes for a group of tourists. He had a cage with a live rattler moving around inside. The cage appeared to be open at the top so the snake could crawl out. As the audience squirmed nervously, the speaker tried to present five minutes of background information about snakes in general before he described the live one in the cage. He remained naively unaware that the audience hadn't heard a word he said!

Though it is sometimes impossible to hide the visual aids (such as an intricate blackboard drawing that must be done beforehand, a large object like a motorcycle, or a large animal), we should make every attempt to assure that materials are *visual* only when we desire it.

Pictures, objects, or printed materials that one or more audience members can look at while the speech is in progress can be used as *handouts*. Avoid handouts during the speech; most of the time they only distract the audience. If passed around, a single handout inevitably means that three or four people are not listening to the speaker at any particular moment; they are looking at the handout or are involved in passing or receiving it. Meanwhile, a person in another part of the room notices the handout's progress and thinks, "I'll bet the speaker is finished before I get to see it." Some people see the handout at the wrong time, after the speaker has already moved on to another point.

A common tactic of business and professional speaking today is to hand out duplicated materials so that everyone can read along while the speaker elaborates on it. While this procedure is productive in certain conference settings, it has a problem: once the listeners have printed materials, the speaker cannot prevent them from reading during other parts of the speech. Many teachers have learned this lesson when they handed back a graded exam at the beginning of the period and then tried to give a forty-five minute lecture.

It is much better to find ways to let everyone see a visual aid at the same time, perhaps by using larger materials or an overhead projector, or by asking people to come up after the speech has ended to see tiny objects or pictures. Presentation of a single document or picture to the entire audience at once is not only cheaper and quicker, but it also directs attention to material at the times and in the manner the speaker prefers.

## The Demonstration

An especially challenging type of speech using visual media is the *demonstration*. A demonstration is not simply the *display* or *exhibit* of visual aids, but rather the *use* of those aids in showing the audience, through the speaker's behavior, a process or procedure. The table below indicates the difference between a visual exhibit and a demonstration.

Notice that the display or exhibit requires only that the speaker set up the aids and assure that they are visible at the appropriate time, but the *aids themselves* supply the key information—they are the message. In the demonstration, the speaker's *body and movement* become a crucial part of the intended message.

Demonstrations have strong audience appeal because they leave little to the imagination. As an instructional device, demonstrations are crucial for topics in arts and crafts, athletics, medical procedures, and equipment operation. However, in any physical process many things can go wrong. What if the speaker must thread a needle? Carefully slice a vegetable with a razorsharp knife? Bring water to boil

| Visual Exhibit | Demonstration |
|---|---|
| A chart showing proper tennis court positions and strategy | A recreation director using a tennis racquet to show proper serving techniques |
| Color photographs of imaginative servings of low-calorie foods | A home economist preparing and mixing ingredients for a low-calorie recipe |
| Slides or films that illustrate techniques of firearm maintenance and safety | A firearms expert dismantling and cleaning a rifle |
| Charts and graphs that show the effects of exercise on cardiovascular functioning | A physical fitness expert doing push-ups, running in place, and then taking blood pressure, pulse, and respiratory readings |
| Showing human models with new hairstyles | A hair stylist cutting a person's hair |

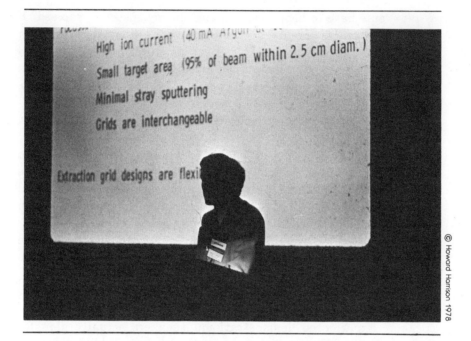

© Howard Harrison 1978

quickly? Comb the hair of a frisky dog? We have seen many well-prepared speakers fail because of unexpected events in the "doing" phase. One speaker demonstrated karate. Because of nervousness, he could not concentrate fully and broke his hand instead of the brick! A woman discussing wine tasting accidentally sent a fifth of cabernet sauvignon crashing to the floor. An ardent golfer swung his three wood and demolished a light fixture. A guitarist broke a metal string and spent several minutes replacing it before he could continue. As a speech instructor, the author could describe numerous horror stories of the demonstration-gone-awry. But almost anyone who has observed presentational speaking in the real world remembers speeches in which unanticipated problems impaired an otherwise productive communication event.

In preparing speeches that include demonstrations, we should remember an important axiom: Whatever *can* go wrong, *will*. We must be able to predict potential trouble spots. Ask yourself beforehand:

What events have to happen as planned for my speech to succeed? If one of these events does not go smoothly, what are my options? What visual materials can become defective? After considering potential trouble spots, try to eliminate them ahead of time. For example, if a speaker anticipates that nervousness will lead to trembling hands, some of the intricate manipulation can be done ahead of time (threading a needle, pin-striping with paints, assembling tiny machine parts, and the like).

Be especially conscious of *time*. Rarely does a demonstration run shorter than expected; it almost always takes longer. Run through the speech ahead of time, precisely as it will be done during the actual presentation. If it is too lengthy, ask again the crucial question: Which portions of the demonstration are really necessary and which are not? Any demonstration should have carefully limited objectives. The speakers who encounter problems are frequently those who tried to do too much in a short time.

Avoid extended *silent demonstration*. Though there are exceptions to this rule, most audiences expect continuous commentary from the speaker. Experienced demonstrational speakers actually plan for filling periods of physical activity with anecdotes or additional information. They know that some people become uncomfortable during these silent phases, and continuity in speaking eases the problem. The speaker who has practiced using the visual aids knows when these moments of silence are likely to occur and can plan accordingly. Anyone who has ever watched helplessly as a speaker quietly struggled with a troublesome visual aid knows how useful supplementary verbal materials can be for this type of situation. While the speaker need not apologize for circumstances beyond his control, he should frankly explain the problem and trust the audience to be reasonable. Audiences are not usually malicious or sadistic people who enjoy seeing a speaker flounder in unexpected problems. Most of us feel real empathy for the speaker in difficulty. Some people will even try to help with the demonstration.

## SUMMARY

Speakers sometimes avoid using audiovisual aids in speech presentations because they require more time, energy, and risk to develop and use. However, they can be an important and even crucial component of the public speaking process. Some technical topics cannot be explained well without them. The multi-channel nature of audiovisual aids can promote the perception, comprehension, and retention of messages and increase receiver attention spans. They can enhance the speaker's self-confidence and facilitate positive audience response. Most important, they are consistent with our increasingly visual culture and with the norms or expectations of audiences in the business and professional setting.

Types of audiovisual aids include the human body, physical objects, models or replicas, electronic media, pictures and diagrams, graphs and charts, maps, and chalkboards. Audiovisual aids require careful use; clear, neat, and artistic results are crucial. The speaker should practice using the aids, with special concern for assuring an unobstructed audience view, maintaining eye contact, and use at the proper psychological points in the speech. In general, handouts should be avoided as visual aids.

Demonstrations involve not just the display of visual aids but also their actual use in explaining a process or activity. They have strong audience appeal, but require even more careful planning and practice than the use of audiovisual aids.

## QUESTIONS FOR STUDY

1.  How do audiovisual aids provide evidence that the speaker has a receiver-centered perspective on public speaking? Could the use of these aids ever suggest that the public speaker is sender- or message-oriented?

2.  What are some advantages and disadvantages of electronic media as visual aids? Of physical objects? Of the chalkboard?

3.  What are some common problems in the preparation and use of audiovisual aids by students in their classroom speech projects?

4.  What are some potential or likely types of audiovisual aids that might be used for the speech topics below?

    Orientation for New Employees
    Hair Styling Techniques

Macrame Made Easy
Gasoline Prices: 1975-80
Summer Travel: See America First
Investment Opportunities in Vacation Property
The New Faces of Architecture

5. What is the difference between visual exhibits and demonstrations? Give some examples of each.

# chapter 7

# MANAGING SPEECH ANXIETY

LEARNING OBJECTIVES

After reading this chapter, you should be able to:
1. List a variety of symptoms of speech anxiety, especially those that are typical of your own experience in giving speeches.
2. Do some self-analysis about the causes or bases or your own public speaking anxiety.
3. Apply several of the suggestions for managing speech anxiety to your speaking projects in the public speaking course.

7

Madeline Evans has never been shy and withdrawn. She is a friendly, outgoing, gregarious person, and was popular in high school and college. But ever since her performance in piano recitals as a child she has feared any audience situation in which her behavior would be perceived and perhaps evaluated by many other people. For example, in high school she carefully avoided competitive sports that might involve spectators, and instead concentrated on gym classes and intra-murals. In college, she decided against majoring in music because all majors had to give yearly public recitals. She also steered clear of public-speaking classes.

Upon graduation with a degree in business administration, Madeline got a good job in a large bank as a management trainee. This bank was similar to most in that it wanted its managers to be familiar with all phases of bank operation, and gave each trainee an opportunity to work in a variety of departments. Madeline's cooperative inter-personal style with other employees, and her general competence, led to several opportunities to advance to higher paying positions with greater supervisory responsibility. However, she turned down several of these opportunities because they would involve frequent presenta-tional speaking—to new employees, to management meetings, or to public groups. She is now assistant manager in one of the branch offices. Her main responsibility is to review and approve all loan and credit applications that come to her desk from the loan officers. Her work demands effective one-to-one communication and no public speaking. Most employees view the assistant manager position as a less-than-challenging step "on the way up." Madeline feels comfort-able in the job and will probably remain in it for several years, despite the lower salary, lack of variety, and limited opportunity for growth.

We have no quarrel with Madeline Evans' decision to stay in her niche, if her work is truly what she would prefer to do. But we suspect that she, along with many other people, has made her career decisions based partly on a preoccupying fear of public speaking. She has chosen to limit her professional development and rewards, to go through her career "with one hand tied behind her back," because the one-to-many communication situation so common to professional people was simply too threatening. It is always unfortunate when people do not achieve their full potential because of inability to deal with their anxiety.

This chapter is about *speech anxiety*, the tension, nervousness, and

sometimes panic that so often accompany the actual speech presentation. Perhaps no problem is more overwhelming for the beginning public speaker. Some students avoid a basic speech communication class, not necessarily because they feel that communication is unimportant, but rather because they are thinking ahead to the inevitable public speaking projects in which they will have to stand alone before the class and present their ideas for the scrutiny of critical listeners. Since this problem is so compelling to so many people, we shall spend some time in this section developing an understanding of this age-old bugaboo and suggesting some strategies for managing it.

## FACING SPEECH ANXIETY

There are two schools of thought about speech anxiety in public-speaking instruction. The first approach suggests that *we should not call attention to our fears by discussing them openly*. People know the degrees to which they are bothered by nervousness in performing situations. Why not just let them deal with it naturally, just as most small children learn to deal with their irrational fear of the dark? The more we think and talk about our fears—this argument goes—the more likely we are to become preoccupied with and perhaps immobilized by them. The best strategy is to "get in there and give speeches," and gradually the speaker will learn to cope with the apprehension of the speaking situation.

If you agree with this philosophy, then there is no reason to read this chapter. Simply go on to something else and forget about dealing consciously with speech anxiety. This chapter is aimed at those who adhere to the second school of thought, which argues for dealing openly and strategically with our nervousness and fears. Its underlying assumption is that *the speaker who knows about speech anxiety, is aware of its symptoms, and understands its effects is better off than one who gives no careful thought to the problem.* Proponents of this approach, including the author, believe that becoming aware of our psychological and physical reactions to a presentational situation can be the most important step in learning to manage them.

Hence we include this chapter for three reasons. First, some people do not speak publicly and will continue to avoid it, even if speaking is in their self-interest, unless they can learn to cope with their fears. Only open discussion can persuade them to try it and provide strategies for managing nervousness. Second, our experience has been that people want to talk about their speech anxiety. While they may fear public speaking, they do not fear telling others how it bothers them. In training situations, we have frequently seen people "come out of their shell" and disclose avidly and in depth their symptoms of anxiety and the ways in which they have tried to avoid public speaking. Talking about their fears becomes a refreshing release of tension. When they learn that others have shared similar feelings, they become more willing to deal consciously with the problem. Third, we have seen significant improvement in speakers' ability to deal with their anxiety after in-depth discussion about the problem and potential remedies. At the very worst, in our experience, people who read and talk about their anxiety may experience no significant improvement, but they do not become less able to deal with the problem. We have seen no evidence that open discussion of speech anxiety causes any harm; our experience with thousands of public speaking students is that it leads to substantial improvement.

The term *stage fright* is often used to characterize the anxiety and nervousness in public speaking. It is probably an intimidating term, because of its suggestion of a theatrical format for public communication. It implies a formal performance with carefully memorized lines and rehearsed movements, just the opposite of the more spontaneous, receiver-centered delivery style we are advocating here. Further, if the speaker thinks of a speech as a staged presentation, the communication task may seem much more awesome and threatening, due to the implied emphasis on pleasing or entertaining an audience with a polished, flawless "performance." Though speech instructors sometimes use the term *stage fright* because of its popularity and common meaning, we caution the reader not to assume that the public speaking event is necessarily analogous to a *stage* presentation.

A term that has replaced *stage fright* in recent speech communication literature is *communication apprehension*. Originally coined by McCroskey, the term encompasses a much broader spectrum of communication behavior than just the public speaking setting (Mc-Croskey, 1970). It refers to all types of "communication-bound anxiety." It is "a broad-based, personality-type characteristic that is characterized by withdrawal from and avoidance of communication" (McCroskey *et al.*, 1975). While research in communication apprehension is very useful for application to the one-to-many situation, the term itself is too broad for our use in a public speaking text. Further, while some people are apprehensive about *any* interaction with other people, we think that most people who are bothered by nervousness in public speaking *do not share similar fears in day-to-day communication events*. That is, the "communication apprehensive person" is not necessarily identical to the "public speaking apprehensive" person.

We prefer the term *speech anxiety*, and shall use it throughout this chapter to refer, as noted earlier, to *the tension, nervousness, and sometimes panic that either accompanies the actual presentation or prompts a person to avoid a public speaking situation altogether*. (Some textbooks title a chapter on this topic "Speaker Poise and Confidence," or something similar, that may appear more positive than "Managing

Speech Anxiety." But the section still refers to the nagging problem that most of us face—the uncomfortable emotions and bodily responses that accompany our public speaking efforts.)

We shall begin with some observations about the public speaking setting and general characteristics of speaker anxieties. From this perspective, we then explore symptoms and causes of speech anxiety and suggested ways of managing it. The reader will not find a handy-dandy set of rules for *curing* the problem. It *is* possible, however, to learn better ways of assuring that it will not impede speech delivery or effectiveness.

## Speech Anxiety in Perspective

**1.** *In the first place, a public communication event should not be a totally relaxed, casual experience for the speaker.* Giving a speech should be a challenge for which we prepare psychologically. Just as an athletic coach worries when the team appears to be too blasé about the approaching game, so the speaker should be concerned if he does not feel at least a twinge of apprehension. If worry and nervousness do not play a part in speech delivery, the actual presentation may be bland and the speaker unenthusiastic. While this premise may be of little consolation for the beginning speaker, we are convinced that experienced communicators come to view speech anxiety as a potential ally in making the best possible presentation.

**2.** *We should realize that speech anxiety is common for most speakers in most public communication situations.* In one survey of 3000 Americans, a team of market researchers asked, "What are you most afraid of?" The most common fear, mentioned by 41 percent of the respondents, was "speaking before a group." "Financial problems" tied for third place; "sickness" and "death" tied for sixth! (San Francisco *Chronicle*, Feb. 12, 1978, p. 46.) While scholars might quarrel with the research methods in this study, the overwhelming conclusion of empirical research into speech anxiety is that, regardless of experience, speakers regularly face the problem of coping with their fears before an audience (Lomas, 1937; Gilkinson, 1942; Clevenger, 1959; Baker, 1964; Klee, 1964; Mowrer, 1965; Phillips, 1968; Friedrich, 1970). When

the beginning speaker assumes that he faces special or unique problems of nervousness, he impedes his speech progress—and he is grossly
inaccurate. Speech anxiety is a *life fact* of public communication, not
an accidental psychological quirk for a few novices.

**3.** *Anxiety is common to nearly any situation in which a person's
behavior is open to immediate scrutiny by others.* Athletes, actors,
ministers, politicians, musicians, singers, teachers, dancers, attorneys,
broadcasters, and many others regularly report apprehension before
and during their audience-centered activities, even after years of
experience.

**4.** *Speech anxiety usually dissipates and sometimes disappears after
we begin the public presentation.* For the football player who can't eat
just before the big game, the first physical contact with an opponent
usually begins the process of fear abatement, and after a few moments
nervousness is no longer a conscious factor. A stage actor, after a few
lines, quickly gets "into the role" and becomes absorbed in her performance. Similarly, we have heard many beginning speech students
report that they can actually feel the nervousness leaving them after
they get into their speech. In a short speech of, say, five to seven
minutes, speech anxiety may not diminish completely, but it is important for the beginning speaker to recognize that for nearly everyone
the process does in fact occur in varying degrees. One reason the
experienced speaker is not preoccupied with speech anxiety is that he
knows from past experience that the symptoms gradually vanish as
the speech progresses.

**5.** *Speech anxiety will not necessarily affect the communication event.*
Some symptoms of nervousness are more distracting or disruptive
than others. Some do not affect the presentation in any discernible way
but merely cause internal discomfort for the speaker. While speech
anxiety may affect the smoothness or fluency of presentation, and
while a speaker with manifest nervousness may not completely fulfill
his speech objectives, it is extremely rare that speech aixiety totally
negates the desired effects of a public presentation. However, if our
apprehension is even a potential impediment to our fulfillment of

public communication goals, we are justified in learning how it affects us and how it can be managed.

## Understanding Our Own Speech Anxiety

Self-analysis and self-evaluation are important to any public speaker. Throughout this book we indicate good and bad speaker behaviors, hoping that readers will apply the information to their own personal speaking styles. That process becomes especially important in the area of speech anxiety, because self-awareness of one's unique responses to apprehension and fear may be the first step to dealing with it effectively. This section will describe typical symptoms of speech anxiety, list potential causes of that anxiety, and finally, provide a self-evaluation test that may help to clarify the range and depth of our fears.

*Symptoms of speech anxiety.* Symptoms are perceptible indicators of deeper psychological or physiological conditions that cannot be observed. The medical profession relies on observation of symptoms to make diagnoses. Similarly, people who are interested in the process of public communication can observe symptoms—in themselves or others —to begin to understand what happens to them physically and emotionally during a public speech.

One indicator of speech anxiety might be called *avoidance behavior*: making decisions and acting in ways to steer clear of public communication situations. Some people regularly decline requests to speak publicly. Others, like Madeline Evans, construct their life style and environment so that the chance of facing an audience will rarely arise. Others back down from previous commitments to speak, as in the case of the speech class student who is regularly and conveniently absent on the day he is scheduled to make a presentation.

Another set of symptoms involves indications of inadequacy, excuses, and apologies. Verbally, this withdrawal behavior can be demonstrated with self-belittling comments like "I'm really no good at this," "I haven't had much time to prepare," or "I'm probably not saying this right, but . . ." Nonverbally, the speaker may suggest inadequacy by a lack of eye contact, unenthusiastic tone of voice, a facial expression showing resignation, confusion, or frustration, and/or a slouched posture.

One way of understanding these symptoms is to identify observable features and behaviors in the speaker that appear to deviate from normal communicator characteristics. One study grouped these observables into three categories (Clevenger and King, 1961). *Fidgetiness* includes such nervous, nonpurposeful movements as shuffling feet, swaying body, swinging arms, stiff arms and legs, a lack of direct eye contact with the audience, and pacing back and forth. *Inhibition* is shown by a deadpan facial expression, trembling knees, hands in pockets, a pale face, nervous hands, and returning to one's seat while speaking. Finally, *autonomia* is the excessive reaction of the autonomic nervous system—the unconscious and relatively automatic body regulator of muscles and glands—producing such symptoms as moistening lips (perhaps indicating inadequate salivation), blushing, heavy breathing, and repeatedly swallowing or throat-clearing.

We must make an important distinction between *observed* symptoms and *experienced* symptoms. What the listeners may actually notice is not necessarily what the speaker is feeling emotionally or physically, and an audience assessment of speech anxiety will probably differ from that of the speaker. Our experience has been that speakers *overestimate* the degree to which they are affected by speech anxiety and the extent to which audiences perceive those symptoms. There is some evidence that audiences tend more often to *underestimate* student fears (Robinson, 1959). Obviously, some of the symptoms are simply not observable to an audience. Listeners cannot see apprehension, anxiety, embarrassment, or self-consciousness; they can only infer them from speaker behaviors that they hear and see. They often do not even notice things that may disturb the speaker and magnify his problem—the slightly quavering voice, unnatural inflection, trembling hands or knees, flushed or pale face, rigid posture, dry mouth, heavy breathing, difficulty in finding the right words. If these characteristics are noticed at all, the degree of nervousness and inner fear they represent usually are underestimated by the observers.

It may be of little consolation to the public speaker to know that the audience does not fully notice the extent of his nervousness. "So what if the audience doesn't *see* it? I still *feel* it, and that's the important thing!" We agree that it is important for the speaker to recognize speech anxiety symptoms when they occur and to learn to predict the ways in which those symptoms might affect the presentation. An analogy might be common physical illnesses, aches, and pains—we learn that these problems are inevitable, that they are uncomfortable, and that there are ways of managing them. Being able to identify and understand the symptoms may not ease our physical discomfort, but such knowledge can soothe our anxiety because we have come to recognize the symptoms as common and predictable. In contrast, we react strongly to symptoms we do not understand or cannot correctly identify. We wonder what is happening to us, and worry that it might be serious. The beginning speaker may be confused and startled by the radical changes in physical and mental functioning; a growing awareness of these changes is an important factor in our ability to accept and cope with our public speaking fears.

*Causes of speech anxiety.* Studying the causes of speech anxiety might be seen as unjustified. In the first place, it can be argued, we have no conclusive evidence that particular events or characteristics are the source of our apprehension. Second, even if the cause could be accurately determined, we would probably find it multiple and dependent on the specific speech situation—a combination of several elements that differ for each person. Finally, the cause is not the issue for most people bothered with speech anxiety; rather, they are concerned with the actual experience of the problem, the feelings, symptoms, or behaviors of nervousness. "Let's change the behavior" —the argument goes—"and we won't have to worry about causes."

While these arguments have some merit, we believe that a discussion of possible sources of speech anxiety can be useful. It helps us examine the bases of our fears and possibly learn to identify apparent contributing factors, so that we can predict the type and magnitude of fear we might face in a particular situation, and perhaps negate its bad effect.

One common explanation of "stage fright" is that it is *learned behavior*. From early development, we've been reminded that any "performing" situation is something to be feared. Before playing a solo in a concert, the third grader is told, "Now, don't be nervous, dear, you'll do a good job." The Little League ball player is counseled by the coach before the big game, "I know you will do well. You won't let the team down; you'll come through." A student hears a friend say, "I'm so nervous! I've got an algebra exam today and I haven't really studied."

Our society is performance- and success-oriented. We emphasize winning. We stress perfection. In so doing, perhaps we also *teach* a fear of failure. A child soon *learns* that to do well in a performance is to receive positive payoffs, and to do not so well is to have those rewards withheld. She also learns that people admire those who succeed and ridicule those who err. Since we view ridicule as a kind of punishment, and since public speaking exposes us to many people who can mock our mistakes, we learn that the public communication situation is a highly threatening experience.

We also learn, incidentally, that when the speech has ended and we return to our seats, the speech anxiety vanishes. But why? People still see us and hear us as we speak in more casual interaction. If we say something foolish, they may still laugh at us. Our self-esteem is just as vulnerable—we are still risking just as much—as when we were standing before the audience. Is it the simple act of moving from a standing position behind a podium to a seated position? Could it be that we not only teach fear of a speech presentation, but also define the limits or boundaries of that performance? That is, perhaps we learn that informal situations are not threatening (at least they are not *defined* as threatening), so that in moving from perceived formality to perceived informality our speech anxiety vanishes.

Another possible cause of speech anxiety is the human instinct to avoid danger or threats to our well-being. This suggests that our physiological responses to an audience situation are similar to those we experience in reacting to unexpected danger—a quickened pulse, rapid breathing, excessive perspiration, tense muscles, and so forth. A possible limitation in this argument is that we quickly return to a more normal physiological state when it is obvious that a threat is not real. For example, if someone comes up from behind and scares us, even though we may react with extreme fright, we quickly return to normal after we learn we have nothing to fear. In a public speech, however, even the adept speaker who has learned that he has nothing to fear may still experience symptoms of fear. It seems logical never-

theless that at least part of our tension is tied to the natural motive of self-preservation and the protection of self-esteem.

More specific potential sources of speech anxiety have been outlined by Beuhler and Linkugel (1962, pp. 36–38). We list them below with our own brief explanations. As you read each one, consider the degree to which it may be a factor in your own communication anxiety.

*Fear of physical unattractiveness.* The speaker believes that he or she is not handsome or pretty or is improperly dressed.

*Fear of social inadequacy.* The speaker fears exhibiting behavior that the audience will perceive as inappropriate or crude. This fear implies social inferiority.

*Fear of criticism.* The speaker may be overly sensitive to, and unable to cope with, negative feedback from the audience.

*Fear of failure.* We discussed earlier this cultural trait; although we know that success is sweet, we preoccupy ourselves with the possibility of blunder.

*Fear of the unknown.* We cannot predict precisely the spontaneous developments of a speech situation. Although beginners may be especially prone to this fear, even experienced communicators may succumb to the uncertainty of public speaking, especially if they have been unexpectedly embarrassed in a previous speech.

*Fear of speech anxiety.* The mere thought of being afraid, of having to cope with the burdensome speech anxiety symptoms, may itself prompt us to fear upcoming speeches.

*Conflicting emotions.* When we must face simultaneously a strong desire to succeed in a task and an equally potent fear of failure, the emotional turmoil may add to our distress; we know that either we speak and face failure, or we don't speak and deprive ourselves of rewards.

*Excitement from anticipation.* The anticipation of a big event, of an intoxicating, ego-enhancing experience, of the opportunity to have many people sit captivated while we present our ideas, may prompt the same physical reactions as when we experience extreme fear.

Buehler and Linkugel also cite character traits as potential speech anxiety sources, suggesting that "the speaker who has developed a full measure of such virtues as *courage, determination, patience, enthusiasm,* and *friendliness*" has special advantages in learning to handle nervousness, while "*timidity, cowardice, laziness, indifference, impatience,* and *unfriendliness*" may impede poise and confidence (Buehler and Linkugel, 1962, p. 39).

Perhaps the seriousness of speech anxiety is ultimately determined by our *self-concept*—the ways in which we think about and evaluate ourselves. Are we happy with who we are? Do we have confidence in our abilities and think objectively about our limitations? Are we proud of our individuality, of those characteristics that make us unique? If so, our speech anxiety may be less intimidating. If not, then apprehension in public speaking may be an indicator of a much more serious problem—a low regard for self.

As we utilize self-analysis in coming to terms with our own communication fears, we might ask several questions that relate to the potential causes noted above. Am I expecting too much of myself? Am I really afraid to fail or to accept negative feedback? Can I unlearn my fear by experiencing speech situations that have positive outcomes? Can I come to understand that rewards for communicative success outweigh penalties for failure? Can I develop a positive attitude about my nervousness, viewing it as an ally in improving my speech effort?

*Evaluating speech anxiety.* A test for evaluating speech anxiety is offered as a final step in understanding your own speech anxiety. This simple evaluation instrument provides quantitative evidence of the degree of anxiety each person reports. Developed by McCroskey, the test is called the Personal Report of Public Speaking Apprehension (PRPSA) (McCroskey, 1970, pp. 276–277). This test is not only useful for gaining an assessment of our current apprehension in public speaking, but may also show changes over time. For example, if you take the test now, you may want to retake it a few weeks or months from now to learn whether you have improved in your ability to manage speech anxiety. The scoring procedure will be explained below, at the end of the test.

This instrument is composed of 34 statements concerning feelings about communicating with other people.

Indicate the degree to which the statements apply to you by marking whether you: Strongly Agree (SA), Agree (A), are Undecided (U), Disagree (D), or Strongly Disagree (SD).

Work quickly; just record your first impression.

|  |  | SA | A | U | D | SD |
|---|---|---|---|---|---|---|
| 1. | While preparing for giving a speech, I feel tense and nervous. | 5 | 4 | 3 | 2 | 1 |
| 2. | I feel tense when I see the words "speech" and "public speech" on a course outline when studying. | 5 | 4 | 3 | 2 | 1 |
| 3. | My thoughts become confused and jumbled when I am giving a speech. | 5 | 4 | 3 | 2 | 1 |
| 4. | Right after giving a speech, I feel that I have had a pleasant experience. | 1 | 2 | 3 | 4 | 5 |
| 5. | I get anxious when I think about a speech coming up. | 5 | 4 | 3 | 2 | 1 |
| 6. | I have no fear of giving a speech. | 1 | 2 | 3 | 4 | 5 |
| 7. | Although I am nervous just before starting a speech, I soon settle down after starting and feel calm and comfortable. | 1 | 2 | 3 | 4 | 5 |
| 8. | I look forward to giving a speech. | 1 | 2 | 3 | 4 | 5 |
| 9. | When the instructor announces a speaking assignment in class, I can feel myself getting tense. | 5 | 4 | 3 | 2 | 1 |
| 10. | My hands tremble when I am giving a speech. | 5 | 4 | 3 | 2 | 1 |

| | | | | | | |
|---|---|---|---|---|---|---|
| 11. | I feel relaxed while giving a speech. | 1 | 2 | 3 | 4 | 5 |
| 12. | I enjoy preparing for a speech. | 1 | 2 | 3 | 4 | 5 |
| 13. | I am in constant fear of forgetting what I am prepared to say. | 5 | 4 | 3 | 2 | 1 |
| 14. | I get anxious if someone asks me something about my topic that I do not know. | 5 | 4 | 3 | 2 | 1 |
| 15. | I face the prospect of giving a speech with confidence. | 1 | 2 | 3 | 4 | 5 |
| 16. | I feel that I am in complete possession of myself while giving a speech. | 1 | 2 | 3 | 4 | 5 |
| 17. | My mind is clear when giving a speech. | 1 | 2 | 3 | 4 | 5 |
| 18. | I do not dread giving a speech. | 1 | 2 | 3 | 4 | 5 |
| 19. | I perspire just before starting a speech. | 5 | 4 | 3 | 2 | 1 |
| 20. | My heart beats very fast just as I start a speech. | 5 | 4 | 3 | 2 | 1 |
| 21. | I experience considerable anxiety while sitting in the room just before my speech starts. | 5 | 4 | 3 | 2 | 1 |
| 22. | Certain parts of my body feel very tense and rigid while giving a speech. | 5 | 4 | 3 | 2 | 1 |
| 23. | Realizing that only a little time remains in a speech makes me very tense and anxious. | 5 | 4 | 3 | 2 | 1 |
| 24. | While giving a speech, I know I can control my feelings of tension and stress. | 1 | 2 | 3 | 4 | 5 |
| 25. | I breathe faster just before starting a speech. | 5 | 4 | 3 | 2 | 1 |
| 26. | I feel comfortable and relaxed in the hour or so just before giving a speech. | 1 | 2 | 3 | 4 | 5 |

27. I do poorly in speeches because I am anxious.     5   4   3   2   1

28. I feel anxious when the teacher announces the date of a speaking assignment.    5   4   3   2   1

29. When I make a mistake while giving a speech, I find it hard to concentrate on the parts that follow.    5   4   3   2   1

30. During an important speech, I experience a feeling of helplessness building up inside me.    5   4   3   2   1

31. I have trouble falling asleep the night before a speech.    5   4   3   2   1

32. My heart beats very fast while I present a speech.    5   4   3   2   1

33. I feel anxious while waiting to give my speech.    5   4   3   2   1

34. While giving a speech, I get so nervous I forget facts I really know.    5   4   3   2   1

---

Source: James C. McCroskey, "Measures of Communication-Bound Anxiety," *Speech Monographs*, 37 (November, 1970), 276.

To compute your score on this test, total all of the numbers you marked in the five columns. The neutral point is a score of 102 (34 questions × a "3" midpoint ranking = 102), but McCroskey found that the mean (average) score for the student–subjects who took the test was about 115. That suggests that if you scored above 115, you reported *more* speech anxiety than the average college students in the initial test. If you scored below 115, you reported *less* anxiety. There is no absolute standard against which to judge the seriousness of your quantified anxiety level. That is, we cannot say for certain at which point a score denotes "serious anxiety," "a cause for concern," or "in need of special techniques to calm fears." We can say that on this test, 68 percent of the students scored between 98 and 132. If you scored above 132, you reported a high degree of anxiety shared by only 16 percent of the original subjects. A score below 98 would put you in the 16 percent of students least bothered by anxiety. Rather than using this test as an absolute indicator of anxiety, we suggest you compare your score over time, by retesting yourself periodically. Or you may want to compare your score with a friend or associate who has also expressed apprehension about public speaking.

In summary, our major objective in this section on "Understanding Our Own Speech Anxiety" has been self-awareness, to look candidly at our feelings and behaviors in the public speech setting, to consider possible causes of our anxiety, and to try to better assess the degree of that anxiety. In the next section, we shall develop techniques for managing our fears.

## SUGGESTIONS FOR MANAGING SPEECH ANXIETY

We have maintained that speech anxiety is inevitable for most people, that it need not detract from speech effectiveness, and that some nervousness may be an aid to the speaker in spurring him to a better presentation. Therefore, we do not urge an attempt to *eliminate* speech anxiety (assuming that were possible). Instead, we suggest that the speaker learn to *control* or *manage* speech anxiety so that its physical and psychological symptoms do not impede the effectiveness of a presentation. (We recall one speaker who thought he had developed a surefire scheme for eliminating fear. About thirty minutes before his presentation, he would down three shots of bourbon. His speeches were free from nervousness. They were also inarticulate, comical, pathetic, and a total waste of the audience's time!)

### Some Common Techniques for Coping with Anxiety

Nearly all speech instructors have pet suggestions for managing speech anxiety, and the author is no different. However, we offer the following list somewhat reluctantly, because the reader may be tempted to view it as a prescription—a set of rules that can lead to predictable results. These suggestions are only strategies that have helped many people, but may not help everyone.

*Develop a message-centered and audience-centered point of view.*  Our anxiety may be magnified by preoccupation with our own feelings and performance. We should center our thoughts on the message content and on our conception of audience expectations. Do members of the audience really expect a polished oration? Are they listening for errors? Usually not. Are they interested in the topic? What do they think of me? We sometimes build up the audience in our imagination as a multi-headed monster waiting to destroy us. Actually, some honest analysis of the audience as a collection of normal individuals with reasonable expectations may be an important step toward meeting them on common terms and without suspicion.

*Learn about public communication theories and principles.*  Twenty years ago, space flight was a frightening prospect. We were facing the unknown. Yet for several years astronauts traveled into space with little observable apprehension. As Neil Armstrong landed the first United States spacecraft on the moon, for example, his heartbeat was within the normal range for everyday activities. One factor in the astronaut's coolness must have been a detailed understanding of space science—orbital mechanics, propulsion theory, communication and navigation equipment, and the like—and confidence in its ability to perform. Similarly, the public speaker can learn much about the variables of a one-to-many communication situation, from ancient theories to the findings of modern behavioral research. This knowledge means the speaker is not confronting the unknown, but has an accurate comprehension of a reasonably familiar environment. One means of developing this awareness is a basic speech course, which can render speech anxiety much less intimidating (Brandes, 1967).

*Seek and accept repeated exposure to public communication.*  To this suggestion we have heard some students and professional people reply, "Get serious! When I finish this training program I'll never speak before an audience again as long as I live!" That is their choice, though not a very practical one. As we have mentioned before, many people willingly impede their personal and professional growth by being reluctant communicators, avoiding public speaking at all costs. Apprehensive speakers not only should accept public speaking opportunities when they arise, but should actually *seek out* such situations. Why? Because *repeated exposure to the one-to-many setting tends to reduce fears and build self confidence.* As public speaking experience increases, we learn to expect certain symptoms and accurately predict their gradual disappearance as the speech progresses.

We stress the *active* involvement of the potential speaker in seeking communication situations. A psychologist we know was directing a therapy program for a client who might be called "severely communication-apprehensive." This person feared any interaction with strangers, and constructed his daily behavior to avoid any contact with all but the closest friends and relatives. The psychologist decided that it was not enough simply to have the person learn to respond to people who confronted him. Instead, one of the therapy activities he prescribed was for the client to *initiate* at least one conversation per day with a total stranger. Though reluctant at first, the client eventually followed the suggestion and after several weeks learned that these transactions were not only manageable but frequently very rewarding. For the same reason, we believe it is reasonable for an apprehensive speaker to *volunteer* to participate in speech presentations.

*Develop positive attitudes.* First, we can encourage positive feelings about our general abilities. Some people tell themselves that they can accomplish their goals, and they come to believe it. For many, the "power of positive thinking" is quite real. Second, we can affirm our expertise on the speech topic. We often know a great deal more about our subject than the audience does, and we should remind ourselves of this fact. Third, we can think positively about our mistakes and about negative feedback. The response of an audience to a mistake in the presentation can be viewed as *new information*. We now know something about ourselves or the speech situation that we did not know before. Negative feedback thus can be viewed as a source of self-improvement and constructive growth.

*Project a positive image.*   The way we look, move, and speak obviously affects the audience's impression of us. When our positive behavior suggests that we expect to do well, the audience is unconsciously led to expect a good performance, which in turn leads us to expect even more from ourselves (Bormann and Shapiro, 1962). If we continually apologize, offer excuses, admit our nervousness, or claim inadequacy, our psychological state—and our performance—will reflect our uncertainty. For many speakers, each apology further damages an already fragile self-concept. To avoid these pitfalls, a speaker should not simply *appear* pleasantly assured before a speech, he should indicate in a casual (but not cocky or arrogant) and positive way what he expects to achieve.

*Carefully select, prepare, and organize the topic.*   Though good preparation is good advice for other reasons as well, it also enhances self-confidence. A poorly prepared speaker has every reason to be apprehensive.

*Recognize the importance of introductory remarks.*   Getting off to a good start can be an important boost; a confused or muddled beginning can be excruciating. Don't rush into it. Pause to arrange your notes and get oriented. Smile. Start slowly and methodically. Seek an early favorable response from the audience—perhaps with an anecdote, a reference to someone in the audience, an acknowledgment of common interests, a rhetorical question. Resist the temptation to begin quickly or to speak rapidly. Positive audience feedback can boost confidence quickly.

*Use a conversational delivery style.*   The more formal our delivery, the more precise and fluent we think we must be. We become physically tense, and even the slightest errors become noticeable. For many people, a more relaxed delivery style can induce relaxation of mind and body as well.

*Use visual aids.*   Visual aids (see Chapter 6) not only improve audience understanding, but also give us a friendly partner during the speech, visual support to a verbal effort. They share the communication burden.

*Use physical techniques to ease tension.* Deep breathing, smiling, stretching, exercising, muscle relaxing, and even meditating are potentially beneficial pre-speech strategies. A deep breath as we begin speaking can also help. Comfortable posture and clothing enhance physical and psychological comfort.

*Share speech anxiety with friends.* While we do not recommend discussing our fears with an audience, frank discussions with others before the speech can be a therapeutic release, a kind of self-disclosure that enhances mutual empathy and the realization that we all share the common human characteristic of speech anxiety.

*Reward yourself for presenting a speech.* Perhaps one reason why public speaking prompts negative feelings is that we have come to associate the activity with negative payoffs. It takes more time and energy than not speaking. It is sometimes accompanied by tension or stress, especially if the receivers provide immediate evaluation of the speaker's efforts. Perhaps the consequences of an ineffective presentation appear to be greater than the beneficial outcomes of an effective one.

Whatever the cause, the perception of public speaking as a *negative reinforcement* may be a significant source of anxiety. Why not develop a system of *positive reinforcement?* Why not reward ourselves for our public communication efforts? Some people treat themselves to dinner out, or new clothes, or a vacation after finishing a challenging project—the prospect of a personal reward helps to motivate more enthusiastic participation in the project. Why not do the same thing with public speaking? A system of rewarding oneself could at least balance the perceived negative factors, and possibly stimulate a greater interest in communicating well. (Notice that this suggestion is in addition to the rewards that evolve from the speech itself—the ego gratification of being noticed and appreciated, the practical results of achieving the speech purpose, and subsequent benefits like promotions, monetary rewards, recognition, and the like. This suggestion

refers specifically to *how speakers reward themselves*, irrespective of the additional payoffs that arise from the situation.)

## A New Approach: Systematic Desensitization

Sometimes when people feel nervous or frightened in a social situation, their anxiety results from a real deficiency in their *personal skills or abilities*. They fear acting in a play or a music recital because they do not have enough experience to do a proficient job. They fear participation in an athletic event because they do not have the athletic ability that most competitors have. They fear a public speech because they've never presented one before. In situations where inadequate skills appear to be the source of one's anxiety, the solution is not learning how to relax—the solution is *improving skills*. Several suggestions in the previous section, for example, focus on becoming a more proficient speaker, thus resulting in greater confidence in the one-to-many setting.

But some public speakers already have good communication skills. They prepare and organize well, they are conversationally fluent, and they have had experience in public communication settings. Yet they still report agonizing, preoccupying fears. They have analyzed their feelings (self-awareness methods) and have discussed their anxiety with others. Yet the serious nervousness persists. Their fears do not gradually diminish during the speech, but continue to impede their communication throughout. The speech event remains a totally negative experience for them.

In the past ten years or so, a therapy program called "Systematic Desensitization" (SD) has been developed and used to help people deal with serious and irrational fears or "phobias" (see, for example: Paul and Shannon, 1966; Mingler and Wolpe, 1967; McCroskey et al., 1970; McCroskey, 1972; Lohr and McManus, 1975). SD has been used in a variety of anxiety-producing situations—flying, taking exams, meeting new people—and has proved useful in easing communication apprehension, including public speaking anxiety.

The program essentially does two things. First, it develops muscle-relaxation techniques. We know that psychological stress is accompanied by physical stress as well, and that we cannot be experiencing both mental tension and physical relaxation at the same time. So the SD program helps the person relax muscles systematically—moving step-by-step in tensing and relaxing hand and arm muscles, facial muscles, chest and abdomen, etc. Deep, rhythmic breathing is also included in this phase. A key objective is, over several therapy sessions, to let the client experience and perceive the difference between tension and relaxation, to recognize tension as it builds and attempt to lessen it. He learns to relax his muscles at will.

In the second phase, the *relaxation behaviors* are paired with the *anxiety-producing situation*, the source of the client's fears. For example, he might be asked to use his new relaxation skills while being shown pictures of the anxiety-producing situation, or while the therapist describes that situation verbally. This second phase might also involve the client's actually confronting a real or simulated anxiety-producing situation and practicing the relaxation techniques in that environment.

Many colleges sponsor SD programs, as do many psychologists and counselors. The programs differ greatly, depending on the time available, the type of fear situation, and the methods and philosophies of the therapist. People who continue to experience significant anxiety despite frequent experience in public speaking settings may want to seek out one of these programs. However, we emphasize again that for *most* people in *most* public communication settings, managing speech anxiety is a matter of awareness, practice, experience, and the other factors suggested earlier. And for most speakers, nervousness can be an important component of a good presentation, a state of mind that helps us to take the speech seriously and get ourselves psychologically "up" for an important communication activity.

## SUMMARY

The term *speech anxiety*, often called *stage fright* or *communication apprehension*, refers to the tension, nervousness, and sometimes panic that accompanies public speaking or causes people to avoid public speaking. It cannot be eliminated, but it can be managed in such a way that it does not impede speech delivery.

Speech anxiety should be viewed as a potential ally to make us psychologically ready for a communication effort. It is by far the most common fear of adults. Anxiety is a common reaction to nearly any situation that can be viewed and evaluated by others. It usually decreases after the speaker begins a presentation. Most important, it need not negatively affect the speech.

The symptoms of speech anxiety differ with each person. Speakers tend to overestimate the seriousness of their anxiety, because they are actually experiencing these symptoms; the receivers usually underestimate the speaker's anxiety, because they cannot perceive (and are not even looking for) many of the symptoms. The causes of anxiety may not be known for certain, but several possible causes can be analyzed by each speaker to try to better understand the reasons why anxiety exists. One's speech anxiety can be evaluated quantitatively with a simple test included in this chapter.

Some suggestions for managing speech anxiety are: develop a message- and audience-centered perspective; become familiar with public speaking theories and principles; seek and accept public speaking opportunities; develop positive attitudes; project a positive image; prepare carefully; develop good introductory remarks; use a conversational delivery style; use visual aids; use physical techniques to relieve tension; discuss your anxiety with friends; and reward yourself for presenting a speech.

A new technique—Systematic Desensitization—is a fear-abatement program by which people with severe anxiety can use programmed physical relaxation and psychological association with the fear-producing situation to cope with the public speaking event.

## QUESTIONS FOR STUDY

1.  Why can it be said that speech anxiety is not only common, but frequently beneficial? Why do we urge that it be *managed* rather than eliminated?

2.  What is the difference between *observed* and *experienced* symptoms of speech anxiety? Why is this distinction important?

3. What are some of the most typical symptoms of speech anxiety that you have observed in the public speaking class?

4. Based on your own experience and on conversations with others, what are the primary causes for speech anxiety in the public speaking class? Do these causes differ in nonclassroom speeches?

5. Of the many suggestions offered for managing speech anxiety, which ones do you think are likely to be the most effective for the beginning public speaker?

# part three

## IMPROVING THE PUBLIC SPEECH

# chapter 8

# MANAGING TWO-WAY COMMUNICATION

**LEARNING OBJECTIVES**

After reading this chapter, you should be able to:

1. State some of the reasons and techniques for pre-speech conversation with audience members.
2. Use the suggestions for seeking and responding to audience messages in question-and-answer sessions in the classroom.
3. List and give examples of some of the unexpected transactions that can develop in any public speech.
4. Explain the potential benefits of obtaining post-speech feedback, along with some problems that may affect that process.

8

The scene was the campus of a major state university. The program was a summer institute for trial judges. The audience was composed of volunteer judges who would be serving as instructors during the month-long session. The official purpose of the meeting was "introductory comments from the director of the institute and a dialogue with participating instructors." The meeting was to last one hour.

When the judge–instructors arrived, they found the room arrangement depicted below. Name tags had been placed on each chair. After most of the participants had found their places, the door opened and the institute director walked in, followed ceremoniously by the associate director and other staff members. This procession moved quickly to assigned seats at the front tables. The arrangement was similar to a courtroom, a church, or a legislative chamber. Before a word had been spoken, the nonverbal message was clear: this was to be a formal meeting.

The director began by introducing himself, and then said, "I am the director of this institute. Welcome to our campus and thank you for coming. I shall now introduce the staff and describe the activities in which you will be participating. . . ." This perfunctory introduction led into a 30-minute speech about the history and purpose of the institute and the policies that would be followed. The director spoke fluently but formally, using neither conversational tone nor humor. When he had finished, he said, "I would now like to learn about your expectations of the program here. Judge Smith, how do you perceive your role as

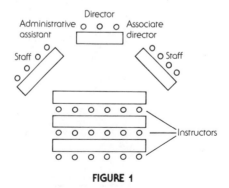

**FIGURE 1**

instructor?" The question caught the judge by surprise, but he gamely provided a one- or two-minute impromptu response. When he finished, the director said, "Thank you, Judge Smith. Judge Baxter, how do you view your role here?" And so it went, each judge trying nervously to say something intelligent and perceptive, and the director moving quickly on tó another person after each response. At the end of the process, the director asked, "Are there any questions?" Not surprisingly, there were none. "Then I shall look forward to seeing you at the opening assembly. This meeting is adjourned." He got up and walked out, his staff following quickly behind. The judge–instructors looked at each other and began to joke about the "dialogue" in which they had just participated.

In Chapter 1 we noted that public speeches involve *two-way communication* according to the degree to which receivers initiate verbal and nonverbal feedback that is perceived and interpreted by the sender. The amount and quality of that two-way process depend on the receptivity of the sender to audience behavior, and on the freedom of the audience to respond to what they hear and see. Certainly, two-way communication existed in the example above, but it was of poor quality and had limited impact on the development of shared meaning in the communication event. The speaker did not let two-way interaction become a significant factor. His lack of spontaneity and his formal speaking style, the seating arrangement, the highly structured "feedback session," and the uncertainty of the audience about what sorts of responses were appropriate, all combined to produce a sterile two-way process.

Though this actual event may not be typical, we suspect that many and perhaps most public speaking today does not maximize the potential of healthy two-way communication between speaker and audience. Whether because speakers have found such transactions bothersome, or threatening, or awkward, or disruptive, or unpredictable, or unproductive, the result is that two-way communication may be the most ignored dimension of contemporary public speaking.

Two-way communication occurs in the public speaking classroom just as it does in other situations. To some extent, it is a function of the instructor's teaching methods and of student willingness to participate. But the quality and quantity of two-way communication depends to a large extent on how the student–speaker behaves, what he does to enhance healthy interaction between himself and his audience. Always present, of course, are the speaker's and listeners' perceptions of each other and the meanings that each assigns to nonverbal factors. But verbal interchange is the heart of two-way communication in classroom speaking. For example, if a student chooses, he may discuss his forthcoming presentation with other students and the instructor before the class begins. These pre-speech exchanges may suggest last-minute alterations. During the speech, the student may have to adapt quickly to an unexpected interruption, like an unsolicited question or comment from another student. He may also have to respond in depth in a concluding question-and-answer session. And when the class period has ended, he may decide to seek additional feedback from other students or the instructor, including the possibility of asking someone to review and criticize a taped playback of the speech. Thus students in the public speaking class should realize that, even in the laboratory environment, the two-way process is an important component, a positive or negative factor in every public speech. The classroom is therefore an ideal environment to begin practicing good two-way communication.

The theme of this chapter is the improvement of spontaneous give-and-take between speakers and audiences. We shall discuss pre-speech transactions; feedback during the speech, both planned and unexpected; and post-speech feedback techniques. We approach this discussion with the assumption that if speaker–audience transactions are a typical part of public communication, then we should understand and plan for them.

## PRE-SPEECH CONVERSATION

Earlier, in Chapter 1, we asked "When does the communication event begin?" It probably starts before the speaker actually delivers the prepared message. Whenever the receivers (audience) perceive and assign meaning to actual or anticipated behavior of the speaker, the communication process has begun. Thus when the speaker arrives at the scene of the presentation, receivers may begin to notice him, evaluate his appearance, and predict what he might say.

© Howard Harrison 1978

Many speech situations include a pre-speech period in which speaker–audience conversation is possible. For example, service-club meetings may include a meal or a business meeting that the speaker also attends. A speech to a high school class may involve meeting the instructor and some of the students beforehand. Political speeches often occur after a cocktail party or banquet. And since any good speaker will arrive well ahead of time to survey the facilities and make final preparations, he is likely to encounter early arrivals who will eventually be in the audience.

One speaker we know confided, "Those people whom I talk to ahead of time bother me with inconsequential, trivial conversation. It upsets my thinking about the speech and makes me nervous. So I just try to avoid people as much as possible." This speaker's avoidance strategy is ill-advised. From the receiver-centered perspective, refusing to converse with people may make them uncomfortable; it may prompt them to create meanings that the speaker they are about to hear is aloof and uninterested in them as people. This reaction can be devastating for the speaker who is trying to sell himself, his ideas, or his product. In contrast, active and cordial pre-speech conversation can create a predisposition among receivers to like the speaker as a person and to attend to the message.

## Functions

What specific functions might pre-speech conversation serve?

**1.** *The speaker can finalize the specific arrangement for the speech*, even if many of those arrangements have been carefully negotiated in advance. Who will introduce the speaker? Does that person have the necessary information? Is everyone agreed on the time limits? Does the audience include people who should be recognized? Should those who arranged for the speech be aware of the speech's purpose or content? Are they aware of any technical support equipment the speech needs?

**2.** *Pre-speech conversation can enhance a speaker's confidence.* We may experience more anxiety if our listeners are a nameless, unfamiliar group of faces than if we have met and chatted with some of them. A minister who was occasionally guest preacher at other churches in the community remarked that he made a point of meeting two or three people ahead of time just to soothe his nervousness in the strange environment.

**3.** *Information we obtain during pre-speech communication can help us adapt spontaneously to the unique situation.* During the speech, for example, we can refer by name to people we met earlier, or we can actually utilize new information picked up in prior conversation. Recently, the author spoke to a group of personnel managers about communication problems in large organizations. During the pre-speech luncheon, the club president told him that at the previous meeting a professor of business administration had discussed supervisor–employee relations. That speech had included information about how the quality of superior–subordinate communication may affect a worker's productivity. This bit of information permitted me to make a last-minute alteration in my speech introduction, to make a friendly reference to the business professor, and to use his idea about worker productivity as a convenient springboard for the main points of the speech.

**4.** *Pre-speech interaction may minimize the "performance" dimension of speechmaking.* Too often a speaker's role is viewed as similar to that of an actor in a play. We do not usually see or speak with the actor before the play. To do so would minimize the distance between audience and actor, making it more difficult for us to perceive the actor *as* the character. Part of the joy of watching a good play is that we can suspend our knowledge of the actor as a real person and make believe that the character is "real." A good performance separates us from Susan Jones, college student and theatre major. Instead, we "see" Anne Frank, gallant Jewish girl who died in a Nazi concentration camp. But a public speech is *not* a theatrical performance. We do not want to perceive the speaker as someone larger than life, someone playing a character who performs in ways that amuse and entertain us. If we are amused and entertained, it should be because a real person has developed a message that was intended to elicit that response. We should see a speaker who, though changing the nature of the communication transaction, remains a person whom we can know, whom we can like, and with whom we can identify. A casual, friendly conversation ahead of time may enhance that personal touch, lessen interpersonal distance, and eliminate the "performance syndrome" during the speech.

Some people dispute this point. They argue that for some well-known speakers, the communication event really is a performance; the mystique of their fame and achievements enhances the impact of the performance. For example, the author heard Robert Kennedy as presidential candidate speak to a stadium audience one week before he was assassinated. Kennedy entered the stadium in a limousine convertible, protected by a phalanx of Secret Service agents and surrounded by various political officials and sundry "beautiful people" who were supporting his campaign. Could it be that the enthusiastic audience response—before, during, and after the speech—was evoked in part by the theatrical dimension of the event? By the magic and mystery of the celebrity who appeared larger than life? Why should someone with the natural appeal of a Robert Kennedy damage the "great man" image with casual, mundane conversation with the audience?

We cannot support this argument. Even famous people, we believe, can profit from being cordial, down-to-earth, and empathic with others. Even famous people can benefit from a speech style that is "talking with" rather than "performing for" an audience. It can just as easily be argued, for example, that Robert Kennedy *did have* a personal, conversational appeal that emerged whether he was speaking to a large crowd or shaking hands with people on the street. Besides, most of us will never be famous, never carry with us the mystique of reputation. Nor will we be very effective with a carefully orchestrated speech performance. When we can participate on the same level as the audience in pre-speech interaction, we lessen the chances that they will expect such a performance from us in the coming speech.

**5.** *Finally, a speaker's willingness to interact before the speech may put the audience more at ease,* especially when they have an opportunity to make comments and ask questions during the presentation. As receivers, we may be reluctant to participate, even when asked directly, if we do not know what to expect from the speaker. Will he embarrass us, make us appear stupid, become rude and judgmental? If we have talked with him beforehand, if we have found him cordial, relaxed, and interested in us as people, we will probably be less apprehensive about participating later on.

This point can be illustrated by considering two typical authority figures in our lives—the teacher and the boss. Do we communicate freely with these people in the formal classroom or work situation? Do we provide open, candid feedback? The quality and quantity of our two-way communication is partly dependent on our previous experience with these people. If we've spoken on a casual, one-to-one basis with our professor, or if our boss regularly stops by our work station and shows a sincere interest in who we are and what we are doing, do we not feel more at ease about initiating comments to them? Similarly, some speakers who honestly seek open two-way communication may not get much if they are perceived as cold, remote, intolerant "experts" or "authorities." Admittedly, some people may prefer that image, like the boss who said, "When I talk with new employees, I *want* them to

fear me; and I don't want feedback!" But a key function of getting to know the audience beforehand is the breaking down of interpersonal barriers that impede later sender–receiver interaction.

## Suggestions

To take advantage of these pre-speech benefits, we make the following suggestions.

**1.** *Be assertive.* Initiate conversations; don't wait for someone to start them. A surprising number of people will avoid taking responsibility for "hosting" the guest speaker, for introducing the speaker to various people in the audience.

**2.** *During speech negotiations, try to arrange for at least one "contact person,"* someone who will arrive early and who can help finalize the arrangements.

**3.** *Smile! Try to convey the nonverbal messages of open, relaxed cordiality.* A speaker who stands grimly against the wall studying his notes and avoiding eye contact with strangers may appear aloof and even threatening to people who might otherwise initiate a conversation.

**4.** *Ask to be introduced to other audience members.* The more people a speaker can meet beforehand, the better. Try to avoid letting a club president or program chairperson monopolize the pre-speech conversation.

**5.** *Ask questions.* Some speakers talk too much about their own backgrounds, opinions, and eventual speech topic. They may bore their audience before the speech begins! Instead, learn more about the people who will be hearing the message. It will not only assist in last-minute adaptation, but will also enhance goodwill with the audience. We all like to talk about ourselves and the groups to which we belong, and we like to know that a speaker is actually interested in us as individuals.

**6.** *Avoid becoming defensive or argumentative,* especially when speaking on controversial issues. Some people, anticipating the eventual speech, may express strong and even provocative opinions. Though it may be necessary to respond directly, it is usually better to be tactful. For example, "I'm glad you are concerned about this problem. I'll have some things to say about it in my speech, and I hope you feel free to express your opinions during the question-and-answer session." The important point is to avoid locking horns too early before having a chance to present a well-prepared message. We should not lose an audience before we begin by appearing closed-minded and judgmental.

**7.** *Use the public speaking class an an ideal place to initiate and practice pre-speech conversation.*

## THE QUESTION-AND-ANSWER SESSION

Two-way communication continues while the speech is in progress. In this section, we shall explore audience comments and questions that are typical and fairly predictable, the kinds of audience-to-speaker transactions that we can expect and even plan for. In the next section, we shall discuss the unexpected transactions that may occur during the speech.

An increasing number of speakers are incorporating a question-and-answer or audience feedback session into their speech planning. Instead of the timid "Gee, I hope nobody will threaten me or clutter my planned remarks with questions," they are instead saying "I want my listeners to understand me, to have a chance to clarify and even disagree with my ideas, and I will be very disappointed if they don't fill the time I've set aside for questions and comments." Thus teachers, politicians, supervisors, and guest speakers at service clubs are seeking two-way communication. Even night club and television performers are interacting spontaneously with the audience as a part of their acts. The author recently talked to an innovative minister who, during and after his sermons, answered questions from the congregation. He said that while some people were bothered by the process (they felt it destroyed the religious mood of the service), most were enthusiastic. "I'm not just a preacher," he said, "I'm a *teacher*. I try to explain and interpret the Bible and theological issues. How can I be effective or know that I'm succeeding unless I permit my listeners to ask questions?" Clearly, the speech event that excludes audience questions and comments is becoming obsolete.

## Seeking Audience Messages

How do we encourage audience questions and comments? In general, we must provide an open communication climate, an environment that suggests that audience responses are appropriate, expected, and a healthy addition to the communication event. But how can this be achieved? We offer several suggestions.

1. *The question-and-answer session should be announced ahead of time,* especially if it breaks the typical pattern or audience expectations of the speech event. If, for example, a professor customarily gives a 50-minute lecture, stopping when the bell rings and walking out, she may catch the audience by surprise when she announces after 30 minutes, "OK, let's have some questions." An appropriate announcement might be: "My prepared comments take about a half-hour. When I'm finished, I hope you'll have some comments or questions." Or a supervisor might say: "As I go through this new procedure, I want to make sure you understand fully. Therefore, please interrupt me with questions whenever you want clarification."

2. *In seeking feedback, the speaker must be believable.* The receivers must believe that the sender really does want honest feedback, that she is not just going through the motions to be polite. Someone once quipped, "The most important thing about communication is sincerity; once you learn to fake that, you've got it made." Not only do we oppose deception—trying to fake sincerity—we also think that most audience members can spot phoniness. They can tell, both verbally and nonverbally, whether a speaker is truly interested in their responses. A perfunctory, unenthusiastic, offhand comment like, "Oh, you can ask questions if you want to," will likely discourage feedback. So instead of

suggesting tricks that will give the *appearance* of sincerity, we believe that the speaker must develop a positive attitude about the give-and-take of audience questions. The process must be viewed as constructive to the main purpose of communication—developing shared meaning. Thus, if the speaker cannot develop this enthusiasm, there is little he can do to prompt open two-way interaction. Speakers who have been dissatisfied with unproductive, lifeless feedback sessions should do some self-analysis to try to learn whether their own behavior was part of the problem.

**3.** *The speaker should positively reinforce good audience comments and questions.* Following are some all-too-typical examples of how some speakers actually *punish* feedback. The professor says, with all the sincerity he can muster, "Anytime you have a question, just ask." The students take him at his word. About halfway through the lecture, a student timidly raises his hand. "Yes, what is it?" snaps the professor, frowning and impatiently glancing at his watch. The student asks a question. "No, no, no!" shouts the professor. "You obviously didn't hear my first point. I suppose I'll have to go over it again for anyone else who wasn't listening." The students have now learned an important lesson; when you ask questions in this class, you get punished. They stop asking questions.

Or a public official is reading a manuscript speech to a community group. A hand is raised and a question asked. The official answers tersely and moves quickly back to the manuscript, giving the nonverbal impression that the question was a bothersome intrusion on his carefully developed flow of ideas. For the rest of the speech he keeps his eyes buried in the manuscript so as not to notice other raised hands in the audience.

Or a fluent, persuasive attorney is arguing in favor of a political reform to a generally supportive audience. One person tries to disagree, giving an intelligent but poorly phrased counterargument. The attorney uses her rhetorical skills, including humor, to make the argument and the person appear foolish. The exchange ends with the rest of the audience laughing at the speaker's cleverness and, probably, at the ridiculous argument from the audience member. Other listeners now know that if they disagree publicly, they will probably be embarrassed.

Sometimes our negative reinforcement of feedback is not as blatant. Simply by being relatively passive to audience response, we may
discourage participation. This passivity becomes, in effect, a negative
reinforcer. Thus, we should be more positive when we seek feedback.
Depending on the speech purpose and situation, the following might be
appropriate:

"Last time I spoke with you, you asked some important questions.
I hope you will continue giving me feedback today."

"Good question, Tom. I'll try to answer it this way . . ."

"I hope you realize that my speech will only take about twenty
minutes and that I'm depending on you to interact with me for the
rest of the hour about anything in my speech that you want to
discuss."

"I had intended to talk about some other things, but you seem so
interested in this point that I suggest I stop here and we discuss it
in more depth. What do some of you think about it?"

"Thank you for so many good comments. I learned a lot today."

"If we don't have time for all your questions, I'll be happy to stay
after we adjourn for you to talk with me informally."

"I don't agree with you, sir, but you've raised an important point
that my program will have to solve if it is to be successful."

"That's an interesting idea. Tell me more."

"For those of you who are unfamiliar with our procedure in this
lecture series, the first half-hour is the speaker's turn; the second
half-hour is your turn to express ideas and ask questions."

In terms of positive reinforcement, we should recognize that some
questioners are very apprehensive about participating. The author has
sometimes been more nervous about asking a question as an audience
member than in actually giving a speech. Thus the speaker may need
to put a questioner at ease. For example, if someone should flub a
question with awkward wording or delivery style, the audience may

laugh or make critical side comments. The speaker might say, "No, please; John raises an important point and I think we need to consider it." The speaker thus *defends* the questioner and *legitimizes* the importance of two-way communication.

**4.** *The speaker should try to discern confusion or disagreement in the audience.* That is, we should not always wait for the audience to initiate the feedback. The speaker who views the communication event as a performance, or who is primarily message-centered, may not be concerned with audience confusion. Rather, he may assume, "If the audience doesn't ask questions, for whatever reason, that's their problem." But the *receiver-centered speaker* considers "shared meaning" with his auditors to be crucial. And this speaker will not rely totally on audience initiative. He will watch for cues—someone shaking his head, a look of confusion on people's faces, a tentative raising of a hand, or even blank stares. Certainly we might misinterpret these cues. But that is why we seek the feedback. "Richard, I thought I saw some confusion on your face a moment ago. Did you want to ask a question?" If Richard says no, that he understands, nothing is hurt and the speaker has proved his active concern for meaningful two-way communication.

**5.** *Ask one or more audience members to help get the questions started.* We are *not* arguing here for the *planted question*, the kind that a speaker carefully arranges and rehearses ahead of time with a particular audience member. For example, we oppose the deception of some political candidates. A supporter asks a "tough question" to which the candidate provides a powerful, dynamic, "spontaneous" response. But there is nothing deceptive about asking one or two people ahead of time to help get the question-and-answer session started. The speaker is not *planting* specific questions; he is merely asking for assistance in getting the two-way process going. Before a public health nurse spoke to a high school class, she talked with the teacher. "Sometimes students are reluctant to be the first person to ask a question. Since it is important to get their questions and comments, would you help me get the process going if no one else does? Perhaps you could comment on any point I've made that you think is especially important to this group of students." This arrangement may prevent the awkward silence that sometimes follows a speaker's request for feedback.

**6.** *Suggest to the audience some areas for questions and comments.* Perhaps some points are more complex or controversial than others and need more discussion. Perhaps some ideas have special relevance to a particular audience. Suppose the city official knows that the audience of home owners is especially concerned with his information about the new freeway construction. He might say, "Would anyone like to comment on the freeway project? Do you have any worries about the current routing?" This technique not only gets the question-and-answer session started, it also avoids getting sidetracked on trivial or irrelevant issues.

## Responding to Audience Messages

As mentioned above, what bothers many speakers, especially inexperienced ones, is not receiving audience feedback, but rather responding to it effectively. One problem is that such responses are usually spontaneous. They are short impromptu speeches to clarify information or refute the speaker's arguments. Inept responses can damage one's total speech purpose, detracting from the impact of the prepared remarks. Another problem is that the way one responds can suggest a relationship with the audience. The speaker may appear angry, impatient, condescending, enthusiastic, appreciative, bored, aloof, or concerned simply by tone of voice, facial expression, and choice of language. It is important that every speaker think strategically about his habitual ways of responding to audience messages.

*How do speakers typically respond?* The most common style is by *providing information*. Either the speaker clarifies previous messages or elaborates with new information.

A second typical response is *defending*. It is appropriate for a speaker advocating a controversial point of view to defend her position when the receivers disagree, to refute opposing arguments and re-support her own. Unfortunately, too many speakers become overly *defensive*. They assume that disagreement with their ideas is an attack on their person. They become aggressive, argumentative, dogmatic, and angry. Even worse, some defensive responses redirect the focus of the question toward the person who asked it. The speaker begins attacking that person: "You obviously weren't listening to my speech." "That's a dumb question!" "How could you possibly believe a stupid thing like that?" "That's just your opinion—I've got the facts." And often, even though these verbal responses are not given, the nonverbal cues prompt the audience to get the same message. Defensive responses are evaluative or judgmental. They suggest good or bad, right or wrong, accurate or inaccurate, effective or ineffective, intelligent or foolish. And it is important to recognize how quickly and easily a judgmental response toward an idea can be interpreted as an evaluation of the person expressing that idea.

A third response category is *probing and paraphrasing*. The speaker asks an audience member for more information (probe) or restates in a few words the question or comment (paraphrase). The problem with too many speakers is that they answer the question or argument *they think they heard*. Not infrequently, their lengthy response prompts the asker to reply, "That wasn't my question," or "That's not what I meant." Why, then, don't we probe or paraphrase more often? One reason is that we become convinced that we heard and comprehended the questioner correctly the first time. Why get more information—why restate the question—if it only wastes time and delays our response? Perhaps another reason is that we are anxious to answer quickly. We like our topic, are enthusiastic about talking about it more in our response, and think that to delay our response might suggest lack of information, indecisiveness, or weakness of our arguments. Thus, while the responding and paraphrasing responses can be immensely useful in assuring shared meaning between questioner and speaker, it is used rarely in comparison to providing information and defending.

*The following strategies may improve our ability to respond effectively to audience questions.*

1. *Avoid defensiveness.* This is easier said than done. Most of us have developed an automatic protective reaction when we think we are being threatened. And the more strongly we believe in something, the more the points of view in our speech directly reflect our identity as a

person, the greater our need to defend those ideas. To implement this
suggestion, therefore, we must analyze the ways in which we habitually respond when people disagree with us. If that self-analysis (or
feedback from others) tells us that we tend to become angry or dogmatic, we should consider less defensive ways of responding. A nondefensive response might be: "That's an important point that you
mentioned. I considered that argument when preparing this speech.
Let me explain why I don't think I can now agree with it." Or "That
argument is something that perhaps we should consider in more depth.
Does anyone else have an opinion on that?" Notice that these responses
do not imply that the speaker has been attacked personally, nor do
they put the questioner on the defensive. Most important, they do not
in any way imply that the speaker is backing down from his own
position. What these less defensive responses do achieve is a focus on
problems, arguments, and ideas, and not on people or personalities.
The speaker who cannot break the habit of automatic defensiveness
may find the question-and-answer sessions the most difficult and
intimidating part of public speaking.

**2.** *Probe and paraphrase.* This technique can assure that the speaker
truly understands the question. It will also help the rest of the audience to comprehend what may have been a poorly worded or inaudible
question. And some speakers have found that this type of response can
"buy time" to consider more carefully the eventual answer. Typical
probes are:

> "Do you think others share this concern?"
>
> "How often has that happened?"
>
> "How do you feel about that?"

A paraphrase might be:

> "I hear you asking for more information about the cost of my
> program. Is that correct?"
>
> "You are suggesting, then, that the general public will not go
> along with this rezoning plan."

Notice that this technique establishes a kind of conversational inter-change—a dialogue—between questioner and speaker, developing a more relaxed atmosphere. The probing-paraphrasing response can be learned. It can become a habit. We can practice it ahead of time and consciously use it in our presentations until it becomes second nature, a routine part of our communication style.

**3.** *Avoid getting sidetracked.* Occasionally a member of the audience will ask or comment about irrelevant details or special concerns that have little to do with the speech purpose. While this person must be dealt with tactfully, the speaker must remember his own speech goals as well as the interests of the audience. The receivers are usually even more impatient than the speaker when the question-and-answer period digresses from the main topic. Perhaps an irrelevant question can be answered briefly, but if the questioner persists, an appropriate comment might be, "I was unable to cover that issue in my speech. But if it is a special concern of yours, perhaps we could talk about it afterward in more depth."

An important exception to this suggestion is if *many people* in the audience want to pursue an issue that the speaker did not cover. The receiver-centered communicator will not hold rigidly to his specific points if it appears that audience interest is clearly on another aspect of the topic. Rather, he will adapt. But in most cases, the receivers will appreciate the speaker's attempts to keep question-and-answer sessions on the track.

**4.** *Recognize the questioner's intentions and feelings.* Effective re-sponses conform not only to the actual subject matter of a question, but also to the personal objectives of the asker. For example, many "ques-tions" are really statements or arguments:

"So how are you going to solve my problems with this proposal?" (Translation: You won't solve my problems.)

"Do you really believe that employees will benefit from this profit-sharing scheme?" (Translation: Employees will not benefit.)

"So what in the world can the ordinary citizen do about this problem?" (Translation: We are powerless to do anything, so you are talking to the wrong people.)

Sometimes key phrases can be a tipoff that the question is really an argument: "Yes, but don't you think . . ."; "Who says that . . ."; "But aren't you aware that . . ."; etc. These comments usually suggest that the person has more to say and wants to talk. The probing or paraphrasing response can help get underneath the question to the authentic idea or feeling. The speakers who can most accurately interpret the true intentions of the questioner can usually provide the most tactful, effective response.

### Confirming and Disconfirming Communication

As a general conclusion to this section, we suggest two terms that have been discussed by Sieberg: *confirming* and *disconfirming* communication (Sieberg, 1976).

*Confirming communication* involves a recognition of another person as a unique human being, not as an abstract entity or "object." It involves acknowledging another's existence and accepting his right to "experience the world" in his own way. Most important, confirming behavior shows "a willingness to be involved" with another person, to participate in a transaction and to accept the fact that that transaction develops a relationship. Confirming communication does *not* necessarily mean *agreement* with another. We can disagree but still accept another person's right to have viewpoints and to interact with us about them.

*Disconfirming communication*, according to Sieberg, denies the positive factors of acceptance, acknowledgment, recognition, transaction, and relationship. It involves such factors as indifference to another person's ideas and feelings, lack of awareness of that person's unique characteristics and goals, attempts to restrict or discontinue another's attempts to communicate, and an unwillingness to establish or recognize a relationship between ourselves and another person.

Sieberg's model, while applying to any kind of communication event, is especially useful in two-way communication between speaker and audience. Any reasonably perceptive receiver can tell when the

© Howard Harrison 1970

speaker is using confirming or disconfirming communication. Notice
how easily a speaker can *confirm* an audience member who has just
asked a question or made a comment. By paraphrasing and probing,
the speaker shows that he wants to understand the message, that it is
important. By smiling, nodding, appearing congenial in facial and
vocal inflection, showing appreciation for the interaction, and even
thanking the audience member for the input, he shows acceptance of
another person's right to exist and to interact. And by seeking continued interaction with the audience, the speaker confirms their legitimate participation in dialogue.

Similarly, *disconfirming* behavior is also readily apparent. The
speaker may cut off someone in mid-question, react judgmentally
about another person's ability to think and communicate, be unwilling
to spend any time in answering the person's question, nonverbally

appear bored or impatient with the questioner, avoid further inter-action with various receivers who are attempting to participate, be evasive or even deceptive in responding to questions, and show anger or hostility toward contrary opinions and arguments.

Perhaps one of the most important reasons why we do not like particular speakers is because of that intangible sense of being discon-firmed, of being rejected as a unique person with a right to participate. And perhaps a reason why we like and respond to some less skilled speakers is that they seem to treat us as people and, whether they agree or disagree, accept and show appreciation for our involvement with them. The question-and-answer session is probably the most important time for demonstrating the speaker's relationship with receivers, for proving our authentic concern for open two-way com-munication.

## UNEXPECTED TRANSACTIONS

The question-and-answer session is not the only time in which two-way communication occurs during the speech presentation. Through-out the communication event, we know that receivers are rarely if ever totally passive. They are constantly engaging in a variety of behaviors, some more noticeable than others, that may affect speech effectiveness. For example, people in the audience may be carrying on private con-versations, a small child may be crying, someone may be staring out the window or falling asleep, another may raise his hand for a ques-tion, and still another may interrupt with applause, laughter, or a comment. Someone may enter the room unexpectedly and someone else may get up and leave. The audience is a dynamic group, in continual activity. And the speaker usually perceives and, in various ways, interacts with audience behaviors.

The obvious implication is that the speaker cannot simply give the speech as planned, but must make regular spontaneous adaptations to the varied responses of the listeners. Unlike the stereotyped professor who enters the classroom, buries his head in notes, reads for an hour, and then walks out, most speakers will be continuously reminded of audience presence.

## Occurrences and Suggestions

The following are some common occurrences, with suggestions for adapting.

*Audience noise or commotion.*  These frequently occur when youngsters are present or when the speech situation involves a volatile emotional issue. Sometimes members of the audience who want to hear will try to silence others, but more often the speaker will have to intervene. Dogmatic statements like "Be quiet while I'm talking!" are usually too antagonistic to be productive, and a more friendly reaction might be: "Perhaps some people cannot hear because of side conversations; we will have time for comments and questions in a few minutes." Such comments should preserve the anonymity of the noisemakers. To single them out might antagonize them to more damaging behaviors. Only when the disturbance persists should the speaker single out people. The key is, be as tactful and accommodating as possible for as long as possible. Do not alienate an audience with an angry command or accusation.

*Spontaneous audience questions.*  Sometimes spontaneous questions from the audience interrupt the speaker's trend of thought. In any speech, we should *decide in advance* whether we want to encourage questions during the planned presentation. If precise timing is not a factor, questions might be handled as they arise (a common classroom technique). However, the speaker should be wary of irrelevant questions that divert the listeners from the speech topic. He should also avoid belaboring a point by accepting too many questions on the same basic idea. A comment like "Perhaps we've discussed this notion long enough and should get back to some of the other things I wanted to mention" will usually have the approval of most of the audience.

If the speaker feels that unsolicited questions during the speech will be disruptive to the flow of ideas, he may want to "contract" with the audience, to agree to answer all questions later on. For example: "I'm going to talk to you for about thirty minutes. Then I shall be happy to spend a few minutes answering whatever questions you might have." If this tactic is used, however, the speaker must reserve that question-and-answer time. We are not amused when the speaker sheepishly concludes, "Well, I see I talked longer than I expected and we won't have time for questions." For persuasive speakers (like a salesperson or politician), this comment can be deadly. Also, a speaker may defer the question to a later point in the speech. "If you don't mind, I'd like to come back to that important question when I discuss the issue later in the speech." That response is fine, so long as the speaker does indeed refer to the question later. An evasive speaker sometimes uses this reply as a strategy for ignoring a tough question. But the person who asked the question (and usually others in the audience as well) will remember what it was and may persist later on, leaving the speaker in a very awkward position.

Using the technique noted earlier—pausing at the end of each main point and asking for questions before moving on to the next— may preempt spontaneous interruptions. But whatever the strategy, we must realize that speaker–audience dialogue is such a growing trend that more and more audiences are coming to assume their right to ask questions at any time.

*The heckler.*   Though feared by many speakers, the heckler is actually rather rare in public communication. Politicians who are being covered by the news media may encounter antagonists who recognize an opportunity to be on television, but most of our speeches involve reasonably well-mannered, considerate people who do not attempt to embarrass or destroy the speaker. However, when a person obviously wants to interrupt, challenge, or heckle the speaker, we cannot ignore him. Remember, first, that *the speaker usually has legitimacy and the heckler does not.* The person at the podium, often with a microphone, has an enormous psychological advantage. Second, many audience members are as embarrassed by the heckler's comments as the speaker is. Hence, the speaker can often count on the audience as an ally rather than an enemy.

The following are some typical responses to the heckler:

"Though you are entitled to your opinions, you've been monopolizing the discussion and I think we should give others a chance to participate."

"It's obvious that you don't want me to talk. Shall we let the

audience decide whether they want to listen to you or listen to me?"

"I'll tell you what. If you will let me finish my speech without interruption, I'll let you have the floor to answer my arguments." (Usually the heckler declines.)

"Sir, you are rude and obnoxious and are wasting the audience's time. I think you should be quiet or leave."

The speaker should probably avoid making fun of the heckler with witty yet biting personal references, as this may provoke more vicious responses. But we must be firm with him. Usually a grateful audience will actually applaud when we do, and they may even assist the speaker in shutting up the challenger. And we dare not ignore the heckler, or the intimidation may increase. Incidentally, some apparently obnoxious people may not be aware of the inappropriateness of their behavior. A brief remark from the speaker to that effect may be all that is necessary to bring them into line.

*Interruptions from outsiders.* These interruptions can come at any time. Waiters may begin clearing tables. A secretary may interrupt to announce an emergency phone call. Someone may enter the room by mistake. A janitor may choose the wrong time to vacuum the floors in an adjoining room. A student may arrive late and may make a conspicuous entrance. A jet passing overhead or an ambulance siren may drown out the speaker.

We should not try to ignore such interruptions, pretending that they don't exist. The audience knows they are there and is usually distracted momentarily. The speaker should therefore recognize the interruption and suggest a strategy for dealing with it. The following are some possible techniques:

"I hope the table-clearing won't be too distracting. Let me know if you can't hear me."

"Would someone shut the door? The hall noise is rather loud."

"Can someone here help the gentleman find the correct room?"

"Would someone volunteer to go next door to tell the janitor that we are having a meeting?"

"Hi! Come on in. There's a seat right over there."

The specific message depends of course on the situation, but some response should be made. The more relaxed and informal the speaker's style, the easier and more appropriate such comments will be.

The suggestions in this section are mainly common sense adaptations to audience and environment. But such practical solutions are frequently overlooked by speakers who are preoccupied with the prepared message. Common sense is only useful at the conscious level, and we urge speakers to develop a systematic procedure or checklist for dealing with both the predictable and the unexpected in any public communication event.

## POST-SPEECH FEEDBACK

Two-way communication need not end when the speaker's presentation ends. In this section, we shall explore an activity that has important implications for public speakers today—obtaining post-speech feedback. The term "post-speech" may be somewhat vague, because it is often difficult to denote precisely when the public speaking event ends. Earlier we suggested that the *communication* process does not necessarily end when the speaker finishes the prepared or intended message, because the receivers may still assign meaning to what they have heard for a long time afterward. And we have also argued that a question-and-answer session following prepared remarks should also be viewed as an integral part of the presentation. Generally, "post-speech" means that the participants in the communication event—speaker and receivers—have ended their formal interaction as a group and have dispersed to other activities; the public or one-to-many transaction has ended. *Post-speech feedback is a process in which a speaker (or agents of a speaker) gathers information about the ways in which an audience received, interpreted, remembered, or acted on the intended message.*

Unfortunately, many speakers are members of the "hit-and-run school" of speechmaking. A political candidate gives some brief remarks and is then whisked away by aides to the next stop. He sees only selected newspaper accounts of what a handful of reporters heard and decided to report, but gets no insight about the meanings that the audience in general assigned to his message. The minister accepts polite smiles and comments of "Enjoyed your sermon, Reverend," as the congregation files out, but gets no in-depth feedback of the speech impact. The teacher lectures right up to the dismissal bell and hurries out of the classroom. The supervisor discusses a new policy with employees, answers a few questions, and then forgets about the event as she returns to other tasks in her busy day. The speaker at a service-club luncheon accepts brief thanks from the president and then apologizes for having to make a hasty exit back to his office.

Some speakers apologize for the "hit-and-run" tendency, blaming it on their busy schedules. Others feel that the communication event is routine and relatively unimportant and therefore does not justify the effort to get feedback. But perhaps many of those speakers are not truly interested in whether their speech purpose has been achieved. Perhaps they are more *speaker-centered* ("How did I perform?") than they are *receiver-centered* ("Did the audience receive and act on my message in the ways that I intended?") This book is based on receiver-centered principles, and the hit-and-run approach denies those principles. Only by seeking post-speech feedback can the speaker truly embrace this receiver-centered philosophy.

### Justification

What can post-speech feedback achieve?

**1.** *It can be a valuable learning tool for improving public speaking.* Some speakers remain inept after many years and hundreds of speeches simply because they have never gotten any notion of their bothersome habits. Others, who present essentially the same message to a variety of audiences, do not get information that might improve that message with each successive presentation. But the speaker who does seek feedback can learn and improve skills with every speech.

**2.** *This feedback can be a guide to policy-making.* Suppose a speaker advocates a new program or discusses various problems and potential solutions. Receiver response can be an excellent guide to what people (voters, taxpayers, employees, home owners, etc.) will accept and support. Policy-makers can anticipate trouble spots in their programs just by listening better to audience response.

**3.** *Feedback can also help determine the* effects *of the public speech.* What did the receivers *do*? How did they *behave* in response to the message? The advertising and television industries rely heavily on post-communication feedback. The Nielsen ratings, for example, tell networks about audience size (how receivers respond to programming). Polls about voting preference, brand-name identification, or actual use of products are crucial to advertising campaigns. Likewise, the speaker who wants the listeners to *use* or *act on* the message in some particular way needs to have some means of knowing what behaviors actually occurred. For example, a speaker who instructs owners of microwave ovens how to use the new appliance should learn whether, over time, the owners have actually implemented the suggestions and techniques.

**4.** *Most important, seeking post-speech feedback helps confirm the receivers as being essential in the communication process.* It tells them: "I think you are important, not just as warm bodies to hear my speech, but as people whom I care about, with whom I want to interact, and who I hope have benefitted from my message." In contrast, it is disconfirming to think that as listeners we are "just another audience" to a speaker, that our uniqueness does not matter. Thus, feedback not only provides direct benefits regarding speech improvement, but also indirect benefits in terms of better speaker–listener relationships.

### Problems in Obtaining Feedback

At least four problems interfere with the feedback process.

**1.** *One of those problems has been discussed before—defensiveness.* The speaker may be afraid of what he might discover. Just as he avoids audience questions, so he insulates himself from any follow-up messages about overall speech effects. Consider someone who has invested many years in teaching. Suddenly he gets nagging doubts about his ability to communicate effectively with students. Instead of finding out about how various lectures are being received so as to change his communication behavior, he avoids interaction with students and widens the sender–receiver gap. He is defensive because the feedback might threaten his self-image.

**2.** *It takes both time and energy to get good feedback.* Since some speeches require significant effort to negotiate and deliver, we may sigh with relief when we finish, forget about the speech, and move on to other things. And people who speak in the context of their busy professional lives may get caught up in other tasks and simply not have time to learn about audience response.

**3.** *A third problem concerns authentic feedback. How do we know that someone's evaluation of our message is candid and accurate?* If it is positive, how do we know that the person isn't just trying to make us feel good or avoid conflict? If the feedback is negative, how do we know that the person listened well enough or was unbiased and thoughtful as he received the message? People in positions of authority have a special problem here. How many people will tell the boss, "Your speech made no sense to me"? Do teachers, who will eventually assign final grades, really hear straight feedback about their courses? Post-speech communication does little good if it does not reflect true audience responses.

**4.** *Finally, feedback may not be representative.* Perhaps a speaker's attempt to get it was not systematic; from two or three random comments afterward, he may falsely conclude that people were persuaded by his remarks. Or from an isolated newspaper account that distorted his central thesis, he decides that nobody understood his point of view. While the speaker's message is interpreted uniquely by each receiver, a general audience response can usually be determined. But it will be misleading unless the speaker can find reliable ways of obtaining enough feedback to be representative.

## Suggestions for Post-Speech Feedback

Following is a list of techniques that audience-centered public speakers use to obtain feedback.

1. *Develop a positive attitude.* View feedback not as a threat to self-image but as a means of achieving better results. Recognize that some of the most effective speakers got that way by trial-and-error, by viewing feedback as new information that will improve future speeches.

2. *Discuss the speech informally with various audience members.* Don't rush off to other activities while the message is still fresh in their minds. Of course, try to remember the problem of unrepresentative sampling. Sometimes the people who are most willing to chat afterward are those who appreciated the speech the most, and may not be typical of the total group. But this conversational technique is often a good starting point for the feedback process.

3. *Tape-record the speech presentation.* Listening to an audio tape of the question-and-answer process might reveal persistent audience concern on certain issues or topics. Viewing a videotape playback can help us experience more accurately what the audience experienced; it permits us to empathize with them and identify trouble spots.

4. *Ask impartial observers to provide a critique.* A judge recently asked members of a college speech department to show up unannounced in the courtroom audience, to observe his communication with trial participants, and to meet with him later to offer some suggestions. Another speaker, a candidate for public office, regularly taped her speeches with a small pocket recorder and asked her colleagues to evaluate them. This technique may be threatening to some, but if the evaluator is someone who will be tactful but honest, it may be the best way to solve the problem of feedback authenticity.

5. *Use questionnaires.* Like the pollsters, a speaker may want to prepare written questionnaires and tally the results. These forms may reveal how the receivers interpreted the message, how much they remember, and what, if anything, they are doing with that informa-

tion. Unfortunately, this technique is often misused. Vague or loaded questions, unrepresentative sampling of the audience, or faulty inferences from the resulting data all decrease the confidence we can place in the conclusions. Therefore, if important decisions are to be made from the results of this post-speech feedback, we should get advice from someone with good background in statistics and testing methods.

**6.** *Observe audience response.* Watch people behave as a result of hearing the speech. If, for example, a trainer instructed employees about operating new equipment, he should spend some time watching them use it in their work. Or if the speaker wants the audience to *understand* a topic, he should listen (another form of observation) to what they eventually say about it or read (observe) what they write. In the final analysis, this technique is the only sure method for determining whether the speech purpose (intended audience response) was achieved.

## SUMMARY

A topic that is often ignored in public speaking classes and textbooks is the process of two-way communication that exists in varying quantity and quality in every one-to-many transaction.

Pre-speech conversation with audience members is the first type of two-way communication. It can help the speaker finalize speech arrangements, enhance self-confidence, improve spontaneous adaptation, minimize the "performance syndrome," and put the audience more at ease. However, good pre-speech interaction depends on the speaker's willingness to initiate communication and to be relaxed and cordial rather than defensive or argumentative.

A second type of two-way communication is the question-and-answer session. Sometimes these sessions are unproductive because speakers do not encourage active feedback from listeners. It should be announced in advance. Furthermore, the speaker should be sincere in seeking questions, should reinforce good audience comments, try to perceive audience confusion or disagreement, and perhaps encourage questions by suggesting key topic areas or by asking an audience member to get things started. Of the several ways of responding to questions, the best ones are probing and paraphrasing *before* actually providing an informative or argumentative answer. Most important, the style of responses should confirm rather than disconfirm the questioner as a person.

A third category of interaction, which the speaker cannot prevent, involves unexpected transactions like audience noise, spontaneous audience questions, rude behavior of an audience member, or interruptions from outsiders. All such transactions must be dealt with tactfully, not angrily, and the speaker may discover that the audience is often an ally in eliminating disturbances and minimizing interruptions.

Finally, two-way communication can be continued by seeking post-speech feedback about the ways in which an audience actually received and responded to the message. Such feedback may cause speaker defensiveness, may be time-consuming, may not be totally authentic, and may not be representative of the total audience. But with careful information-gathering techniques and a sincere interest in getting objective feedback, the speaker can use each speech effort as a basis for improving all future efforts.

## QUESTIONS FOR STUDY

1.  When does the "public speaking event" actually begin in terms of a student's presentation to the speech class?

2.  During the pre-speech period, does the student in the speech class have any advantages or disadvantages that speakers with more unfamiliar audiences might not have? Explain.

3.  When questioned or challenged by other students in the speech class, what are some strategies or guidelines to follow?

4.  What are some unexpected events or transactions that have occurred in public speeches that you have observed? What would you have done to deal with them?

5. What are some real or hypothetical communication events in which obtaining post-speech feedback is especially important? Assuming that your instructor provides critiques after each presentation, what are some additional techniques that you can use to obtain additional feedback?

# chapter 9

# IMPROVING INFORMATIVE MESSAGES

**LEARNING OBJECTIVES**

After reading this chapter, you should be able to:

1. Explain several characteristics of the informative process, especially in terms of typical informative speeches that might be given in the speech class.
2. Use different types of informative materials in public speaking projects.
3. Modify the language of an informative speech in terms of accuracy, appropriateness, and vividness.
4. Incorporate several of the techniques for maintaining audience attention in your classroom projects.

9

Hundreds of times every day, human beings send and receive information. An alarm clock reminds us—none too gently—that it is time to wake up. A TV announcer reveals that skies are cloudy and rain is expected. Family members discuss their plans for the day. Friends share the latest gossip. Teachers instruct students, supervisors direct employees, professionals advise clients, and associates share information to make decisions. At the end of the day, family members return to describe their activities, while the six o'clock news brings them up to date on world events. Although information exchange occurs frequently and in many forms, we rarely stop to think about the process.

*Informative speaking* (also called *expository speaking*) is the most common type of one-to-many communication. It can be defined as *a process in which a speaker creates and transmits messages to receivers so as to be understood, to develop shared meaning*. The speaker seeks audience *cognition* (the process of gaining knowledge, of comprehending, or learning), regardless of the listeners' attitudes about the information.

All of the preceding chapters should assist the speaker in developing and delivering informative messages. Those of special interest in this regard are Chapter 3—Gathering and Organizing Materials; Chapter 5—Delivery Strategies; Chapter 6—Audiovisual Aids; and Chapter 8—Managing Two-Way Communication. The purpose of this chapter is to refine our informative skills and to discuss the informative process in more depth and develop suggestions for improving it. This special emphasis is increasingly important in public speaking today. A growing number of professional people have discovered that informative presentations are not infrequent, accidental occurrences in their work, but rather are frequent, essential responsibilities.

We have divided Chapters 9 and 10 between *informative* and *persuasive* speaking. It is useful to note here the distinction between these two terms. Using persuasion, a speaker seeks to influence the listener's beliefs, attitudes, values, and behavior. Persuasive objectives have not been achieved if listeners merely understand ideas or facts. They must instead respond to the persuader's message with agreement, with conviction, and usually with a particular behavior or action, before persuasive communication can be termed successful. While information is still a crucial part of the persuader's message, the

© Howard Harrison 1978

goal goes beyond simple information exchange and shared meaning.

This distinction between informative and persuasive communication is useful for the public speaker, because it helps in isolating the speaker's communicative goals and assessing the best methods for achieving them. For example, suppose a political candidate is planning two speeches on his programs for the elderly. The first speech is to be delivered to a group of campaign workers. His purpose here would not be to persuade them of the programs' value or of his ability—the listeners are already convinced of that. Rather, he simply wants to assure that when the volunteers speak to voters, they can describe the programs in accurate detail. The objective here is understanding, cognition. The second speech is to be delivered to the "Gray Panthers," a senior citizens' activist group. Here the objective would be persuasive, because the candidate seeks belief, support, and votes. Notice the significant differences that would have to exist between the two speeches on the same topic. Thus, the candidate's awareness of the informative–persuasive distinction would be useful.

A good case can be made, however, for the claim that on a deeper level there is no meaningful distinction between informative and persuasive communication. As Berlo suggests: "There is reason to believe that all use of language has a persuasive dimension, that we cannot communicate at all without some attempt to persuade in one way or another" (Berlo, 1960, p. 9). Winterowd adds that "there is no such thing as neutral language" (Winterowd, 1968, pp. 1–2). He means that the speaker cannot construct a message so precisely worded that it will be understood in exactly the same way by everyone. Each listener will decode and respond to the language symbols in a unique, personal, subjective way. Suppose a teacher in a classroom utters this declarative sentence: "The weather report says the temperature outside is 76 degrees, with clear skies." One student might think, "Yeah, and I wish I were out there instead of in here." Another might respond, "Gee, it sure seemed hotter than that during lunch hour." A third might argue, "No, it isn't clear; I can see some dark clouds forming." A fourth might complain, "Couldn't we discuss the weather some other time and get back on the subject?" Even this simple informative message affected each listener in a different way. It changed the students' attitudes ever so slightly, in ways that would not have occurred had the teacher *not* commented on the weather.

As another example, a speaker is describing, say, the internal combustion engine. While his objective is to assure that the audience understands how the engine works, he is also suggesting, at least indirectly: "Please be interested in my speech. Like me as a person and appreciate my efforts to inform you. And when I've finished my message, use the information I've given you in constructive ways." Hence, all speakers attempt, to a greater or lesser extent, to *influence* listeners' emotional or psychological states, whether the main objective is to achieve understanding, modify beliefs, or change behavior.

It can be argued, then, that all communication is persuasive; all communication is designed to influence the receiver. From a theoretical perspective, we agree that the informative–persuasive dichotomy may be somewhat misleading. We therefore hope that the public speaker will recognize the inherent persuasive content in any informative message.

From a practical standpoint, however, we believe that the major functions and outcomes of informative speaking are unique and distinct from the persuasive. It is possible to inform without persuading (as with the politician who describes his program, but cannot convince the Gray Panthers to vote for him) and to persuade without informing (as with some emotionally loaded advertising). When the primary communication goal is instructional or expository, the speaker faces special problems. The remainder of this chapter examines these concerns and explains some approaches to informative communication. Chapter 10 covers the persuasive aspects of public speaking.

We shall examine, first, the general characteristics of the informative process that make expository speaking an especially challenging activity. Next, we shall discuss methods of making such speeches clear, and perhaps striking or vivid, with well-chosen materials and effective language. Finally, we shall discuss factors that help assure audience interest and attention to informative speeches.

## CHARACTERISTICS OF THE INFORMATIVE PROCESS

Before developing specific techniques for improving informative speaking, we think it is important to provide some general characteristics of the informative process. Appreciation of the points below may motivate the speaker to be especially diligent in speech preparation and delivery.

### The Process Is Complex

Speaker–audience interactions are composed of five identifiable stages, all critical to the presentation's effectiveness.

1. *The speaker must gain the audience's attention.* Listeners must be focused on the message. Attracting their interest can require significant effort, as will be noted later in this chapter.
2. *The second stage is reception.* Transmission of the message must be effective. The audible symbols (spoken words) must be articulated clearly and with sufficient volume to permit accurate reception of all intended sound.

3. *Audience comprehension is the third stage.* The listeners must understand the received message in about the same ways the speaker intended.

4. *The fourth phase, retention and recall, involves the listeners' ability to store and remember the speaker's message.* Computer specialists use the terms *information storage and retrieval*, and note that recorded information is useless unless it can be located and recalled quickly and accurately.

5. *Finally, application is the use of recalled information for practical purposes.* The ultimate objective of any informative speech—from a professor's lecture to a cooking demonstration—is to impart facts and ideas that can somehow be applied. Whether the information is used for solving a puzzle, answering exam questions, operating a machine, or creating new ways of understanding the world, the inherent value of information is that we can *do something with it*, that we can *respond* in productive ways.

The complexity of the informative process is increased because *audience feedback* intervenes throughout. Feedback is especially crucial during the first three stages—attention, reception, and comprehension—but at the same time difficult to read clearly. For example, if a member of the audience is looking the speaker squarely in the eye, does that mean that he is paying attention? Not necessarily. His thoughts could be a thousand miles away. If the listener is not cupping a hand to his ear or straining forward in his seat but sitting back passively, does that mean that he is receiving the audible signal clearly? If he nods pleasantly, does that mean that he understands and appreciates the message? Many "instructors" in our society—such as teachers, parents, and supervisors—are often surprised when feedback in these first three stages appears positive, but a failure in recall, the fourth stage, proves that at least one of the first three was defective. The listener wasn't paying attention, couldn't hear, or didn't understand; recollection of the message proved incomplete or inaccurate. Even if feedback shows that the receiver *can recall* information, we still have no assurance that he can *apply* it until we get more feedback. A business manager, unimpressed by a new employee's recitation of the courses he had taken in college, remarked, "I don't care what you know; I want to see what you can do with it."

## Receivers Are Selective

The informative speaker's message must compete with hundreds of other bits of information in the environment at any point in time. And it is physiologically impossible for receivers to process every bit of sensory information available to them. They pay attention to some events and ignore others. This selectivity affects the informative process in four ways.

**1.** *Receivers engage in selective exposure.* We decide many, though not all, of the events in which to become involved, to which we may be exposed. Which movie to attend or television program to watch are common exposure choices. No public-service program on TV can inform us if we choose not to watch. Even if our supervisor were to tell us, "Be in the conference room at 9 a.m. tomorrow for a training program," we could still decide whether to attend. Though a decision not to attend may have severe consequences, *we do have a choice.* Even most so-called "captive audiences" are not truly captive. They have not been dragged in forcibly and tied down to their seats. Except perhaps for school children, audiences can decide not to attend or can leave. They are present because they have considered the comparative payoffs between exposure and non-exposure, between participating in this event and forgoing a different one. While some audiences are less "voluntary" than others, nearly all have engaged in the process of selective exposure.

**2.** *Audiences practice selective attention.* Having decided to expose themselves to a particular event, they focus only on a portion of the available phenomena in the environment. That focus might be on the speaker's behavior, or it might not. Sometimes receivers may shut out the external environment altogether and get lost in the internal environment of their own minds, as in daydreaming. In the latter part of this chapter, we shall suggest several techniques for improving receiver attention on the intended message.

**3.** *Audiences engage in selective interpretation* (sometimes called *selective perception*). That is another way of saying that "meanings are in people, not in messages," that each receiver processes a particular bit of information in unique ways. Each interprets or "makes sense out of" the messages received. This selectivity is the classic problem of two or more people who hear the same message but interpret it very differently.

**4.** *Receivers exhibit selective retention.* They remember some messages and not others. The reasons for selective retention are varied. One cause may be genetic; some people simply cannot remember certain types of information, like lists of numbers or spatial arrangements. Another cause may be psychological; we may not remember some messages that we received while in an extreme emotional condition, or that remind us of other unpleasant events. But perhaps the most important reason for inadequate retention is that we have not been rewarded for recalling particular information. We have not had to use it and have not been given positive payoffs for retaining it. Whatever the reason, informative speakers who overcome the first three types of selectivity may fail in their objectives unless the receiver can remember important messages.

**5.** *A factor that affects all four types of selectivity is information overload,* a condition in which a receiver cannot effectively process all the relevant or important information in a given environment. Either too much information is being sent too quickly from a single source (like a rapid-fire lecturer with detailed information), or competing messages are being sent simultaneously by two or more different sources (like listening to a television program and talking to someone at the same time). Information overload can also occur when we must listen to one message while we are emotionally upset and preoccupied with other things. When it occurs, we may discontinue our involvement in an event (*selective exposure*); tune out one or more of the messages (*selective attention*); assign meaning differently because we are receiving only a small part of the total message (*selective interpretation or perception*), or be unable to recall portions of competing messages (*selective retention*).

## Extensive Information But Limited Time

The good expository speaker usually confronts a dilemma, probably an inevitable one. He knows the topic in depth and therefore knows how

broad and complex the subject really is. He knows that limited information on a broad topic can be deceptive. Furthermore, the speaker
usually likes the topic and enjoys talking about it as much as possible.
However, the informative speaker rarely has enough time to discuss
the topic for more than a few minutes; the constraints of the speaking
situation require significant limitation of content. Thus the dilemma:
Should he try to tell as much as possible, even if he must speak rapidly
and go overtime, so the topic gets the coverage it deserves; or should he
establish limited objectives, helping the audience understand the few
points but possibly distorting the overall picture he'd hoped to provide?

We favor the second alternative. (A rereading of the "Narrowing
Topic and Purpose" section of Chapter 2 may be useful here.) The
speaker with limited goals may caution listeners that they are not
getting all the available information and therefore should not draw
certain conclusions. At the same time, the audience may appreciate
the speaker who has made a few manageable points meaningful and
interesting.

Some informative speakers have the advantage of several days
and even weeks to present information. The college classroom, military training, and management development programs are examples.
For most of us, however, the information/time dilemma remains a
common problem.

## Infinite Presentational Choices

The previous chapters provide many options for adapting a message to
a specific audience and context. The fact that so many expository
messages by different speakers are so similar in form and style, or that
each speaker tends to fall into habitual and relatively unimaginative
patterns of speech development and delivery, do not negate the basic
fact that we have many alternatives.

For example, this textbook is a type of informative communication. The author experimented with various organizational plans and
language styles before deciding on what was eventually selected. If the
book is revised someday, new forms will be considered, based on feedback from readers. But textbook authors, including this one, have
become too locked into traditional patterns of message development
and presentation. Most of us are not imaginative enough; we fail to

consider the truly infinite alternatives available to us. Similarly, informative speeches may not achieve their fullest potential because the speakers have given too little attention to developing the most effective combination of words, structure, delivery style, and supporting materials. The next two sections will explore some of the informative devices, materials, and language styles that are alternatives for the informative presentation.

## DEVELOPING INFORMATIVE MATERIALS

The speaker should consider the best ways of making information clear. The objective is not to convince or move to action, but rather to assure that shared meaning occurs. What are some of the choices?

### Definition

The use of definition, frequently an essential step in the informative process, is a common expository device. Unfortunately, speakers often move quickly into their topic, wrongly assuming that key terms are already familiar. Listeners become confused and lose interest. If the speaker perceives the problem, he must awkwardly backtrack with hastily contrived definitions. Because of this common difficulty, many textbooks and lectures begin with a clarification of key terms.

Several definitional methods are available. Probably the best approach—particularly when dealing with a complicated term—is to use a combination of several methods.

The obvious choice is a *dictionary definition*, generally accepted as accurate, concise, and thorough. A disadvantage is that this may introduce other unfamiliar terms. However, dictionaries are the place to begin in developing good definitions. For the *jargon or technical vocabulary* of various professions, a definition taken from professional documents or literature may be used.

*Synonyms*, which are often found in a dictionary or thesaurus, are words very close in meaning to the word we wish to define. For instance, we may say that "honesty" and "ethics" are synonyms for

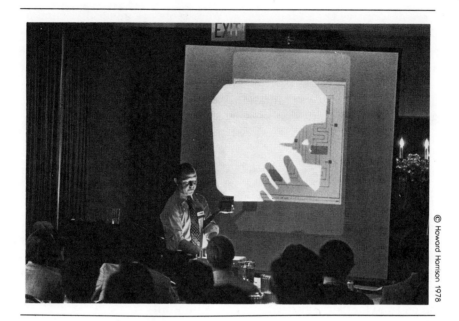

© Howard Harrison 1978

"integrity." We should avoid, of course, using synonyms that are equally unfamiliar to receivers.

When we define by *negation*, we explain what the word does *not* mean. For example, a speaker whose topic is "victimless crimes" may identify crimes to which he is not referring, acts that do have victims —burglary, rape, arson, and so on. By itself, a definition by negation may not be adequate, but when included with other types of definition it can be very effective.

Another popular method is *contextual use* of a word or phrase, usually done by putting the key term in a sentence. For example, we could say: "Because John F. Kennedy's mere physical presence generated enthusiasm, and because his words almost magically elicited wide popular support, he must be considered one of the most *charismatic* leaders of our time."

Sometimes we can clarify meaning by tracing the origin or *etymology* of a word. For instance, the word "democracy" comes from the Greek *demokratia*, which means "people rule," a term that may be more descriptive then "democracy." Word roots are generally found at the beginning of the dictionary definition or in etymological dictionaries. They are particularly useful for suggesting subtle implications or for developing the history of a concept.

Definition by *classification* shows the relationship of the unfamiliar term to other more familiar things that fall into the same group. Since we know about the class, we can generalize certain similar qualities or characteristics to the unfamiliar thing. To define "porpoise," for example, it is important to know that it is a mammal, thus enabling us to think correctly of the animal as being more like a dog or bear or human than like a fish, which it is not.

Finally, we can use an *operational definition* that explains a term according to its function or behavior. Modern behavioral and scientific researchers use operational definitions to identify more accurately what it is that they are watching and measuring. Hence, a vague term like "responsibility" can be defined by describing *specific human behaviors* that are "responsible"—caring for one's children, showing up on time for work, participating in community activities, and so on. More and more trainers are using operational definitions in their instructions, because they specify precisely the response (skill or behavior) that the employee should exhibit. For example: "Be friendly and courteous with our customers. By that I mean, when someone enters the store, you should walk up to them with a smile on your face and . . ."

Five *guidelines* are essential in constructing definitions.

1. Is it *consistent* with generally accepted meanings of the term? While it may be necessary to correct misunderstandings, the definition should remain basically in harmony with other common interpretations.
2. Is the definition too *restrictive*? We would be misleading if we defined "democracy" solely in terms of "voting." "Democracy" is a much broader concept than that.
3. Is the definition *overinclusive*? Does it suggest too many additional members of a particular class? For example, we should not define an automobile simply as a vehicle with four wheels. Many things that are not autos—such as trucks, children's wagons, and bicycles with training wheels—would fit that definition.

4. Is the definition *circular*? Circularity occurs when a word is used to define itself. For instance, defining "earnestness" as "the quality of being earnest" is circular.
5. Does the definition *facilitate understanding*? Since the purpose of a definition is to clarify, it should be simple enough that it is easily understood and improves our appreciation of the speaker's attempt to adapt to us as receivers.

## Example or Illustration

An example or illustration (a longer example, usually involving narrative) helps the receiver *visualize* something more clearly. In Chapter 10, on persuasive speaking, we shall refer to examples as a potent form of support for arguments. But throughout this text we have used examples as informative devices. Several chapters have begun with real events involving real people. Some of the suggestions throughout the chapters have included real or hypothetical illustrations that demonstrate how the suggestions can be put into practice. Had we relied only on description and explanation, the text would be less interesting and more difficult to understand.

Complex processes and ideas that are difficult to describe in the abstract can be made concrete with examples. (And here we use one to reinforce the previous statement.) Suppose an informative speaker is attempting to explain a socialistic economic system. After providing definitions and explanations, he offers an extended illustration of an actual family in Sweden, a socialistic democracy. He shows how they earn their money, pay taxes, purchase consumer goods, acquire jobs and housing, and so on. The reference to real people in their everyday activities adds both interest and clarity.

Three *guidelines* should be considered when preparing an example.

1. Is the example *clear*? Good examples should relate directly to the idea. Informative speaking is no place to develop subtle, indirect implications; examples should be concise and immediately relevant to the listeners in terms of what they are intended to show.
2. Is the example generally *representative* or *typical*? The speaker should consider those examples that occur frequently and closely reflect typical characteristics of the concept being explained.

3. Are *enough* examples provided to achieve clarity? Frequently one example is not enough.

## Comparison and Contrast

As noted in Chapter 3, "comparison and contrast" can serve as a general organizational plan. But this is also a convenient device for clarifying informative speeches. By showing the similarities and differences between two or more objects or ideas, the speaker can make fine distinctions not possible with a simple explanation of a single object or idea. For example, a science teacher might explain the physical principles of an orbiting satellite by comparing it to a ball on a string. A political scientist might make the characteristics of "conservatism" clearer by contrasting the programs and voting behavior of conservative office-holders with those of liberal politicians.

Comparison and contrast achieve informative objectives when certain *guidelines* are followed.

1. At least one of the things being compared must be *familiar* to the receivers. Comparing the human brain to a binary computer, a kind of analogy, does no good if the audience understands neither.
2. The speaker should be *selective* about which characteristics need to be compared. Potentially hundreds of phenomena may be alike or different in two separate things—such as, say, the Soviet Union and the United States—but only a few of these phenomena are relevant and useful in achieving the speaker's purpose.
3. The comparison and contrast should *not be too obvious*. The technique should be used to clarify complex information, not to bore the listeners by belaboring obvious likes and differences.

## Analysis of Structure and Process

Another basic type of informative device is an analysis of structure and process in which an activity, event, or object is broken into component parts, stages, or steps. The speaker should use this method when an explanation of the overall or general function of something is potentially unclear. Organizational plans like space order and time order lend themselves to this technique especially well. Suppose a driving instructor believes that students become better drivers if they know not just how to operate a vehicle, but also understand how it works; he thus develops an informative message describing the location, function, and potential problems of the car's components.

Some *guidelines* may be helpful.

1. Clearly *identify* and thoroughly *explain* all major parts and steps. An incomplete analysis breeds misconceptions about how the overall process works.
2. Draw *relationships* between the parts or stages. Most are interdependent; they affect each other. In the automobile example above, we do not really understand a car's mechanical functions simply by knowing what the components are. We must also know what they do in relation to each other.
3. Be *selective*. In suggestion 1 above, the *major parts or steps* for a beginning driver would not include the upholstery or the paint job. These elements might be important in a speech about "Car Care," but not "Safe Driving Habits."

### Audiovisual Exhibits and Demonstrations

The use of audiovisual supports and physical demonstrations has already been discussed in depth in Chapter 6. These techniques have become indispensable in much informative speaking today. They provide additional channels of communication by which comprehension, retention, and recall are more likely to occur. Rarely could a speech purpose not be enhanced by use of such informative materials. Review Chapter 6 for suggestions on their use.

## IMPROVING THE LANGUAGE
## OF INFORMATIVE SPEAKING

Language is, of course, the primary symbol system by which speakers transmit messages. Through language the speaker goes beyond merely expressing ideas. First, language provides a host of additional information about the speaker. The way we use language can suggest our educational background, our mood, and our attitudes about ourselves, the speech, the receivers, and the occasion. It may also give cues about our lifestyle and relationships. Second, language provides any communicator with an infinite range of choices about how to combine the symbols in unique and meaningful ways. As we develop these patterns and styles in sentences and paragraphs, we are perhaps applying our own trademark to our work. In spite of these choices, however, we tend to develop habitual and unconscious linguistic preferences. We use the same words and phrases again and again. The process of choosing language becomes unconscious, too routine and unvaried. Speakers thus forget about the significance of their unique language behavior.

Three general characteristics of language should be part of every speech, whether informative or persuasive: accuracy and clarity; appropriateness; and liveliness and vividness.

## Accuracy and Clarity

*Accuracy* is the specificity and precision with which language is used to compose messages. *Clarity* is used here to denote the degree to which the language can be reliably decoded by receivers. Thus, if I am accurate, the words I use will leave as little ambiguity as possible in describing the world, or my thoughts and feelings. If I am clear, then receivers will interpret about the same meanings from the verbal message that I intended.

What can speakers do to improve accuracy and clarity?

1. *The first step is to expand and diversify vocabulary.* This should be an ongoing process throughout our lives. Unfortunately, several forces are acting against it. One force is television, which—in both advertising and programming—aims at a grade school language level. Another factor is the educational system. Students are rarely challenged to expand vocabulary, and textbooks often accommodate their readers' present level rather than pushing them beyond it. Business and professional organizations, also, too often consider language abilities as a given and, instead of requiring that people improve, channel them into a niche where their communication skill level will be appropriate. In short, as a culture we are too tolerant of limited language skills; as individuals we have learned that we can survive without exerting the effort to build our word power.

As informative speakers, however, we want to achieve accuracy and clarity with receivers who usually do not know as much as we do about our topic. Further, time is usually limited and word economy is necessary. Finally, in our technological society, fine distinctions in meaning may be crucial to achieve understanding and accomplish our goals. The only solution is to improve our vocabularies. Learning new words and practicing new language patterns can significantly improve accuracy. The message becomes more precise and specific. We may want to develop more careful wording of main points and definitions and rehearse the delivery of complicated explanations to assure clarity or shared meaning.

**2.** *Simplify sentence structure.* Too many informative speeches include long, involved, complex sentences. The sentence you are now reading contains only ten words. Conversational speech rarely exceeds sentences of twelve to fifteen words. Yet many informative speakers today seem to thrive on complex sentences. The author examined several examples of jury instructions—informative messages that judges deliver to the jury before they deliberate. These messages typically had 30- and 40-word sentences, and 70- or 80-word sentences were not uncommon! Many speakers quote from technical or professional documents that are equally wordy. Grammar and syntax may be needlessly complex. Take this excerpt from an informative speech:

> Given the current inflationary pressures that have provided impetus to speculative buying, and recognizing, of course, that the disproportionately high rate of return on real estate investment has rendered impotent any intended dampening effects of increases in the mortgage interest rates, it is unlikely that we will experience anything less than at least a maintenance of current high borrowing and investment activity in real property with commensurate high returns.

Translation: "Real estate investment will yield high returns."

**3.** *Use redundancy and elaboration.* Using *redundancy* means to express an idea more than once. It may include *restatement* (using different wording) or *repetition* (using the same wording). Redundancy may be an *internal summary*, grouping together a series of ideas to remind the receivers what has been covered so far. We have all heard speakers, some of them teachers, say, "Now listen carefully, because I am just going to say it once." But the receiver-centered informative speaker should say it more than once, both to add emphasis and to better assure clarity.

The use of *elaboration* provides greater depth and detail to information. Each new sentence builds on what has preceded it. We caution, however, against overelaboration, a common fault of story-tellers or of speakers with poor organization of extensive materials. But some messages are neither accurate nor clear because the speaker has taken too many verbal shortcuts or made too many assumptions about what the receivers already know.

4. *Good informative language should include previews and transitions.* Many messages involve a procedure or process. Others explain complex ideas that must be built in logical steps. Receivers must be reminded where the speaker has been and where he is going. The old saying is still valid: "Tell them what you're going to tell them; tell them; then tell them what you told them."

## Appropriateness

*Appropriateness* is a general characteristic of speech style that refers to using language in ways that are suitable and acceptable to the speaker, the receivers, and the context. It includes standards of taste, norms, and expectations. The receiver-centered approach assumes that we will use accommodation when developing messages, a goal that does not require us to sacrifice our opinions but does require that we adapt to audience standards in terms of how we present those opinions. Though some informative language is clear, it may still yield negative responses if inappropriate.

First, we should *consider our choice of words*. Will jargon or technical language, even if understandable, cause audience discomfort? What kinds of slang terms are likely to be acceptable? What about mild profanity? The use of either slang or profanity, even though part of one's conversational style, can impede shared meaning because the receivers react emotionally to the words themselves. Further, even when we use terms that an audience accepts, they may not approve of our using them, because they know we do not speak that way normally.

We appear phony or seem to be making subtle judgments about the character and intelligence of our listeners. A visiting speaker at a high school assembly used terms like "I can dig it," "far out," and "that really freaked me out!" He did not realize that, like most slang, those phrases were no longer popular, and that the students recognized their use as a pathetic attempt to "relate" to a younger group with whom the speaker rarely interacted.

Second, we should *consider the appropriate tone of our message.* By *tone*, we mean the general attitude or mood we wish to suggest about ourselves, our topic, or our relationship with the receivers. Some informative messages might include language that is light, relaxed, or even humorous. Others might be heavy, precise, and serious. For example, an orientation speech to new employees might be friendly, light, and chatty. But a later message to those same employees about the use of expensive, dangerous equipment might include language that is strict and specific, since personal safety is at stake.

Tone should be based in part on the nature of the relationship between speaker and listeners. If the relationship is very structured and formal, as in the case of a staff assistant presenting official information to a group of managers, the language should perhaps not be too friendly or casually conversational, as it might be with a group of equals. The formality and precision of the language can tell receivers very quickly about the type of relationship the speaker thinks is appropriate in a situation.

A more personal mood can be developed by emphasizing our awareness of the sender–receiver relationship. Use of first person (I, we, us) and second person (you) is more personal than third person (they, one, the individual, an employee). Notice the difference in mood between "I think you should notify me when you cannot come to work" (first and second person) and "The employee shall notify the supervisor when he or she cannot come to work" (third person). A cordial, interactive mood can also be established by language that tells the receivers something about the speaker—his feelings, background, experiences, and so on.

### Liveliness and Vividness

The final characteristic of good informative language goes beyond clarity and appropriateness. Liveliness and vividness are essential to what may be called "the artistry of public speaking." Unfortunately, relatively few speakers develop expository materials in language that is imaginative, lively, and memorable. But those who have spoken in language that creates distinctive mental images have been especially successful. They let their imagination run free and develop novel or unusual ways of expressing ideas.

**1.** *Use active rather than passive voice.* Active voice places emphasis on the person and the action (subject and verb)—for example: "John Smith developed this new procedure." Passive voice emphasizes the object or focus of the action: "This new procedure was developed by John Smith." The difference is psychological as well as structural. Active voice focuses quickly on people and behavior, adding vitality and interest. The passive voice gives more immediate attention to ideas and things and may require more awkward, cumbersome wording which lacks directness. Good writers try to use the active voice almost exclusively; good speakers should do the same.

**2.** *Avoid triteness.* Common, worn-out phrases—called cliches—may be clear, but are so overused and familiar that they do little to make a message striking. The phrases below are typical examples of triteness:

> And so, without further ado . . .
> And now, a man who needs no introduction . . .
> And in conclusion, just let me say . . .
> Thank you for that heartwarming applause . . .
> That reminds me of a story . . .
> as American as apple pie
> hold your horses
> dead as a doornail
> a giant among men
> as old as the hills
> as pretty as a picture
> tried-and-true
> up-to-the-minute
> that's nothing to sneeze at
> show our true colors
> right as rain

food for thought
take the bull by the horns
like a bull in a china shop
putting the cart before the horse.

Anyone who has heard frequent public speeches can easily add to this list.

**3.** *Employ creative figures of speech.* This suggestion may not be appropriate for many business and professional audiences in routine informative speaking situations. But it can enliven speeches to audiences of outsiders at special events.

The *simile* is a very brief comparison of two different things that share one trait in common. It is generally expressed through the use of "like" or "as": "The house looks like a giant mushroom"; "The room is as colorful as a garden."

A *metaphor* is like a simile except that the comparison between two things is implied rather than stated: "The building is a steel cocoon which isolates its occupants from the outside world." The listener knows that the building isn't really a cocoon and the people in it are not insects, but they share a common characteristic.

*Hyperbole* is a deliberate, blatant exaggeration: "It seems as far from San Francisco to Salt Lake City as it does from the earth to the moon." While no one believes it is that far, the phrase may enliven the notion that to get from one place to the other requires a long, hard drive, or that the social ambience of the two places is very different.

The opposite of hyperbole is *understatement*. Describing World War II as a "minor disagreement" would be a blatant understatement that would emphasize what a massive and horrible conflict it was. The British are masters of understatement, like the RAF pilot who remarked after the Battle of Britain, "Had a bit of a scrap there!" The classic example comes from Mark Twain: "The reports of my death are greatly exaggerated."

Another figure of speech is *personification*, or the application of human qualities to animals, objects, or concepts: "The television receiver has a cold, unblinking eye"; "The cozy farmhouse opened its arms to the weary travelers."

Although figures of speech are excellent ways to add vitality and a literary flavor to potentially dull, tedious concepts, their general impact is more to *emphasize* rather than to truly *clarify* information. The use of too many may impede efficient informative communication; simple, sparing use is a good guideline. If the same imagery can be carried throughout the speech, so much the better. But avoid mixing metaphors, such as "Don't let the deceitful face of success stab you in the back" or "My desk was a forest of paperwork that I swam through like jelly."

A final pitfall is the overuse of exaggeration. Our society has become inundated with superlatives. To say something is the biggest, highest, or greatest no longer has much effect on audiences who have been numbed by constant overstatement. Use exaggeration infrequently, and consider the alternative of understatement to emphasize the significance of something.

## AUDIENCE INTEREST AND ATTENTION

Perhaps the most awesome challenge in public speaking, at least from the speaker's perspective, is maintaining audience interest and attention. Most of us would rather have receivers disagree with us than be bored with our presentation. In this section, we shall explore the troubling problem of keeping receivers attentive to what we say.

Informative presentations are especially challenging in terms of audience attention. Of course, interest may lag in persuasive speeches, too. Therefore, this section is relevant to *any* presentational speaking, regardless of purpose.

### General Principles about Audience Attention

1. *The primary responsibility for maintaining attention rests with the speaker, not the receivers.* We are not suggesting that a person in the audience has no responsibilities for assuring a productive communication event. The listener should make a sincere attempt to hear and understand the message, and should be civil to the speaker and respect the rights of others. However, we cannot accept the familiar complaint from public speakers that "those rude people just wouldn't pay atten-

tion to my speech!" It is a flimsy excuse, an attempt to shift the blame for dullness. After all, the audience, often participating involuntarily, has limited means of contributing to speech effectiveness. In contrast, the speaker has wide latitude and the choice of infinite combinations for presenting a message. It is the speaker who has opted for a particular speech structure, content, and style. It is the speaker who must accept the consequences of his choices.

**2.** *Few messages or speakers are innately interesting.* While some general topic areas seem to have natural attention-getting qualities (crime, war, sex, wealth, high adventure), the ways in which those topics are developed will have the major impact on audience responses. Speaking situations rarely permit us the luxury of choosing exciting topics. We speak on topics that we *must* speak on, topics of the moment that evolve or are chosen for us, regardless of their inherent appeal. Similarly, the speaker is also a "given." We are who we are, and very few of us are natural attention-getters. We cannot wish on ourselves a charisma that will hold audiences spellbound or a natural fluency that guarantees to keep them awake.

**3.** *Audience attention is both incomplete and ever changing.* Total or absolute attention on a particular event in our sensory field is very rare. Suppose we draw a continuum, a scale from 0 to 100 percent. We can think of one end as representing no attention whatever to a particular phenomenon, and the other end as perfect concentration on that phenomenon without a shred of attention elsewhere. Such complete attention occurs only with sudden dramatic events that stand out from other events (an ear-splitting noise, a painful injury, or events that prompt deep emotional responses, for example). And total attention is very brief, perhaps lasting but a few seconds. Hence, achieving perfect attention is unrealistic. "Please give me your undivided attention," actually means "Give me most of your attention."

Furthermore, the listener's attention level is in constant flux. It may vary during the presentation from intense absorption in the message to daydreaming about other things. No two audience members are likely to experience the same interest intensity at the same time. Thus the speaker should not be overly concerned if one person is nodding and smiling, another is taking notes, a third is staring out a window, and a fourth appears drowsy. As one comedian noted, "I don't really worry that I'm turning them off until people get up and leave— *in groups!*"

**4.** *Attention declines rapidly after a few minutes of speaking.* If more people would remember this obvious principle, we would have fewer long-winded professors, preachers, politicians, and banquet speakers. Short speeches are more productive than long ones, and speakers who are tempted to talk longer than, say, thirty minutes should recognize that their efforts will quickly become counterproductive. The more they talk, the less they will achieve.

**5.** *Ability to focus intently on a message depends on physical and psychological levels of activity.* Too much activity, and we have difficulty settling down enough to concentrate; too little activity, and we cannot exert the necessary effort to listen carefully. Teachers who work with hyperactive children report that their first task is not to give an instruction, but rather to get the child calmed down enough to pay attention. An evangelist at a revival meeting, a politician at a noisy convention, or a teacher on the last day of school should not expect the audience to attend carefully to a well reasoned message.

Similarly, the activity level can be very low; people who have been sitting quietly for a long time, or who are digesting a big meal, or who are fatigued and depressed will pose a challenge. The speaker may literally have to wake them up before getting into substantive speech content. In general, a balance of activity level between hyperactivity and lethargy is a precondition for an attentive audience.

**6.** *Audiences exhibit different types of attention.* Weaver and Ness list three types—involuntary, voluntary, and habitual (Weaver and Ness, 1963, pp. 206–208). *Involuntary attention* occurs when we make no conscious decision to perceive an event, but rather attend to it simply because it is the most obvious or intense element in the larger environment. For example, we may hear a loud siren, see a bright light, feel a sharp pain, or smell an unpleasant odor because they are obvious and unavoidable. Advertisers know the potency of involuntary stimuli and use colors, lights, and sounds that easily dominate competing messages. The problem with this type of attention is that it is short-lived. A loud noise may get our attention briefly, but we quickly lose interest. If the noise is repeated, it soon becomes monotonous and we tune it out. Some audiences dislike involuntary attention-getting techniques because they appear to be gimmickry rather than relevant messages.

*Voluntary attention* occurs when the listeners force themselves to attend, when the decision to listen or not to listen has important consequences. For example, while we may not be naturally interested in income-tax laws, we may attend to a speech on that topic because it could save us money. Even voluntary attention will not continue indefinitely, however, as the effort required to concentrate on the message may eventually outweigh any expected gains of listening.

*Habitual attention* contains elements of the first two types. From past experience, we know that a particular type of message is one to which we usually pay attention. It stands out from other types of speech events and at the same time contains information that is important to our needs. For example, we may listen to a professor's lecture or a supervisor's instructions simply because we are accustomed to doing so. Our concentration demands no special effort (involuntary), even though we are consciously attentive (voluntary). The speaker who develops a reputation for being interesting and at the same time imparts information of real importance can develop the habitual attention pattern in the audience.

**7.** *The speaker's main goal is always message effectiveness—comprehension, retention, and application.* Maintaining attention is an important means to that end, but it is not an end in itself. Once a speaker discovers that he has the ability to keep listeners on the edge of their chairs, he may be tempted to put on a show of his speaking expertise. But the ultimate test of good public communication is not whether people say "I enjoyed your speech," but whether the speaker has made a difference in their thinking and behavior.

### Suggestions for Maintaining Audience Attention

As noted, most speakers have to plan for audience interest; it does not come naturally. Following is a list of factors that may help create interest and maintain attention. But they do not guarantee success. The artistry and creativity with which they are developed, combined with their adaptation to a particular audience, will ultimately determine the speaker's success.

*Vital information.*   We attend to messages that appear crucial to our well-being. How does the topic directly affect us? If we fail to hear or heed the message, what might be the consequences? "What I am about to tell you may save your life."

*Animation.*   Moving objects attract attention better than still ones. Movies are more attracting than slides. The animated speaker or animated visual aids can be part of almost any informative communication situation. Incidentally, animation is also useful in minimizing the effects of speech anxiety. Movement is a tension release.

*Visual stimuli.*   The most interesting visual stimulus is probably color. Notice, for example, how disappointing black-and-white television becomes after we have become used to color. Other attracting visual effects include sharp definitions, contrasts in tones and hues, and interesting forms or shapes.

*Auditory stimuli.*   In Chapter 5 we discussed the vocal dimension of speech delivery, noting that vocal inflection affects meaning. Here we add that vocal emphasis also affects attention. We know the tedium of the speaker who drones on in a quiet monotone. An abrupt change in vocal characteristics, like a sudden pause, an increase in volume, or the precise and forceful articulation of a key statement can improve attention. At the very least, a naturally varied conversational style can help sustain interest levels.

*Familiarity.*   Have you ever seen a movie that was filmed in a location that you were familiar with? There was the actor walking where you had walked, and you said, "Hey, I've been there!" Or you were in a conference with total strangers. A casual acquaintance walked in, and suddenly he or she became the most important person in the room, the only spark of familiarity in a strange environment. When an audience begins to tune out an abstract message, a reference to something familiar may bring them back. However, it also may be true that "familiarity breeds contempt," and the overuse of this technique may be counterproductive.

*Newness.*   Just as we like to recall the past, so we are intrigued with new things. New acquaintances fascinate us, new products lure us, new ideas and activities preoccupy us. The fascination with space flight, with its almost incomprehensible gadgetry, is an example of a topic that can sustain attention with newness. Though the ability to introduce novelty into the speech may be limited by topic, even the inventive phrasing of old ideas into new and exciting language is a possibility for any speech situation.

*The bizarre or unusual.*   As a factor in maintaining attention, the bizarre or unusual is closely related to newness. Audiences cannot resist the odd or extraordinary, as evidenced by popular films and magazines that show strange lands and people. The continuing success of Ripley's "Believe It or Not" and the fascination with science fiction and the occult are also examples. But these materials are usually topic-dependent, and their overuse may impede a focus on common here-and-now problems.

*Suspense.*   As with a good mystery novel that we cannot put down, the feeling of uncertainty, of suspense, has enormous potential in holding interest. We cannot resist finding out how a story ends. Some of the most successful public speakers rely heavily on the extended narrative, a story with plot and characters. Sometimes suspense can be developed without a story, as with the speaker who promises early in the speech to reveal some vital information and waits until the last minute to do so.

*Conflict and antagonism.*   Remember from grammar school days an occasional playground argument that ended in a fistfight? When it began, someone would yell "Fight! Fight!" and from every direction students would come running to watch. We simply cannot resist paying attention to competition or hostility. Thus a political debate is

© Howard Harrison 1970

more interesting than a single speech, and a persuasive speech on a controversial subject is more compelling than an informative one that describes everyday activity. The speaker who dispassionately analyzes an issue is less appealing than one who contrasts competing arguments or refutes opposing ones. The teacher who simply explains ideas may not be as interesting as the one who plays "devil's advocate" with the opinions of students.

*Humor.*    Audiences enjoy humor in a speech if it is truly funny, is not offensive to the audience, and applies to the topic. Good humor seems to gain almost total attention. For example, though some students cannot remember a lecturer's main points, they can recall almost verbatim the jokes and stories. If humor is to be a tool for *sustaining* attention, it should be periodic throughout the speech. The speaker who begins with two or three jokes and then lapses into dry prose for the next hour will have gained little attention with the humorous introduction. Finally, just as some people "can't tell a joke," so some speakers cannot use humor effectively, and we should frankly evaluate our innate ability to use this device.

*Emotional materials.*   In Chapter 10 we will explore the persuasive potential of appeals to emotion. Listeners become especially attentive when they hear information that is shocking, frightening, romantic, poignant, sad, or sentimental. An emotional audience is neither indifferent nor bored. But the question in informative speaking is whether they grasp the main ideas. Since the informative objective is shared meaning, materials that stimulate an emotional response should be used infrequently.

*Specifics.*   Our everyday lives are filled with concreteness, with tangible people and things. Much of our conversation deals with specific behavior, actual events, and well-defined environments. Informative speakers often deal with intangible ideas, however, and the minds of listeners may wander unless the speaker can make abstract concepts concrete. Using real names of real people in specific activities can significantly improve audience tolerance for abstraction.

*References to audience members.*   We like recognition. We like to hear our names mentioned. Some speakers are especially adept at using specific audience members as examples. The person mentioned shows interest, as do others who know him. Teachers use this technique in a devious way—to call on students who aren't paying attention. Personal references sometimes backfire, especially if the speaker's information about the listener is inaccurate or if that person prefers to remain anonymous. It can also cause resentment in those who feel they should have been mentioned. Used carefully, however, this technique can assure that at least some people are paying very close attention.

*Audience participation.*   Passive audiences are more likely to lose interest than active ones. If the speaker encourages active verbal or physical responses, receivers have to be attentive in order to participate. For example, the speaker might ask for a show of hands, ask particular people to stand up, ask specific questions for people to answer, or select people to help in a demonstration.

*Receiving audience feedback.*   It is frustrating to be part of an audience in which everyone but the speaker realizes that the speech is dragging. On the other hand, it is rewarding to us when a speaker notices our lagging attention and tries to do something about it. As speakers, we must be receptive to feedback. If it is obvious that most of our receivers are inattentive, we should consider strategies for bringing them back, like taking a break, asking for questions, eliminating some of the prepared remarks, and/or adding vocal variety and bodily movement.

*Variety.*   This is by far the most important factor for sustaining attention throughout a lengthy speech. Variety or change assures that no single attention-getting device will lose its effectiveness through monotonous repetition. Careful planning will suggest the use of several different interest appeals for any particular speech.

## SUMMARY

Informative (expository) speaking is a one-to-many communication process in which a speaker creates and transmits messages to receivers so as to achieve cognition or shared meaning. The distinction between informative and persuasive speaking may be misleading, because all communication has some persuasive intent. However, since informative speech purposes are more limited in terms of audience response, we discuss the topic separately from speeches designed to convince and actuate.

The informative process is complex, involving five identifiable stages. The speaker's task is challenging because receivers are selective in the ways they attend to, interpret, and retain information. Further, the speaker has limited time to present information and has infinite choices about how to develop the message.

Some of these choices involve the kinds of informative devices and materials that can be used. One device is definition; any idea or term can be defined by a variety of methods. Others include: the example or illustration; comparison and contrast; analyses of structure and process; and audiovisual exhibits and demonstrations.

In addition to these general strategies, the informative speaker has great freedom in language usage. One objective is accuracy and clarity; it can be achieved by effective vocabulary; simple sentences; redundancy and elaboration; previews and transitions. A second objective is appropriateness, determined by the norms and standards of the speaker, the receivers, and the situation. We must use suitable words and develop an appropriate mood for the specific event and intended speaker–audience relationship. Third, informative language should be lively and vivid, especially through the creative use of figures of speech.

Perhaps the most compelling problem of the informative speaker is maintaining interest and attention. Audience attention levels vary and are the speaker's responsibility. Since few messages or speakers are innately interesting to all audiences, we should develop conscious strategies for maintaining attention: the use of vital information; animation; visual and auditory stimuli; familiarity; novelty; suspense; humor; specifics; audience involvement; and variety.

## QUESTIONS FOR STUDY

1. Why can it be said that all language is persuasive—that even an expository speech includes attempts to influence an audience? In a typical informative speech, what are some of the persuasive messages that a speaker would be sending?
2. What problems do the characteristics of the informative process pose for the speaker, especially the student in a speech class? How does the speaker solve those problems?
3. Using some of the different methods suggested in this chapter, how might a speaker *define* the terms below?

   | | |
   |---|---|
   | democracy | love |
   | college | recreation |
   | family | money |

4. What is appropriateness? How does the receiver-centered speaker incorporate that concept into the language of the speech?
5. What are some of the factors that determine how well an audience pays attention to the speaker? Based on your own experience as a listener and a speaker, which two or three methods of maintaining attention listed in this chapter seem to be most effective?

# chapter 10

# IMPROVING PERSUASIVE MESSAGES

**LEARNING OBJECTIVES**

After reading this chapter, you should be able to:
1. Recognize and define major types of reasoning that are used in public speaking.
2. List and give examples of several logical fallacies.
3. Utilize the three types of evidence or supporting material in classroom speech projects.
4. Discuss the terms "suggestion" and "motivational appeals" as categories of nonrational strategies.
5. Develop ways of improving your own source credibility in the public speaking classroom.

# 10

An old legend tells of two statesmen in ancient Greece. Both were fluent, polished orators. And they were political opponents. One was a dove, arguing for restraint in military adventures and accommodation of potential enemies. The other was a hawk, claiming that only strong, aggressive military action could assure the security of the Greek states. Both orators took the stump to argue their cases before the public. The legend says that when the first man, the dove, finished speaking, people said, "Listen, how well that man speaks!" But when the hawk finished speaking, people shouted, "Let us march!"

This legend is not documented fact. But it is certainly plausible and realistically depicts a common phenomenon in public speaking today. Some speakers possess a glib fluency that brings appreciative comments from receivers. "Boy, that was really a good sermon!" "That was one of the best summations to the jury I've ever heard." "She really told those commissioners a thing or two." "Have you ever heard a more dynamic speaker?" We are frequently impressed by striking speech "performances," by people who have mastered techniques that assure audience attention and appreciation. And these speakers are rewarded for their efforts—people compliment them, seek them out for further communication events, and often pay them well. A kind of notoriety may accompany the speaker who can hold audiences in rapt attention with a dramatic and powerful presentation.

Most of us do not possess such exceptional public speaking abilities and never will. We can learn to do a solid, competent job of communicating with an audience, but we will probably never become spell-binding. Public speaking will be an important facet of our lives, but rarely so much so that we are preoccupied with the artistry of presentation so that people will be in awe of our prowess. The speaker who strives primarily for audience appreciation will probably need some natural personal skills and not a little luck to achieve the desired response.

But one who gains audience approval of presentation skills will not necessarily achieve the more functional purpose of most public speeches—to obtain a practical, functional response from listeners. It does little good to be appreciated if the listeners do not think or do as we suggest. If the people in the congregation love the sermon but do not change the way they live; if the jury, despite the defense attorney's polished summation, still finds the defendant guilty; if the commissioners vote against a proposal despite an advocate's outstanding support—then approval of one's speaking skill is faint praise indeed.

In this chapter we shall be concerned not with how much receivers appreciate the sender's delivery skills ("Listen, how well he speaks!"). Rather, we shall focus on methods that better assure the desired response ("Let us march!").

*Persuasive communication* may be defined as *a process by which a sender attempts to influence the thinking and behavior of receivers.* We all participate in persuasive communication every day. And most of us are pretty good at it. Since infancy, when we learned that by vocalizing (crying) we could influence our parents to feed us or generally make us more comfortable, we have developed verbal and nonverbal strategies to help us get desired responses from others. A small child learns that an emotion-laden "Please, Daddy," accompanied with the appropriate facial expression and outstretched arms, can achieve what a more straightforward "I want that" never could. So-called "courting behavior," as two people become acquainted with and attracted to each other, is dependent on various types of persuasive messages. And success in your work life will to some extent depend on the ability to get others to see things your way.

Because of the wide experience and general competence most of us have in using persuasive communication, we shall not attempt further discussion of the role of persuasion in human affairs. Rather, we shall present materials that can provide new insights, develop more systematic thinking, and reinforce what we already do—influence the thinking and behavior of other people.

This chapter will contain four main sections. First, we shall explain some general premises about persuasive speaking. Second, we shall discuss the logical dimension of persuasion. Third, we shall identify nonrational factors of the persuasive message. And finally, we shall explore the persuasive factors that reside in the speaker and the setting, regardless of the intended content of the verbal message.

People whose careers depend on achieving specific results through regular persuasive speaking—and many of us fall into that category—should not stop with a public speaking course, but should study such subjects as "argumentation and debate," "management and personnel psychology," "theories of attitude change," "advertising and marketing techniques," and similar courses. But we hope that when you finish this chapter, you will have a better idea about your own strengths and weaknesses as a persuasive speaker and know some tangible ways of improving.

## PRINCIPLES OF PERSUASIVE SPEAKING

Just as with informative communication, persuasive messages should be prepared and delivered with some awareness of what happens during the persuasive process. How do people come to change their thoughts and behaviors in a communication event? In this section, we shall explain a few of the important principles that should guide the persuasive speaker.

1. *Persuasion is best viewed as a response to messages.* We noted earlier that anyone who initiates communication with others seeks a response from them. The receiver-centered model of communication assumes that how listeners respond to a speech determines the degree and quality of communication that has occurred. Yet many people tend to think of persuasion as something that one person *does* to another, much as one person might hit another, or feed him, or douse him with water. The problem with this view is that the persuasive speaker might assume that it is possible to develop the same type of cause–effect relationship that exists with other physical processes: If I hit you, a bruise will appear; if I feed you, your body will process the nutrients; if I throw water on you, you will be wet. *If I transmit messages that you can perceive, you will be persuaded.* But this latter cause–effect link does not necessarily follow. Even my most well constructed, fluently delivered message may not achieve the response I intended.

Rather than viewing persuasion as something that one person does to another, we should think of it as a process in which one person attempts to elicit a specific response, and one or more people respond in various ways. Persuasion occurs when the receivers say it has, when their verbal or nonverbal behaviors show us that we have achieved our purpose. Viewed in the common stimulus–response approach to human behavior, the stimulus is the persuasive speaker's message (anything perceived by the receiver) and the response is the receiver's thoughts and behavior. This distinction is important, for it explains why the "best-laid plans" of many speakers do not achieve the expected results. The outcomes of persuasive communication accrue not only from the speaker's message and context, but also from the complex variables in the receiver. Awareness of this distinction may make us more willing to try to understand our receivers as complex individuals and to interact with them to get feedback about how they are responding to our message.

**2.** *The persuasive process is reciprocal.* The senders and receivers of persuasive messages reinforce and respond to each other's behavior. Stated differently, the persuasive speaker who seeks change in other people is likely to be changed himself. That change may be more gradual and less dramatic than sometimes occurs with audience members, but in the long run it can be just as significant in the speaker's life. For example, people who have run for elective office for the first time often report that, as a result of having talked to audiences about the important issues of the day, they have themselves changed their attitudes or become more committed to various causes. They also note that receiver responses not only changed their speaking styles, but also their opinions on various issues.

Conditioning experiments with laboratory animals might be seen as an analogy of this reciprocal process. Each time a light goes on, the rat jumps up on a pedestal and the human experimenter drops in food as a reward. He assumes that the rat is now "conditioned." But the rat might be thinking, "Hey, everytime the light goes on, all I have to do is jump up on the pedestal and this guy will drop in food. I really have him conditioned!" Who is affecting the thinking and behavior of whom? Indeed, in persuasive speaking as in any other form of human interaction, we are interdependent with others. We are at once both persuaders and persuadees. We should consider the ways in which our own behavior is a response to audience behavior.

**3.** *Responses to persuasive messages are generated by both rational and nonrational factors.* Homo sapiens has been termed the "reasoning animal" because we are capable of thinking logically, analytically, abstractly, rationally. We are able to solve puzzles—such as landing men on the moon and returning them safely to earth—because of the efficient use of our rational faculties. To let nonrational factors enter into certain kinds of decisions is to invite disaster. For example, the astronauts could not have completed the crucial retro-rocket burn for earth re-entry by basing the decision on hunches, whims, or feelings. The "human factor" had to be eliminated from the precise mechanical process of firing the retro-rockets. Perhaps as products of the scientific culture, we may pride ourselves on our ability to make other kinds of decisions on rational grounds, even though such decisions are not necessarily based on the physical laws of science.

Persuasive speakers should recognize that while their messages may truly be "reasoned discourse," the receivers will respond to the messages in part on nonrational grounds. The listeners may be affected by their own feelings and beliefs in ways that render the logical development of the speech irrelevant.

Notice that we use the term nonrational, not irrational. *Irrational* means that a person or message is unreasonable, not endowed with reason, lacking a logical component. *Nonrational* means "not based on or relying upon reason"; it does not mean that something "doesn't make sense," but only that the logical dimension is not a factor in how it is perceived. For instance, someone might buy a car because it "looks attractive, luxurious, and sporty," and makes him "feel good." It might *make sense* to buy that car if, say, his business requires that he be seen in a nice car—the rational basis for buying it is to improve business. The nonrational (not irrational) basis is aesthetic taste and pleasurable emotional reaction.

Just as a receiver responds to persuasion in part through nonrational factors, so the decision to present a speech may be partly nonrational. The logical reason we might speak is to achieve a specific, practical purpose. A nonlogical stimulus to speak might be our desire to enhance good feelings about ourselves as productive people.

**4.** *It is difficult, and perhaps impossible, to accurately predict or interpret a receiver's response to a persuasive message.* Persuasive speaking is to a large extent an artistic process. It will never be totally scientific.

Why? Because we are dealing with a complex system of innumerable components that interact in a unique context at a particular point in time. True, we are attempting to become more systematic about predicting receiver response. Computer technologists, voter analysts, and advertising and marketing specialists have improved their ability to elicit desired audience responses *in the aggregate*. That is, we might learn to predict fairly reliably ahead of time how various groups in the electorate will respond to a particular candidate. For example, "Based on our opinion surveys and prior voting behavior, we believe that about 70 percent of the union members in Illinois will support Senator Braxton's medical insurance proposal." But we cannot predict how person A, on September 30, 1980, will respond to speaker B's particular message on a particular topic in a particular setting.

Furthermore, once we have observed that response, what does it mean? What caused it to occur? How do we *interpret* it? If I present a speech urging you to buy my product, and if I learn later that you have bought my product, can I assume that my message elicited your behavior? Perhaps you disliked me and were not moved by the message, but a friend of yours whose judgment you trust had also bought the product, liked it, and urged you to buy it. And perhaps even you do not know for certain why you bought it. So what does your response to my message mean? Should I continue giving the same speech to others, assuming that it was effective in your case?

When the persuasive speaker analyzes the receivers and attempts to guess at their response to various stimuli, he should be as systematic as possible. However, he should also recognize that complexity, spontaneity, and even artistry intervene to make any prediction or interpretation of audience response a less-than-accurate process. We can improve our adaptation to specific audiences, but we can never perfect it.

## LOGICAL BASES OF PERSUASIVE SPEAKING

Our ability to develop reasoned or logical communication is primarily a product of our intelligence and our cultural experience. Most people have developed over many years an intuitive notion of "what makes sense." We evaluate logic every day, both in casual interpersonal transactions and in our school and job activities. Though some people do not try to think very hard, nearly all of us can reason things out if we are willing to exert the mental energy.

Despite this natural ability that develops as we mature, we can *learn* to think better, more carefully, more systematically, more logically. And we can *learn* to apply our logical thought process in the preparation and delivery of persuasive speeches. How do public speakers typically use logical techniques to construct persuasive messages? This section will provide some insights to help improve the rational bases of our communication. It is an attempt to systematize what most of us do in more unstructured ways in everyday living.

## Reasoning

*Reasoning* can be defined as *the process of inferring conclusions from premises*. That means that given certain conditions in our environment, conditions that we perceive and give meaning to, certain conclusions can be inferred. An inference occurs, for example, when we see someone hunched over a table, hear him crying, and notice an opened letter drop from his hands to the floor. We *infer* that he has just received bad news in a letter. We may be wrong; he may be sad about something else, and the letter is merely incidental, but that does not deny that we have used our logical thought processes to arrive at a conclusion. We have used reasoning. The use of reasoning in communication is sometimes called *argumentation*, which Freeley defines as "the art and science of using primarily logical appeals to secure decisions" (Freeley, 1971, p. 2).

*Certainty and probability.*   In many forms of human endeavor, the reasoning process yields *absolute or certain conclusions*. That is, given the rules of the conditions being observed, the conclusion must follow in a prescribed way. An example of certainty in reasoned conclusions can be seen in the area of computer programming. A computer is a piece of electronic machinery that operates according to how it is structured. The electrical impulses that pass through its wiring obey physical laws. The givens of electronic circuitry and the properties of

© Howard Harrison 1978

electricity combine to form a set of "rules" by which the computer functions. The programmer knows these rules and can use reasoning to determine precisely what the machine can and cannot do. Any "surprises" that confront the programmer are not really surprises at all, but rather are gaps in her knowledge of the rules or of what is happening inside the machine. But the computer is *not* operating randomly or accidentally. It follows the rules. Good reasoning from these rules allows the programmer to predict accurately what will happen when she supplies it with certain kinds of inputs.

The logical process used in the preceding example is the reasoning of science and mathematics. Absolute or certain conclusions also are obtained when premises are combined by some arbitrary set of rules. These conclusions are not necessarily *true* (they are not necessarily consistent with what we judge to be reality), but they are *valid* because they follow the rules of reasoning. For example, suppose I argue that the fastest any commercial airliner can travel is 650 knots. Therefore,

I reason, the quickest anyone can travel on commercial carriers between New York and Los Angeles is about five hours. My conclusion may not be *true* (perhaps commercial airlines can and do fly faster, or perhaps SST's are now flying that route and cutting flight time to about two hours). However, my conclusion is *certainly or absolutely valid*; it follows from the "givens" of the argument.

It would be comforting to think that most issues in persuasive speaking could be reasoned through with certainty, either because they followed natural laws (as with the computer) or because the premises from which conclusions were drawn were *assumed* to be accurate (as with the airline). But that is not the case. Most reasoning in persuasive speaking deals with *probability*. Our goal is to convince others that our conclusions are *more likely* to be accurate statements about reality than competing conclusions. For example, suppose a speaker argues that "excessive Federal spending causes inflation." She reasons, on the basis of various types of evidence and economic premises (themselves probability statements) that the conclusion is "true." But she really means that the conclusion is *probably* true, while her opponent will use reasoning to suggest that it is *probably* false.

As speakers we need to recognize that if it were possible to determine an absolute conclusion from accepted rules or premises, persuasion would simply be a process by which we take our receivers through the logical steps. But because we are dealing with probabilities and with premises (rules) that some receivers may not accept as givens, persuasion becomes more an artistic process in which we try to construct messages that are likely to convince them that our arguments are probably true. Deduction and induction are two common terms used in reasoning.

*Deduction.*   *Deduction* relates to the discussion above about certainty in reasoning from premises; conclusions follow logically, or according to the rules of reasoning, from these accepted premises. The classic example of deduction is the simple syllogism:

| | |
|---|---|
| All men are mortal | (Major premise) |
| Socrates is a man. | (Minor premise) |
| Therefore, Socrates is mortal. | (Conclusion) |

Notice that if the two premises are accepted as true, the conclusion is certain or definite; it is the *only* conclusion that can be inferred. The conclusion provides no *new* information, but merely rearranges the information already given in the premises. The Socrates example is *valid* reasoning. It also illustrates why we sometimes say that *deduction reasons from the general* (all men) *to the specific* (Socrates).

The syllogism above includes a major premise or generalization that describes a category of things, in this case "all men." It has thus come to be known as a *categorical syllogism*. Other forms of deduction are the disjunctive syllogism and the conditional syllogism.

The *disjunctive syllogism* contains a major premise with mutually exclusive alternatives—*either* this *or* that, but not both.

> Either we get new tax support or we must close the school.
> We will not get new tax support.
> Therefore, we must close the school.

The most common flaw in the use of disjunctive reasoning is that other plausible alternatives are omitted. For example, "We can economize by cutting out some programs and laying off employees, so that even if we do not get more tax support we will not have to close the school." And some alternatives are not mutually exclusive; they can coexist. An opponent of our *either–or* argument can sometimes refute with a *both–and* approach. "Both low taxes and quality schools are possible."

The *conditional syllogism* assumes an *if–then* relationship between two conditions: If A, then B.

> If the legislature does not adopt no-fault insurance, then insurance
>    rates will rise.
> The legislature will not adopt no-fault insurance.
> Therefore, insurance rates will rise.

Notice that the major premise of this syllogism usually involves a cause–effect relationship. Refuting that relationship will destroy the logical validity of the argument. Causal reasoning is discussed later.

Public speakers use deduction regularly. But it is only effective when the receivers accept the truth of the premises. For example, a politician recently argued that the new cattle grazing restrictions on public lands should be abolished, because they hurt the ranching business. The deductive pattern was:

Any policy that hurts ranching should be abolished.
The new grazing policy hurts ranching.
The new grazing policy should be abolished.

His argument was logically valid. It followed the rules of deductive reasoning from a general premise to a specific conclusion. Ranching audiences accepted the conclusion as truthful, because they accepted the premises. But environmentalist audiences rejected the conclusion, because they denied *both* premises. They claimed that ranching should not be the highest priority in land-use policy (denying the first premise), and that the stricter grazing policy would not hurt ranchers anyway (denying the second premise).

*Induction.*   This form of reasoning relates closely to the earlier discussion of probability. With *induction*, conclusions are arrived at by reasoning from specific cases. For example, the proponent of the new grazing policy might try to refute the politician's claim thusly:

Rancher A follows the new grazing policy and is still making a
   profit.
So is Rancher B.
So is Rancher C.
So are Ranchers D, E, and F.
Therefore, ranchers who follow the grazing policy can still make a
   profit.

Hence, if deduction is reasoning from general to specific, induction can be thought of as reasoning from specifics (cases A, B, C, D, E, F) to the general (ranchers as a class). Unlike the deductive pattern, in which the conclusion has to be true if the premises are true, the conclusion in the inductive pattern is, at best, only *probably* true, even if we accept all the specific cases.

Receiver acceptance of a speaker's inductive conclusion and the degree to which it is probably true depends on many factors, some of them the intangibles of receivers' backgrounds, attitudes, and perceptions. But three common tests of the acceptability of the conclusion are *sufficiency, typicality,* and *negative instances* (Ray and Zavos, 1966, pp. 72–74). The *sufficiency* criterion demands that the number of specific instances be large enough to yield a reliable generalization. "There are over 11,000 ranchers who must follow the new policy. Are 6 examples enough to tell us how the entire group will probably fare?" *Typicality* requires that the examples be representative of other members of the total class or category. "Ranchers A through F all live in Wyoming, where the rangeland has excellent vegetation. What about other parts of the West, where rangeland is drier and has sparser vegetation?" To meet the *negative instances* criterion, there must be no examples that contradict the conclusion; if there are such examples, it must be explained why they do not conform to the others. "Rancher G lives in the same region as Ranchers A through F. Rancher G followed the new policy and went bankrupt last month." "But Rancher G has never made a profit and has been in debt for many years; the new land policy had nothing to do with his business failure."

*Variations.* In actual practice, a persuasive speaker mingles deductive and inductive patterns. For example, suppose the major premise in a syllogism (deductive) is "Women are equal to men as business executives." That premise would probably not simply be asserted as true, but would be supported by specific cases (inductive) in which women have successfully performed the duties of an executive role.

We use other terms to describe variations in the reasoning process. One such term is *reasoning by analogy.* A comparison is made between one case that is familiar and another that is less familiar—the argument is that what is true in the known case will also be true in the other. "The group health plan has been successful in Corporation A; it will be successful in our corporation as well." Speakers who use this pattern must assure the receivers that similarities between the two cases are significant and critical to the comparison, and that differences between the two cases are insignificant or irrelevant to the comparison.

Another pattern is *reasoning from sign.* Literally, when we observe one event we take it as a *sign* of another, related event. We identify the relationship between two variables—one is an attribute or characteristic of another. Having observed one of those variables, we make inferences about the other. Medical doctors use this method when they observe symptoms and draw conclusions about the type of disease that probably exists when such a sign is present. Conversely, we might reason from the *absence* of a sign. "There has not been a single complaint since Harry became supervisor; he apparently works effectively with his staff." An inference is faulty if a sign is not necessarily an attribute of the other variable, if the relationship is not inherent. "So we have a high unemployment rate; that does not necessarily indicate a lack of capital investment in the economy." Or there may be other signs that contradict the observed symptom. "True, we've had no complaints from Harry's employees, but absenteeism is much higher, and we've had problems of low quality work."

Another very common pattern among persuasive speakers is *causal reasoning*. It establishes a cause–effect relationship between two or more events; when one event occurs, another event will also occur. Sometimes we reason from a *known cause* to a *probable effect*: "The new industry will bring in 5,000 new employees (*cause*); the current housing shortage will thus become critical (*effect*)." Or we can move backward, from known effect to probable cause: "It's not surprising that student scores on the SAT have declined significantly (*effect*); what do you expect of the television generation that does not read? (*cause*)."

A common flaw in causal reasoning is failure to note multiple causes or multiple effects. "Why blame low scores on television? Aren't teachers and parents really the cause of low student aptitudes in reading and math?" Or: "A housing shortage is only one possible effect of new industry; there might be a boom in housing, because building contractors predict increased demand for it." Another problem with this pattern is that perhaps two or more events are not causally linked. The familiar joke, "I washed my car today; that's why it rained," illustrates this problem. Finally, even if the cause–effect relationship is assumed to be accurate, both events must be significant or relevant to the conclusion being claimed. "Sure, adopting the new program (*cause*) will force us to borrow money (*effect*). But we were planning to do that anyway, whichever proposal we approved. So your argument that we can't afford the program does not follow."

It is useful for speakers to analyze their patterns of reasoning. But remember that *most people who think carefully about developing a persuasive message develop a logical plan spontaneously and naturally*. As mentioned earlier, we all seem to have at least some intuitive notion of what makes sense. The preceding discussion is thus intended not as a "first course" in elementary logic, but rather as a review of available options.

## Evidence

Evidence may be simply defined as *information that generates belief in premises or conclusions*. It generates *proof* of propositions. The objective of the persuasive speaker is to provide the kinds of evidence that are likely to cause a receiver to consider a proposition proved. The process of developing proof is not something that a sender does *to* a receiver. Rather, proof exists in the minds of the receivers. Technically, it is inaccurate for a speaker to say, "Based on this evidence, I have proved that such-and-such is the case." Instead, the *receivers* must respond, "Based on the evidence we have heard, we think there is adequate proof of this conclusion."

In other words, evidence is data that evokes an audience *response* that something has been proved. This distinction is crucial. Just as some communicators are surprised when their intended meaning is not shared by a receiver, so persuasive speakers are surprised when their carefully developed evidence does not elicit audience belief in their arguments. We need to remember that evidence that is convincing to us might not be persuasive (it might not prove the proposition) to others. As in other communication situations, therefore, the persuasive speaker should rely on feedback to determine whether his evidence actually proves what he wants it to prove.

Evidence (also called *supporting materials*) can be discussed in four general categories: explanation, examples, statistics, and testimony.

*Explanation.* When explanation demonstrates how an event occurs, how a process works, or why a condition exists, it becomes a type of evidence. Explanation is a kind of description which, because it appears to receivers to be plausible, provides evidence that helps prove a conclusion. For example, suppose a speaker wants to persuade receivers that solar energy is a desirable method for heating homes. One device she uses is an explanation of the solar heating system—its components, how it is built, and how it functions. When she has finished, the receivers are more likely to believe her conclusion: "Solar heating systems work; it is mechanically or physically possible to heat a home with the sun as power source." Notice that the speaker could not stop here. She would still have to demonstrate its desirability. But her first step is to convince skeptics that a system is at least workable, and explanation evidence can do that.

Explanations can describe events or conditions that have already occurred, or they can suggest things that might possibly occur (hypothetical). The latter method can be seen in arguments developed by ecologists, who use explanations to show "what will happen in the future if we adopt this program." Conclusion: The program will be harmful. Since these explanations often depend on cause–effect reasoning, some people prefer to think of them as "arguments" or as "lines of reasoning" rather than as evidence. But we think that it is more convenient to view explanation as a form of supporting material by which a speaker generates belief in a conclusion.

*Examples.* A broad category of evidence, *examples* include specific instances, analogies, and illustrations. Even some explanations discussed above could overlap into this category. A *specific instance* is a relatively short description of one thing. *Analogies* are comparisons between two things in which similarities in a particular characteristic suggest similarities in other areas as well. An analogy can function both as a form of reasoning (see previous section) or as supporting material for a broader premise. When an analogy is *literal*, it compares things of the same class, as when Detroit is compared to Minneapolis in terms of urban problems. When an analogy is *figurative*, it compares things in different classes, as when a business organization is compared to a living organism in terms of what both need to survive and grow.

An *illustration* is actually a type of specific instance, except that it is more lengthy and provides more detailed information. A typical illustration is an extended *narrative*, a story with characters and plot.

The illustration may be *real* or *hypothetical*. The real or factual illustration is usually more potent in generating proof of propositions, but the hypothetical approach can be effective if the events described are plausible, if they are interpreted by the receivers as things that happen all the time or would be likely to happen under certain circumstances.

Examples are usually very strong evidence, because they are believable. The receiver can visualize an object, condition, or event. Suppose a speaker wants to convince the audience that the child abuse problem is especially serious because it is legally very difficult to intervene to protect battered children. So she uses an illustration of a real second grade teacher who regularly noticed terrible bruises on one of the children, reported it to authorities, testified against the parents, and was eventually sued by those parents, lost the case, and had to pay damages. It would be difficult for listeners to deny that trying to protect abused children can be very risky.

The main disadvantage of examples as evidence is based on the nature of inductive reasoning. Remember that induction argues from specific instances to a general conclusion. It is difficult to convince a skeptic that two or three examples are anything but "isolated" and "not typical of the general rule." A receiver may brush aside even the most compelling instances, analogies, or illustrations because there are too few to establish a general rule or condition. Despite this problem, most logical messages rely to some extent on the use of examples.

*Statistics.* Quantified data that summarize many specific instances are called *statistics*. In this scientific age, statistics have become perhaps the most common form of evidence. Instead of having to describe case after case to arrive at a convincing generalization, a speaker can achieve the same effect simply by providing a number or series of numbers that quantify all of the cases in a single category.

While the advantages of using statistics as evidence are obvious, the disadvantages need to be weighed carefully. Do the statistics distort the truth because they are taken out of context or because they ignore other contradictory data? Are complex statistics, perhaps representing involved mathematical relationships, easily understandable by receivers? Will receivers become too easily bored by a lengthy recitation of "facts and figures"? Will some receivers react negatively to any quantification, because they believe that most speakers have mastered the art of "lying with statistics"? The persuasive speaker thus needs to consider not simply the *logical validity* of statistics in supporting conclusions, but the *persuasive impact* of certain types of statistics with particular audiences. The author has observed debates in which a speaker with only two or three compelling, dramatic examples was more convincing than his opponent who had voluminous statistics. Perhaps the ideal strategy is to combine cogent examples and statistics to provide both qualitative and quantitative support for conclusions.

*Testimony.* A statement of one's opinion or a description of one's perceptions is called *testimony*. When used as evidence in a persuasive speech, testimony may either be verbatim (a direct quotation of someone's spoken or written words) or paraphrased (a general summary of someone's words). *Eyewitness testimony* is a statement by someone who actually observed a particular condition or event. This type of evidence is the basis of courtroom persuasion, but can also be useful in other areas of public speaking. For example, a speaker who argued that violence in the high school classroom is becoming a serious problem quoted several witnesses—teachers and students—who had observed actual cases of assault and violence. *Expert testimony* is a statement by someone with special information, background, and credentials to make a judgment (provide an informed opinion) about an issue or condition. The expert may not have actually observed particular events firsthand, but has studied a topic area in enough depth to be a reliable commentator. In most persuasive speeches on current issues, especially when some policy change is being recommended, expert testimony will be important evidence.

When the other types of evidence are used, two factors are important in determining their effectiveness—the persuasive speaker's ability and the quality of information in the evidence. But with testimony, a third factor becomes important. The person giving the testimony, the eyewitness or expert, affects the ways in which receivers will perceive and interpret the information. Testimony can thus be a blessing or a curse. The information it reveals may be more or less credible, depending on who says it. Like statistics, testimony should be selected in part on the ways in which receivers are likely to be impressed by it. In jury trials, lawyers are careful to instruct their own witnesses to speak, dress, and groom appropriately so that their testimony will be received more favorably. A persuasive speaker should be equally concerned about the "persuasive images" of the people she quotes in her presentations.

*Tests of evidence.*   In addition to one's intuitive sense of what makes evidence good or bad for particular audiences, we offer several guidelines to help in selecting the best possible supporting materials. However, in each business and professional area, as well as each issue or topic, there will be special criteria for what constitutes good, reliable evidence in a particular case. For example, the legal profession has extensive rules of evidence. Economists and accountants consider certain types of statistics more relevant than others. Therefore, the list below is a general one. Several points are borrowed from Freeley, a good source for more in-depth study of the use of evidence (Freeley, 1971, pp. 97–110).

1. Does *enough* evidence exist to support the conclusion?
2. Is the evidence *clear* to the audience? Are most receivers likely to understand it quickly and easily, especially in terms of what conclusions the evidence is intended to support?
3. Is the evidence *consistent*? Is it *extremely* consistent with other information that exists? (Does other evidence tend to corroborate or refute the evidence in question?) Is it *internally* consistent? (For example, does the first part of an eyewitness' account jibe with later parts of his same story?)
4. Is the evidence *verifiable*? Can a speaker go back to original sources to check on the accuracy of statistics, examples, or testimony? Can someone other than the speaker, like a political opponent or a member of the audience, gain access to the same information?
5. Is the source of the evidence *competent*? Has printed material from which examples or statistics are taken come from someone qualified? Is testimony given by someone who observed and was mentally and physically able to report that observation accurately, or whose background equips him to provide competent opinions?

6. Is the source of the evidence *reliable*? Is someone who testified trustworthy, truthful, and unbiased? Do printed materials have a good reputation for fairness and thoroughness?

7. Is the evidence *relevant*? Does it support the conclusions that the speaker claims it supports? Does it lead logically and directly to the conclusion?

8. Is the evidence *statistically sound*? Are statistical criteria followed rigorously—such as accuracy, appropriate classification, valid sampling procedures, statistically significant results, reporting in context, and fair visual representations?

9. Is the evidence *recent* or current? This judgment is obviously relative; it depends on the topic. A business executive, attempting to persuade colleagues to adopt a particular investment program, needs up-to-the-minute statistics. In contrast, an advocate for prison reform might need not only reasonably recent evidence about current conditions, but may also use historical materials about past failures in the system.

10. Is the evidence *adaptive* to the information and interest levels of the receivers? Sometimes a speaker with the same topic and purpose must use significantly different supporting materials when speaking to different audiences, like the anti-smoking advocate who used primarily statistical evidence with a group of older smokers, and used extended illustrations with a teen-age group.

Testing the evidence in a persuasive speech is an ongoing process that begins while compiling information and continues through audience feedback phases. Whether speaking or listening, we should think critically about the logical links between the claims being made and the materials that support those claims.

## Logical Fallacies

We conclude this section on the logical bases of persuasive speaking with a brief discussion of logical fallacies. A *fallacy*, generally speaking, is faulty or unsound reasoning; it is drawing inferences that are not warranted either in terms of the rules of reasoning or in terms of the evidence used to arrive at conclusions.

Unfortunately, though fallacious reasoning may be bad logic, it often achieves intended results in persuasion. That is, some speakers either unknowingly or by design use fallacies that some receivers find convincing. We may be amused by some of the examples below because they appear to show naive and shallow thinking, but they are nevertheless typical of logical errors committed by many, many public speakers.

**1.** *Ad hominem*. Also called the "genetic fallacy," *ad hominem* attacks the person making the argument rather than the argument itself.

> "I can understand why my opponent makes that claim; what can you expect from someone who didn't even finish high school?"

A subcategory of the *ad hominem* fallacy is called *guilt by association*, in which one is judged by the company one keeps.

> "How can we believe someone like Jones? He's a member of a radical socialist group that has threatened to overthrow the government!"

While one's associates might indicate bias, and detract from general credibility, the guilt by association fallacy does not deny the rational content of the argument that person advances.

**2.** *Appeal to ignorance*. This fallacy occurs when a speaker claims that some event did not occur or some condition does not exist because "no one here has ever heard of it."

> "We must maintain the testing and grading system if we are to motivate students to do their best work. After all, who ever heard of students working hard on their American history books unless there was a test coming up?"

**3.** *Straw man*. The straw man fallacy occurs when a speaker creates an argument or an issue that is different from the opposing point of view, and then attacks that argument. The successful refutation of this straw man may suggest to some that the speaker has actually destroyed an opponent's argument, when actually the refutation has avoided the real issue or claim.

"I have shown that my program would not be too expensive and should therefore be adopted." (The program had never been opposed because it was too expensive, but rather because it was impractical and unworkable.)

**4.** *"Two wrongs make a right."* Since childhood, when we tried to justify hitting our playmate because "he hit me first," we have heard the familiar response, "But two wrongs don't make a right." Yet some advocates are guilty of this fallacy anyway, suggesting a course of action that is no worse than what others have done.

"We admit that there may have been some unreported contributions to our campaign fund, but after all, the other party has been doing that for years."

**5.** *The "bandwagon" technique.* This fallacy seeks acceptance of a course of action because "everyone else is doing it." Logically, we should do things because they make sense (because they yield positive results), and not just to follow the crowd. Yet politics and advertising both utilize this technique with notable successes.

"Dozens of delegates have decided to switch their votes to Grimsley for governor. I hope you will switch, too."

Notice that the bandwagon technique could be based on a logical premise—"When many people switch to a new product, it is because the product has developed a reputation for doing what we say it does." But that premise needs logical support, especially in terms of proving that the product is good, and cannot be demonstrated simply because many people use it. They may have other motives—it's cheaper, they feel peer pressure, they want to be part of the "in crowd," and so on.

**6.** *Post hoc, ergo propter hoc.* Literally, this fallacy argues "after this, therefore because of this." It is a type of faulty causal reasoning. The fallacy is the basis for many primitive superstitions. A person would do something "bad," and then a flood would occur. The people would assume that it was the prior act that caused the flood. It continues today, when we argue "This bad thing happened because God is punishing you for stealing." *Post hoc* reasoning is popular in politics.

> "No sooner did the Democrats come into power than inflation jumped to its highest rate in twenty years."

Notice that there may actually be causation between two sequential events. Perhaps, for example, Democratic policies are linked to inflation. But it is the characteristics of those *policies*, and not the mere fact that they preceded the inflation, that establish any alleged causality.

**7.** *Arguing in a circle.* Circular reasoning is unsound because two or more conclusions, unsupported by reasoning or evidence, are used to establish the logical validity of each other.

> "Hemingway is a great author; just look at *For Whom the Bell Tolls*." [Later]: "Of course *For Whom the Bell Tolls* is a great novel; it was written by Hemingway."

**8.** *Begging the question.* The question is begged whenever the speaker assumes as true or false, good or bad, some of the very questions at issue.

> "We can't let the government tell us how to build our homes and our places of business. Why, that would threaten our free enterprise system!"

Notice that the speaker is assuming, without support, that (a) the free-enterprise system exists, (b) that it is beneficial, (c) that the government policy would, in fact, threaten it, and (d) that sacrificing any free enterprise would be harmful. Some audiences might make the same assumptions and accept the speaker's question-begging. But more skeptical receivers certainly would require more logical basis for assuming as true some of the critical points at issue.

**9.** *Inconsistency.* A speaker commits the fallacy of inconsistency when he makes a claim at one point of the speech and then logically contradicts himself with another claim later on. At least one of the claims cannot be true, and the speaker is thus inconsistent.

> "If we adopt this program we will need to hire people to staff it, thus providing jobs and alleviating the unemployment problem." [Later]: "The program will be efficient; it can be operated with minimal manpower needs." (If a relatively small number of people are needed to staff the

program, then it will not do much for the unemployment problem. But if
many people are hired, then it is not as efficient as claimed.)

**10.** *False dilemma.* Also called the "black-and-white fallacy," the
false dilemma claims fewer alternatives than actually exist. Usually,
the speaker reduces the alternatives to two, both bad (a dilemma). The
dilemma is false because there are other alternatives that have not
been considered, and one or more of these other alternatives may be
beneficial.

> "Sure, we have problems with the rapid growth of this city. But how would
> you like the alternative of no growth—a stagnant economy and unem-
> ployment?" (A third alternative is controlled growth, which protects
> employment and minimizes social problems of rapid growth.)

**11.** *Hasty generalization.* This fallacy is associated with the inductive
reasoning discussed earlier. The speaker has presented insufficient
evidence (specific cases) to warrant the general conclusion.

> "I've shown three people who have used my techniques and have success-
> fully quit smoking. I hope you'll try this proven method, too."

**12.** *Faulty extension.* Sometimes a speaker reasons well from premises and evidence to a conclusion, but then tries to extend that conclusion to applications beyond reasonable limits.

> "My opponent has claimed that this retraining program will help unem-
> ployment and boost the local economy. But will it help the elderly who are
> retired? What about the sick or disabled who can't work at all? I question
> how much social benefit this will have. (The program is not designed to
> solve all economic problems, but is beneficial for some of them.)

**13.** *Irrelevant reason.* This fallacy occurs when the premises and
evidence are irrelevant (do not logically apply) to the conclusion.
Sometimes called a *non sequitur* ("it does not follow"), this fallacy
usually leaves receivers scratching their heads in confusion because
they see no logical link.

> "Too many of our children are out on the streets with no purpose and no
> future. Our schools are a mess. There is low morale among teachers. Elect

Smith for School Board. (There is no logical link between school problems and Smith's competency to serve on the Board.)

The foregoing analysis of fallacies is by no means complete, but reflects some of the more common logical flaws in persuasive speaking. People who are truly interested in improving their speech presentations will, during message preparation, carefully analyze the logical elements to assure that these common fallacies are avoided.

## NONRATIONAL BASES OF PERSUASIVE SPEAKING— THE MESSAGE

In the first part of this chapter we noted that people respond to persuasive messages both rationally and nonrationally. They may use their reasoning ability as a basis for thinking or doing, but they may at the same time respond according to their motives and their feelings, according to nonrational bases. We believe that persuasive speeches should have a logical basis. But we also believe that in order to achieve a persuasive purpose, a speaker must consider those nonrational factors that tend to make a message more persuasive to a particular audience.

The degree to which receivers respond to rational versus nonrational factors differs according to the speech context, the topic and purpose, and the nature of the audience. For example, if a receiver is an executive who is primarily concerned with making a profit, and if the speaker is an employee urging that the company develop a new product line, the message should probably be developed totally on well reasoned, well evidenced arguments. But if that same rational executive were a receiver of a different message in a different context—for example, as the father of three children, listening to a school counselor urge more parental involvement in their development—he might be responsive to more nonrational factors. In this section, we cannot prescribe the emphasis that is placed on emotional factors. Rather, we simply identify some of the typical nonrational elements in a persuasive message and remind the reader to remember the unique, situational factors of every speech event.

Persuasive speakers have come to use two general strategies in

developing nonrational appeals in their messages. First, they use suggestion. Second, they appeal to the needs and the feelings of the receivers.

## Suggestion in Persuasive Speaking

*Suggestion is a process in which a person responds to a message (thinks or behaves) without rational thought or deliberation, and sometimes without any conscious awareness that such a response has occurred.* Suggestion occurs when the sender of a message identifies an appropriate response, but does not supply *reasons* or *evidence* to justify that response. The message becomes the stimulus for the receiver's subsequent thought or behavior. Howell and Bormann call suggestion a kind of "button-pushing" that prompts a conditioned or "unthinking" reflex in the receiver, so long as that receiver has no contrary impulses or reasons to respond otherwise, and so long as the receiver sees the stimulus as something relating directly to his interests (Howell and Bormann, 1971, pp. 214–217).

Suggestion occurs frequently in advertising, both political and commercial. A candidate might be shown talking with elderly people, listening carefully to their comments. The suggestion might be: "This candidate is concerned about people, especially those who need effective government support." But that conclusion is neither stated nor supported with rational argument. A few years ago, a full-page color photograph appeared in a weekly magazine. It showed an elderly couple in a bright red convertible, smiling at the camera. Underneath the photograph was a quotation from George Bernard Shaw: "Youth is such a wonderful thing; what a crime to waste it on children." That was the entire ad. No evidence about the car's performance or cost or beauty. Yet the message was clear to most receivers. "If you buy this car you will feel young."

Public speakers use suggestion because it is frequently effective, because it is more striking or memorable than some reasoned discourse, because it saves time, and because it is difficult to refute by argument—logic cannot easily negate a response that suggestion has already stimulated. Some suggestion in public speaking is *direct*; the message tells precisely which response the sender is seeking. It is usually a relatively straightforward assertion like "Vote for Grimes" or "This program will work for us." Some suggestion is *indirect*, because it only implies but does not explicitly state the desired response.

Howell and Bormann provide several techniques of both direct and indirect suggestion (Howell and Bormann, 1971, pp. 222–234). Direct *positive* suggestion can be used in speeches simply by making forceful statements like "The abortion laws are unfair to the unborn" or "Study hard for this exam." Direct *negative* suggestion is probably less effective than positive, because the speaker must indicate what response he does *not* want from the receiver. In noting that undesired response, the speaker must risk planting it in the receiver's mind, perhaps prompting a positive response to it instead. For example, when parents use direct negative suggestion like "Do not open the cookie jar," they almost guarantee that children will open it. Speakers should thus rely primarily on positive suggestion.

A third type of direct suggestion is *autosuggestion*, in which a person stimulates himself to think or do something. By forcefully saying, "I feel good," we might actually begin to feel good. And as speakers, if we can get receivers to repeat our comments, they may themselves be positively affected. For example, when the Reverend Jesse Jackson speaks to young Black audiences, he asks them to shout with him again and again, "I am somebody!" He thus helps them persuade themselves with autosuggestion.

Indirect suggestion has many forms. One type Howell and Bormann call *simple implication*. It may be a more tactful or diplomatic way of saying something which, more directly stated, might offend someone. The respondent can read into the message the speaker's intention. Of course, this indirect method is less reliable, because the speaker must depend more on the receiver to interpret the intended meaning. An example of simple implication occurred when an instructor wanted her students, a relatively older adult group, to study carefully for the exam. Instead of using direct suggestion like "Study thoroughly for this exam," a comment that might have appeared to be treating adults like children, the instructor instead said, "Since the material we have covered is especially important in our everyday lives, the upcoming exam will be the most thorough and rigorous of the semester." The message was the same—study hard! Any listener could have accurately understood the implication of her comment.

A second type of indirect suggestion is *countersuggestion*. The technique depends on people doing the opposite of what they are told. The message suggests one course of action, and the receivers think or behave counter to that suggestion. Countersuggestion is the basis of literary satire. A familiar case is the Uncle Remus fable in which Br'er Rabbit says, "Do anything you want to me, but *please* don't throw me in that there briar patch." Of course, Br'er Bear and Br'er Fox do exactly that, and Br'er Rabbit ends up right where he wanted to be. In public speaking, suppose a speaker wants quick action on his proposal and senses that his receivers are impatient to do something quickly. He may suggest, "Of course, we don't have to adopt my proposal now. Perhaps we should proceed with more caution, studying the problem further and perhaps having a committee report." Someone is likely to respond, "No, I'm sick and tired of studying it to death. I want to move on your program now and stop wasting valuable time."

Countersuggestion can backfire. A very skeptical or hostile audience may find the unintended response most appealing. Some receivers might innocently take the suggestion at face value and miss the speaker's true intention. Effective countersuggestion requires artistry and a good understanding of receiver characteristics. But when it works, countersuggestion is potent because the *receiver*, not the speaker, has "decided" on the appropriate response.

A third category is *word manipulation*. By slanting a message with carefully selected positive or negative words, a speaker can elicit a desired response. For example, during the war in Vietnam the Pentagon carefully selected the term "protective reaction strikes" rather than "bombing raids" to describe the B-52 missions. The words may be ambiguous, like the "buzz words" of which politicians are so fond because they permit each receiver to take the most favorable possible meaning. One state governor said, "I favor a legal system that has speed, fairness, and justice." Who can disagree with that? And how many different meanings could be ascribed to it? Like countersuggestion, word manipulation may not succeed with a wary or argumentative audience. And if it is used to distort or deceive, it is suspect on ethical or moral grounds. But careful wording of key points of the speech can sometimes be as persuasive as the most carefully supported argument.

A fourth type of indirect suggestion involves *humor*. Sometimes the conclusion or point of a joke, or the implication of a witty remark, becomes an accepted statement of reality, of "the truth." For example, if a speaker tells a joke about a foolish government bureaucrat. One meaning that a receiver might unconsciously ascribe is that the bureaucracy in Washington is made up of foolish people with unsound policies. The speaker may thus have achieved the desired response without establishing a logical basis for proof. Humor can be useful for many other reasons—maintaining attention, minimizing speech anxiety, or putting the audience at ease—but it can also be an effective type of suggestion.

Another category is the *common ground* approach, in which a speaker praises the audience members, notes points of similarity between himself and his listeners, compliments the listeners' organization, or refers to acquaintances in the audience.

Speakers may also use the *yes response* technique as a form of indirect suggestion. It is based on the theory that if people get used to answering "yes" to a series of questions, they will be more likely to say "yes" to the most important final question. The early questions must be phrased carefully to assure that the affirmative pattern is well established before arriving at the last question, the "bottom line" of the speaker's persuasive purpose. Salespeople use the yes response approach frequently, asking customers nonthreatening questions like "Do you think you'd like to own a sofa like this?" or "Do you think a quality sofa like this is worth its sale price of $499?" and then concluding with a request like "Why don't you let me write up the order and we'll have it delivered tomorrow morning. Okay?" The public speaker can develop the main points of the speech in the same way, building on each positive response to the eventual conclusion. The risk, of course, is that a particular question might prompt a "No," thus destroying the persuasive progression.

Finally, the use of *multiple options* can be a form of indirect suggestion. Instead of seeking only one possible response, the speaker develops several related options and asks the receivers to assist in selecting the best one. The options may not differ greatly, and any one of them may essentially fulfill the speaker's intent. If the audience thus concentrates on the best of the options, they tend *not* to consider whether all should be rejected. They feel as if they are a part of the process, that they are not being persuaded but rather are helping the speaker solve a problem. For example, instead of saying "I'd like you to help solicit funds for the United Way campaign," the speaker says, "There are at least four methods we might use to meet this year's campaign goal. As I discuss each one, please consider which would be the best approach." Phrased this way, it appears that deciding *whether* to conduct the campaign is no longer an issue, only *how* it should be conducted.

### Motivational Appeals in Persuasive Speaking

Nonrational factors in the persuasive message often involve the receivers' attitudes, values, and needs, the psychological or emotional components of decision-making. A useful term is *motivational appeals*, which Andersen defines as:

> . . . stimuli designed to create a tension, to elicit a feeling or affective response from a receiver. Motivational appeals are directed to the wishes, wants, desires, goals, and needs of the person. These needs and wants are not necessarily logical (nor necessarily illogical), rather they exist either as the result of inherent predispositions or the conditioning of the self by the society and one's experiences. Appeals to emotions are clearly one part of the area of motivational appeals (Andersen, 1971, p. 146).

In this section we shall discuss some of the more common motivational or emotional appeals that speakers frequently use and that have been effective in eliciting desired responses.

The persuasive speaker will probably never be able to predict the receiver response accurately. There will never be a science of persuasion in the same way that we have come to think about the physical sciences like mathematics, biology, and chemistry. But over time, an experienced speaker will learn to recognize the salient features of various audiences and to develop messages that enhance persuasive goals. Experienced salespeople, lawyers, politicians, members of the clergy, and even teachers have learned to utilize certain appeals that generate intended responses fairly consistently.

© Howard Harrison 1969

*Receivers' needs.*   Let us first consider appeals that speakers use to suggest things that the receivers *want*, their *needs*. There are several types of needs.

1.  *Self-preservation and security.* We want to be safe, to protect ourselves and our loved ones, to avoid danger and pain, to acquire property, to seek and maintain good health, and anything else that assures our survival as individuals and as a species.
2.  *Affiliation and esteem.* We need to be involved with and appreciated by others. We need love and affection, companionship and friendship, trust and loyalty, physical and sexual attraction and beauty, admiration, recognition, and approval. Related appeals apply to our desire to be like others, to conform. Thus, appeals to obedience and imitation are frequently effective.
3.  *Freedom.* Despite the need to affiliate and conform, we also want to be relatively unrestrained by others, to be autonomous, to explore, to seek adventure, to satisfy our curiosity and creativity without being told how to think and what to do.
4.  *Pleasure and fulfillment.* We want happiness, to enjoy experiences and people and things. We need to believe that our lives are meaningful, that we are being fulfilled by what we do. Aesthetic enjoyment can be as important a need as physical or material pleasure.
5.  *Power and control.* We want to be able to influence or affect our environment, to control the behavior of others, to achieve mastery over the events in our lives. Though we may want freedom for ourselves, restricting to some extent the freedom of others (causing them to behave in ways that help us) can better fulfill our own wants. We want to be strong and to compete in ways that demonstrate our skill and our mastery over others. Or we may want to fight and destroy to make the environment better for us.
6.  *Achievement.* We want to accomplish something, to complete tasks, to be able to say "I did that." We want to make a difference in our own and others' lives by our personal efforts.

*Positive and negative appeals.*   When speakers can show that receiver responses to the message can fulfill some of these needs, then persuasion may occur. We can also look at persuasive appeals in terms of the way we *feel*, the *emotional or affective states which, if aroused, may prompt the desired response*.

Some feelings are generally positive and desirable in terms of the receiver:

| | |
|---|---|
| love | sympathy, compassion |
| happiness, contentment | trust |
| awe, wonder, reverence | pride |
| joy, elation, ecstasy | desire, passion |

The persuasive speaker may appeal to positive emotions in two ways. First, he may suggest that if the receivers respond a certain way, they will experience some of the positive emotions. The *appeal* of the message is that, if followed, the receivers will feel good. The second approach is the more common way of viewing emotional appeals; the speaker attempts to arouse the positive emotions so that the receivers will respond as intended. The emotional appeal becomes a means to an end rather than an end in itself. Whether these *positive* emotions become *constructive* emotions depends on the eventual behaviors that result.

Negative emotions include:

| | |
|---|---|
| fear, anxiety | revulsion |
| anger, rage | revenge |
| hate | sorrow |
| resentment | disappointment |
| envy | depression, discouragement |
| jealousy | guilt, regret |

Many persuasive speakers have learned that appealing to negative emotions can be very effective. It may be relatively innocent, like a football coach exhorting the team to become angry at the opponents and seek revenge for the previous year's defeat. But using such appeals can be insidious, as with Hitler's campaign of hatred, anger, and resentment of the Jews. Like positive emotional appeals, these negative emotional responses can lead to constructive or destructive outcomes.

An example demonstrates how both positive and negative motivational factors can become important parts of a persuasive message. A

IMPROVING
PERSUASIVE
MESSAGES

291

speaker is urging middle-aged men to become active in the YMCA's sports and physical fitness programs. He makes seven main points.

1. Risk of heart attack is high among the middle-aged, and this risk increases with lack of exercise. (*fear, self-preservation*)
2. Sports activity is great fun. (*pleasure*)
3. Improved fitness permits people to do many things they were previously incapable of doing. (*freedom, adventure*)
4. Improved physical fitness has been shown to improve mental or emotional well-being. (*avoidance of depression and anxiety*)
5. The YMCA programs permit frequent activities with others and the chance to make new friends. (*affiliation, companionship*)
6. Participation leads to loss of excess weight, improved strength and agility, and improved performance in various sports. (*achievement*)
7. Competitive activities give participants a chance to play in tournaments and to win. (*power, pride*)

We suggest three concluding points about motivational appeals. First, we are motivated by both positive and negative factors, whether these factors originate in the environment or within ourselves. And we have learned to influence others by using both. For example, from early childhood we learn to recognize the "carrot and the stick" methods of persuasion. The carrot is positive reinforcement of good or desired thoughts and behaviors; the stick is negative reinforcement of bad or undesired responses. As children we get cookies if we've been good and a spanking if we've been bad. As adults, we may put money in a savings account to buy something that gives us pleasure and pay money to the IRS to avoid going to jail. The supervisor may praise a worker, increase his pay, or promote him for good work, and fire or threaten him for bad work.

Both positive and negative reward systems have achieved desired responses. In persuasive speaking, we favor positive appeals, those that suggest beneficial results of thinking or behaving in the intended ways. Good persuaders may utilize both sides of the coin, but in general we should stress the positive as much as possible.

Second, notice that while many of these appeals can be developed through suggestion, many result from logical argument. I may prove to you, through valid reasoning and evidence, that smoking and a high cholesterol diet will probably shorten your life-span. But that conclusion evokes an emotional response—probably fear—that becomes the basis of your response, possibly changing your smoking and eating habits.

Finally, the effect of motivational appeals always depends on the individual receiver and on the culture and situation in which the communication event occurs. Persuasive speakers should never be surprised when intended responses do not occur, or when successful appeals to some groups do not achieve results in others.

## NONRATIONAL BASES OF PERSUASIVE SPEAKING— THE SPEAKER

In this concluding section, we shall discuss what is often the most important determinant of whether persuasive responses occur—the nonrational appeals that exist in the speaker. Regardless of what the verbal message happens to be, many receivers alter their thinking and their behavior simply because of how they perceive and give meaning to the speaker as a person. The ancient Greek rhetoricians called this factor in persuasion *ethos*, and defined it as *the proofs that exist in the speaker*. Modern theorists have used such terms as *source credibility*, *image*, and *reputation* to refer to the ways in which the speaker enhances or detracts from the persuasive purpose.

### Principles about Ethos

1. *There will always be a relationship dimension in any public speaking situation.* Sender and receivers make judgments about each other. They decide whether or not they like each other, conform to norms of behavior around each other, and develop strategies for dealing with each other. One receiver relationship with a sender might be, "I don't like that woman, I am skeptical of what she suggests, and I shall make it a point not to associate with her afterward." Though this is a negative response, it nevertheless establishes a relationship. As persuasive speakers, we hope that most of our sender–receiver relationships will be positive, not only because it boosts our ego but also

because it increases our persuasiveness. We hope that receivers will respond in this way: "I like that speaker. She seems to be a knowledge-able person, committed to what she is saying. I think I trust her." But whatever the relationship happens to be, it will always develop. It is a given in any speech.

**2.** *Some ethos exists before the speaker begins the presentation.* It is *antecedent*, based on audience perceptions of the speaker (or what the speaker represents) that have occurred in advance of the presentation. It may be notoriety, our tendency to give credibility to people we have seen on TV or in the movies, to people in the news, to celebrities. It may be that we have heard about the speaker from others—"You are really going to like our guest speaker tonight; I've heard him before and he has some exciting ideas." It may be that the person's creden-tials, job, or title prompt us to anticipate an immediate credibility. "Our speaker tonight, a Ph.D. in biochemistry and accomplished pilot, is the first woman to be selected as an astronaut in the Space Shuttle program." Or for most of us it may simply be that our receivers know us, work with us, and have heard us speak before. That prior relation-ship may establish antecedent ethos.

**3.** *A speaker must continue to earn or derive ethos during the actual presentation regardless of prior reputation* (over which we have little control). Whatever positive judgments may have preceded the speaker, those perceptions can be quickly negated after the speech begins. Perhaps it is a disturbing *nonverbal* characteristic—a nervous tic, an unpleasant vocal inflection, unattractive clothing, or awkward ges-tures or mannerisms. Or it may be the *verbal* content. The speaker says things that suggest lack of preparation or knowledge, lack of moral principles, lack of concern for audience well-being. Only the receivers can determine which factors improve or detract from prior ethos.

**4.** *Some listeners attempt to disregard positive or negative factors of ethos and concentrate on the message.* For example, jurors might at-tempt to disregard a lawyer's awkward, unpleasant style or a judge's monotone in giving instructions and concentrate on the logical or informative verbal content. A group of scientists at a convention may attempt to listen to the incompetently delivered paper of a noted physicist. A manager may realize that despite his antagonism for a colleague, he will try to listen objectively to the colleague's plan for a new company program. Whether these receivers actually do totally disregard nonlogical appeals in the sender is doubtful. Since the "message" includes *all* speaker and context characteristics that the audience perceives and gives meaning to, and since receivers can never know for sure why they make the judgments they do, it is probably foolish to assume that any of us, in any situation, really ignore factors of ethos.

**Suggestions to Improve Ethos in Speechmaking**

What can the speaker do to improve persuasiveness by improving ethos? We offer several suggestions.

**1.** *Try to exhibit the qualities on which source credibility is based.* Some of them are:

Competence: Is the speaker qualified to talk about this topic?

Candor: Is the speaker telling the truth?

Benevolence: Does the speaker like us? Is he interested in our well-being?

Trustworthiness: Can we depend on this speaker?

Attractiveness: Does the speaker look and sound good? Does he have a pleasant personality?

Similarity: Does the speaker think and do things that we also think and do? Are we alike in any respects?

Communication skill: Does the speaker have effective speech style and fluency? Do we consider him to be a "good speaker"?

Since meanings and "persuasiveness" exist in the minds of receivers (speakers are not innately persuasive; the audience decides whether they are or not), they will determine whether these qualities accurately describe the speaker. But the speaker can *suggest* those characteristics by the things he does. For example, he can describe his background and display complete and current information to suggest *competence*. He can note experiences and feelings that are typical of what listeners think and feel (*similarity*). He can dress and groom in a way consistent with receiver expectations and standards of good taste (*attractiveness*). He can develop a consistent history or reputation for telling the truth and, during the speech, frankly discuss the bad with the good (*candor*). In other words, the audience determines source credibility, but the speaker's appearance and behavior are key factors in this process.

**2.** *Try to like the audience as people.* This suggestion usually becomes consistently easier to implement in the public speaking class as a student gets to know the others as people, and possibly as friends. In other settings, however, it may be difficult to like the receivers—not that we necessarily dislike them, but that we have no prior experience or basis for feeling positive affiliation for them. It may be hard to display warmth to strange, nameless faces. Yet some of the most successful politicians in terms of ethos or charisma have seemed to exude a sincere warmth and affection for their audiences. They like campaigning because they like people. The same is true for some teachers, members of the clergy, and supervisors. Simply stated, we believe them more readily because they appear to like us.

As receivers, we can usually spot insincerity and we can usually tell quickly whether or not others like us. To develop a liking for the audience, speakers might try to get to know them better beforehand. But the speaker who says "I want to persuade these people, but I just don't like them very much and I don't think that attitude will change," should not be surprised that his personal appeal is minimal.

**3.** *Determine in advance what antecedent ethos might exist.* During pre-speech negotiation and conversations, find out what the receivers know about you. Consider any prior experience with them, like having worked together before. What will the introduction say about you? Most important, consider any antecedent impressions that will have to be changed after the speech begins. For example, if a speaker believes that, because of her title or reputation, some receivers consider her aloof and unapproachable, she might try to begin the speech with some personal experiences that establish common ground, that show her to be a real, down-to-earth person just like them. On the other hand, some speakers may think that their perceived reputation establishes a distance between themselves and the receivers, and that this distance establishes a kind of mystique that actually improves their persuasiveness. To become too chummy and familiar might actually destroy their appeal. Whatever judgment the speaker makes, he should assess his ethos with a particular audience.

4.   *Consider nonverbal factors of source credibility*. Return to the discussion in Chapter 1 on nonverbal communication. Think carefully about each of the categories there and apply them to your own appearance in a persuasive speech.

5.   *Always adapt to the unique audience and situation*. The advice we gave regarding logical and nonlogical *message* appeals applies to the speaker's image as well. The receiver-centered persuasive speaker will adapt not only the verbal message, but his own appearance and behavior as well.

In conclusion, the nonrational appeals that exist in the speaker may have some logical basis. For example, it could be logically argued that the *reason* a speaker has an outstanding reputation is that he is competent, that he has done his job well. The absence of a reputation may logically point to a lack of competence, especially if other people who do the same thing for the same length of time usually acquire positive reputations. Thus, while we may not *reason through* our judgments of source credibility, those judgments may have an implicit logical basis.

## SUMMARY

Persuasive communication is the process in which a sender attempts to influence the thinking and the behavior of receivers. Persuasion can be viewed as a response to messages; it occurs when receivers actually behave in ways that the sender intended. The process is reciprocal; senders and receivers reinforce and respond to each other's behavior. These responses are generated from both rational and nonrational factors. But it is difficult to predict or interpret accurately a receiver's response to a persuasive message, to know precisely what it will be or what it "means."

Logical bases of persuasion include both reasoning and evidence. *Reasoning* is the process of inferring conclusions from premises. Whereas some reasoning processes, such as mathematics, yield *absolute* or *certain* conclusions, most reasoning in persuasive speaking involves probability; the conclusions are more or less likely to be accurate or true than competing conclusions. Deductive reasoning is based on logical rules about moving from general premises to specific conclusions. Inductive reasoning involves general inferences based on observation of specific events in the environment. Both types of reasoning, and their variations, are combined to develop most persuasive messages.

*Evidence* is information that generates our belief in premises or conclusions. It generates proof in the minds of receivers. Evidence includes explanation (description of how an event occurs), examples (specific instances, analogies, and illustrations), statistics (quantified data that summarize many specific instances), and testimony (statement of opinion or description of perceptions). Depending on the audience, a speaker should subject evidence to several tests of its validity and persuasiveness. The speaker should also guard against several logical *fallacies* (faulty or unsound reasoning) that can impede persuasive purposes.

Persuasion also has a nonrational basis. One nonrational technique is suggestion, a process in which a person responds to a message without rational thought or deliberation. Another is motivational appeal, a message that elicits an affective, feeling, or emotional response based on receivers' attitudes, beliefs, and values. These appeals may involve motives like self-preservation and affiliation, or feelings like love, fear, or joy.

A final category of nonrational bases is *ethos* or source credibility —the proofs that lie in the speaker as a person. Some ethos is antecedent; it exists in the receivers' minds before the speech begins. But for most speakers, ethos is derived from the actual speech behavior; it must be earned. The better we understand the criteria by which receivers ascribe ethos to a speaker, and the better we adapt to those unique criteria in each communication situation, the more persuasive we will be.

## QUESTIONS FOR STUDY

1. Why do we think of persuasion as a response to messages? As reciprocal? As both rational and nonrational?

2. What are some similarities and differences between deduction and induction? Why can it be said that the two types are interrelated and that most speeches include both types?

3. What are some common tests of evidence? Based on these tests, what is the general quality or reliability of evidence that is typically used in persuasive speeches in your classroom?

4. What are some motivational appeals that might be appropriate (depending on the audience) in the speech topics listed below?

   Improving the Airport
   Take a Speed-Reading Course
   The Energy Crunch: Let's Take Action Now
   Vote Against National Health Insurance
   Toward a More Effective System of Public Education

5. Assume that you were planning to give speeches to a variety of audiences about contributing to the United Way campaign. What might be your initial *ethos* as determined by the receiver groups below? What might you have to do to improve credibility?

   The local Rotary Club
   A group of high school students and teachers
   A senior citizens group
   The League of Women Voters
   Fellow employees in a factory or office

# chapter 11

# ADAPTING TO THE COMMUNICATION CONTEXT

**LEARNING OBJECTIVES**

After reading this chapter, you should be able to:

1. List some of the typical variables in the physical setting that can affect the speech presentation.
2. Explain how a typical speech in the classroom environment would have to be modified and adapted to more specialized communication events.
3. Utilize suggestions for adapting to special communication contexts in any nonclassroom speaking you may do.

**11**

Upon graduation, Will Denton got a job with his university's Alumni Association office. Realizing that he would have to give frequent speeches to many different groups, Will enrolled in a public speaking class. He gave four speeches during the semester, all with an audience of students in the classroom environment. He improved his preparation and delivery skills, and by the end of the course felt very comfortable with the room, the instructor, and the group of listeners whom he had come to know personally.

Then he confronted the "real world." The Alumni Association began its fund drive for the athletic program—money for scholarships and a new field house. Will was asked to head the campaign. Within a two month period, he delivered his speech and slide presentation many times, including the following contexts:

to a group of 800 people at a Booster's Club banquet

at a luncheon of about 12 executives of local companies in a student union meeting room

at an outdoor picnic of 150 alumni preceding a football game

in a televised half-hour program on a local station called "Your University Today"

to the Alumni Association's Board of Directors (about 5 or 6 people) in a conference room

to a Kiwanis Club breakfast meeting, 30 people in the back banquet room of a restaurant

to a group of 20 alumni volunteers who themselves were preparing to give their own presentations on the fund drive

on a panel with 3 other speakers, each requesting funds at a meeting of a charitable foundation.

Will discovered that he had to alter his presentation for each new context. For example, at the outdoor picnic he could not give the slide presentation, and on the panel presentation he was limited to only five minutes. His own speaking style and the amount and type of two-way interaction with the audience also varied with each speech. When the

campaign ended (successfully, by the way), Will Denton realized that he had now completed a much broader education in public speaking than the speech class had offered.

In Chapter 1, we presented a simple model of the communication process. One of the components of that model was *context*, the situation or environment in which the communication transaction occurs. Context can include such factors as physical setting, audience backgrounds and expectations, the speech purpose, time limits, communication channels that are available, and any other feature that can be perceived by the participants and given meaning.

Since every public speech is unique, and since the context of any presentation has dozens of specific features that can potentially affect speech outcome, it is unrealistic for a public speaker to learn how to adapt to all of the hundreds of situations that may arise. However, in this chapter we shall cover a few of the more important factors and describe special public speaking contexts that pose unique problems.

## THE PHYSICAL SETTING

A noted historian was asked to present a one-hour speech as part of an evening lecture series. The man was a fluent speaker with a superb grasp of historical materials. He had color slides of the site of a famous battle and had numerous examples and anecdotes to hold attention. His audience included people who enjoyed historical subjects. They also knew of the speaker's several books; his reputation and credibility were well established. Many ingredients were present for a successful communication event. Yet the speech failed, with the audience leaving two hours later shaking their heads. Why? The reasons lie in the speaker's neglect of the environment. He *assumed* that everything would be appropriately arranged for him, and appeared only five minutes ahead of time. This is what happened.

The room scheduled for the speech was already occupied by another group, an administrative foul-up. The program chairman hurriedly arranged for another room in an adjacent building. The audience and the speaker filed out of the building together and found the alternate room locked. Luckily, a brief search turned up a janitor who opened the door. As people settled into their chairs, the speaker began to look for an extension cord for the slide projector. The janitor again came to the rescue, but members of the audience had to help pass the cord under their chairs to reach a wall socket. Volunteers from the audience also had to bring in more chairs from down the hall, because this new room was not as large as the one originally scheduled. The speaker finally began about thirty minutes late, but his problems had just begun.

The new room had a podium but no reading light, and when the house lights were turned off for the slide presentation, the speaker could not read his notes. He moved near a red exit light to see the notes, and was then too far away to point at various features on the screen. The microphone was attached to the podium, and the volume kept changing as he continually moved from the podium to the exit light to the screen and back to the podium. Sometimes he was uncomfortably loud, and sometimes he was barely audible.

Finally, the speaker had not arranged in advance for someone to operate the slide projector (his projector had no remote or automatic slide-changing mechanism), so the program chairman, who had never operated such equipment before, agreed to run the projector. To change slides, the speaker called out "Next, please," and the audience waited awkwardly as the chairman-turned-projectionist struggled with the next slide, sometimes getting it in upside down or backward. The planned hour lecture took about an hour and a half, and the chairman called off the previously announced question-and-answer session.

Here was a good speaker with an interesting topic, clear visual aids, and an enthusiastic audience—yet he failed in his communication effort because of poor management of the environment. This true story is typical of many speeches that fail due to unexpected problems.

In this section we shall explore some of the typical physical features of speech context which speakers frequently must deal with.

## Seating Arrangement

One of the most common elements is seating arrangement. In many cases, the arrangement is fixed and the speaker must adapt to it. Classroom desks are often bolted down, as are theatre-type seats typical of auditoriums. The best strategy here is usually to encourage

listeners to sit as close to the front as possible. This suggestion should be made before the presentation begins, as many people are reluctant to move after getting settled in a particular place.

The general objective in most fixed seating situations is to get people as close together as possible without discomfort. A kind of psychological closeness often develops along with physical proximity. Listeners become more aware of the nonverbal and verbal behavior of others who are close by. They may feel more a part of a cohesive group and thus experience less inhibition. The reverse is also true: the speaker who wants to evoke enthusiastic response from a small audience scattered around a large auditorium faces a nearly impossible task.

More and more public speaking settings today have variable seating—classrooms, conference rooms, television studios, banquet rooms, and the like. That means that someone (not always the speaker) can exert control over the arrangement. An obvious concern with these adjustments is vision. Can everyone see the speaker? Is it also important that receivers see each other? Another concern is participation. Will the arrangement enhance or discourage interaction? Most important, what does the arrangement "say" nonverbally about the speaker? Is he relaxed or formal? One-way or two-way oriented? Innovative or traditional? Psychologically close or distant?

The figures below display some typical arrangements of variable seating.

The arrangement shown in Figure 1-A is especially useful for demonstrations and for encouraging audience participation. Figure 1-B is typical of business conferences and workshops in which the participants need to write and review printed materials on their tables. Figure 1-C is one of the better arrangements for banquet speaking. Food service is simpler and quicker at small tables than at long ones, and aisle access is clear. Most important, only one person at each table has to turn around to see the speaker, compared to many luncheon or dinner speeches in which nearly half the audience must either rearrange their chairs or sit with their backs to the speaker. Figure 1-D is a good arrangement when the focus of the presentation is not the speaker, but rather visual exhibits like films or slides. All seats are aimed directly at the front and the speaker moves off to one side. Figure 1-E is an improvement on the traditional long "Board of Directors" table for smaller group presentations and briefings. These events usually involve interaction among all participants, so the modified arrangement permits everyone to see everyone else easily and also gives an unrestricted view of the speaker, who may be seated or standing Figure 1-F, the traditional arrangement, has some people too close, others too far, and nearly everyone looking at the backs of other people's heads.

## The Podium

Another important context factor is the podium. The decision about whether to use a podium is often preempted by the facilities, as with a pulpit in a church or fixed speaker's stands in legislative rooms or auditoriums. And the loudspeaker system often requires that the speech be presented from a set location. But use of the podium is frequently optional. Some speakers use it more out of habit than need.

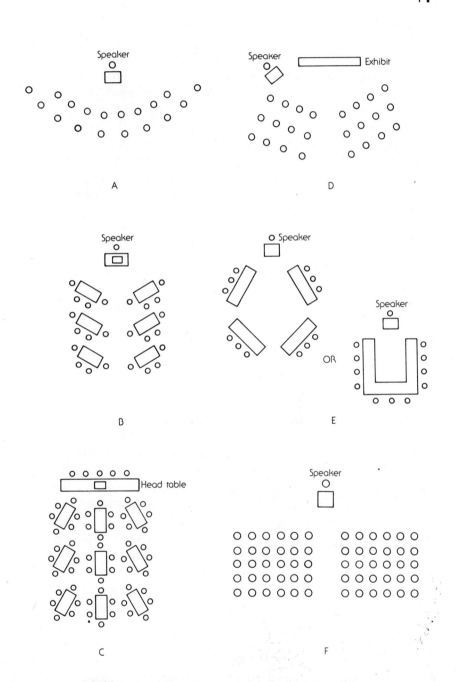

**FIGURE 1**   Some Typical Arrangements of Variable Seating

Several questions should be answered before using the podium. Is a small portable lectern available? Will a table be a suitable substitute as a place for notes and visual aids? Will the podium impede natural movement? Will it restrict audience vision? Will it become a crutch for the insecure speaker? Does it assist or restrict the speaker from achieving the desired audience response? Many speakers have learned that if one of their goals is to evoke audience enthusiasm, inspiration, or commitment, active animation away from the podium is essential. How many successful evangelists, teachers, political campaigners, salespeople, or even entertainers do we see remain in one place? These people usually move continuously. If amplification is needed, they use hand or lavalier mikes. Who would we be most likely to believe and trust—the speaker who remains behind the podium and whom we can see only from the shoulders up, or that same speaker out in the open before us? And which situation would be more likely to prompt us to view the communication event as a two-way transaction rather than a performance? It is easy to see why the use of the podium is one of the most important decisions in the speech setting.

## Temperature and Lighting

Temperature and lighting are also variables of setting. The speaker who refuses to consider these factors ("That's the janitor's job") may well be limiting speech effectiveness. If temperature cannot be easily modified (if the air conditioning system is broken, for example) the speaker might want to shorten the planned speech, seek another location, or even postpone it. We should not kid ourselves about receivers' willingness to tolerate discomfort and *still respond to the message*. Though students, for example, might suffer through a lecture in a hot classroom if an exam is approaching, many speeches in uncomfortable environments are actually counterproductive.

While lighting may be a given, the speaker should try to avoid overlighting the area where he will deliver the message. That area should not contrast significantly with the audience area. A darkened audience area, as in a banquet hall or auditorium, accentuates the undesirable impression of the "public speech as a performance." It also discourages receiver responsiveness; audience participation is more likely in an evenly lit room.

### Electronic and Mechanical Equipment

A fourth aspect of physical setting is electronic and mechanical support equipment—speaker systems, projection screens, recording systems, electrical outlets, extension cords, pointer devices, writing equipment like chalk or felt-tip markers, and so on. In discussing visual aids in Chapter 6, we noted the importance of advance preparation. But sometimes a speaker must work with what he finds in the actual setting. Testing the microphone in advance is absolutely essential. So is assuring that visual materials can be seen easily by everyone. Like the ill-fated speaker in the opening of this chapter, even well prepared communicators are surprised by physical factors they confront when they first arrive.

### Suggestions

Physical setting can work in favor of the speaker. These suggestions may help.

1. Get information about the setting during the speech negotiation process (see Chapter 2).
2. Arrive early.
3. Try out all equipment.
4. Consider last-minute rearrangement of seating.
5. Survey the area for potential distractions.
6. Be committed to audience comfort; try to empathize by sitting where they will sit.
7. Be willing to adapt spontaneously after the speech has begun.
8. Seek audience involvement in arranging and modifying the setting.

## SPECIAL PUBLIC COMMUNICATION EVENTS

Students in a basic public speaking class learn to conform to a standard, fairly predictable laboratory environment—they present short speeches to a captive audience of peers and a teacher-evaluator in a familiar and usually accommodative classroom setting. While useful educationally, this format lacks many of the important elements of real-world public communication. As we know, public speaking today does not necessarily involve a familiar environment, nor a small and manageable audience that shares with the speaker a common purpose, nor a neat set of evaluation criteria (standards of effectiveness), nor the freedom of each communicator to select topics and purposes. Instead, speakers must be willing and able to adapt to a great variety of contexts, using the basic skills developed in the classroom in many new and challenging ways.

In this section, we shall examine some of the special ways in which public communication occurs.

## The Conference or Business Meeting

Al Swanson is a mid-level manager for Transport Services, Inc., a large shipping company. As the company has grown, the problems of processing orders and keeping track of vehicles and loads have become too complex to handle efficiently. The company needed a new computer system, and asked Al to survey the computer industry to determine costs and capabilities of the various systems. He was then asked to make a presentation to the Board of Directors, summarizing his findings and recommending three computer companies for eventual demonstrations and bids. Al was also told that he would have no more than 30 minutes to present his report, despite the fact that his research had taken more than three months.

The example above is typical of the kinds of speeches that occur in a business conference. Though some conferences closely resemble the small work group, they may take the form of a one-to-many communication event. While 10 to 20 people listen, one speaker with special information or expertise develops a comparatively complicated topic. Members of the audience are usually insiders in that they share the same language and background with the speaker, and some of the same interests. The message in this setting thus does not need to make so many compromises toward simpler language, nor to explain in great depth the concepts that the audience should already know. The speaker may cover more material more quickly because of audience expertise. Interest in the topic also is likely to be higher because of special audience backgrounds, so devices to maintain attention may not be so numerous or necessary.

The conference speaker may be constrained by strict time limits. A fairly common instruction is: "At the next meeting, we'd like you to discuss your new proposal; you will have 8 minutes." And the chairperson really does mean 8 minutes, not 9 or 10. The speaker must also be more concerned with precision or content; oversimplifications or minor errors are usually noticed. Message organization is equally important, for busy professionals have little patience with the rambling speaker.

Guidelines for the business meeting presentation include:

1. Adhere to the topic, purpose, and time limit. Avoid digressions and overelaboration.
2. Visual aids and handout materials are especially useful, since this type of presentation frequently involves technical information and complex statistics.
3. Two-way communication is essential; leave time for questions.
4. Speakers in a business conference often know specific audience members much better than in most public speaking situations; careful adaptation to specific people—their backgrounds, expertise, attitudes—is therefore more important.
5. Be especially concerned with accuracy and thoroughness; "insiders" are less tolerant of sloppy or incomplete information that they may know as well as the speaker.
6. Modifying the physical setting may be easier in this situation; as a member of the organization, the speaker may be very familiar with the speech location and the potential for arranging it.

## The Briefing

Every Monday morning at 9 a.m., the professional staff of the state-supported Mental Health Institute meets to be briefed on the week's activities and relevant policy matters. Georgia Markley, as assistant supervisor of the facility, is responsible for conducting the briefing. She knows that the meeting, though crucial for effective interstaff communication, is viewed by the participants as an irritating but indispensable ritual, a necessary evil that takes time away from what really interests them in their work. She also knows that appointments begin at 10 a.m., so the briefing can only last about 45 minutes, regardless of the amount of information to be discussed. Finally, Georgia knows that audience members with special information may have to comment on some of the topics, and that these remarks may be unprepared, poorly presented, and take too much time.

Like the example above, a *briefing* is a relatively short (60 minutes or less) message that condenses a large amount of current information into capsule form. The usual objectives are to provide background materials, to describe situations and events, or to give instructions for future events. The briefing may provide feedback on how a particular project was carried out (sometimes called a *debriefing*). Briefings may occur in one-to-one or small group situations and be relatively informal, but they are also useful in audience situations. The stereotyped briefing is the old war movie scene of a RAF wing commander telling the bomber crews of the day's mission over Germany. Actually, such speeches are not usually so dramatic and occur on an everyday basis in many professions and organizations.

The keys to a good briefing are *accuracy* and *brevity*; anything less, and the whole purpose of the activity has been negated. A good strategy is to include outlined or excerpted printed materials and perhaps some pictorial visual aids to accompany the oral message. The speaker should expect to be interrupted regularly with audience questions unless he indicates that he will leave time for audience feedback at the end. In some situations, the speaker has freedom to delete topics or data in the interest of manageability. However, a good briefing often demands that the speaker present all relevant topics, because they are crucial to understanding an event or activity. If the speaker has only 15 minutes to present about 30 minutes of material (a frequent problem), he must economize in language and elaboration rather than arbitrarily eliminating relevant points. This task of condensing large amounts of information is the fundamental challenge of briefing.

The suggestions for the business conference presentation in the previous section generally apply for the briefing as well. Additionally:

1. Try to predict which items are likely to prompt active audience response, and plan for more time on those points.
2. If a particular audience member has special information that can assist in the briefing, arrange with that person ahead of time and stress the importance of brevity.

3. Too many briefings appear to be a random "checklist" of topics with no apparent structure; organize the announcements and topics into groups that have some logical progression.
4. Prepare a conclusion for a briefing just as in a regular speech; a summary or a recommendation may be appropriate here.

## Classroom Instruction

As a secondary education major with an emphasis in physical science, Adam Clayton took various courses in classroom methods, including testing procedures, course planning, and experiential learning activities. What he did not do was learn how to give lectures or presentations to a group of high school students. He thought that such lectures were too traditional for the kind of teaching he wanted to do, believing that classroom discussion of readings and laboratory projects would be the primary learning methods. He soon discovered that it was necessary to develop textbook materials in more detail and to provide additional information about various projects. Reluctantly, he began giving two or three instructional messages (lectures) per week, even though he had never had any training or experience in public speaking.

Adam's experience is similar to that faced by thousands of teachers who have learned that knowledge in a content area and in teaching methodology do not assume effective one-to-many presentations to students. Entire courses are devoted to classroom teaching methods. Though some of these courses include practice in presentational skills, we believe that any instructor should try to develop his public speaking skills in more depth. Here we provide some overviews about that special communication event.

The classroom instructor has several advantages—a captive audience, predictable facilities and environment, a series of meetings, reasonably large blocks of time, and usually some legitimacy in that the listeners tend to presume special speaker expertise. Whether in the public or private schools, business and government, or special training programs, however, the instructional speaker still must adapt to several problems.

An obvious advantage of having more time is that the informative speaker can cover topics in more depth and obtain more reliable feedback on communication outcomes. But the paradox of having plenty of time is that the speaker may waste too much of it. He does not prepare information carefully and economically. Too often the result is a rambling, disjointed message with irrelevant information, careless presentation or delivery, and limited audience appeal. Planning is just as important regardless of the available time. For example, if a speaker spends two of the eight hours allotted for a 25-member training session in casual meanderings and without planned teaching techniques, she has wasted 50 "people hours" with her poor preparation. She may also have bored her listeners. Or when a classroom teacher sheepishly admits, "I didn't have time to prepare any lesson for today, so let's just discuss the textbook," he may be indirectly suggesting that class time is not very important and that haphazard conversation serves as an acceptable substitute for prepared activities and objectives.

Unlike many informative situations, the classroom does not usually confront the speaker with continuous pressure to communicate well. Instructors get so used to the informal environment that they may not be psychologically "up" for the communicative effort. But we believe that the setting is no less important because of its familiarity and informality. Rather, we argue that an informative speaker can no more justify wasting the time of 30 students or trainees than he can justify rambling through a shoddy report to a corporate board of directors.

Another problem is that the classroom may be less suitable for maintaining continuous attention. As any teacher knows all too well, the captive audience may lose interest quickly, and the speaker must make special efforts to bring them back. Because the speech content is not usually as compelling as that discussed in, say, a business or professional setting, the teacher must be creative in developing interesting presentational techniques. Visual materials, variety in instructional activities, and the encouragement of group participation are some of the common devices to surmount this problem.

Suggestions for improving classroom presentations include:

1. Divide the presentation into short segments, offering frequent opportunity for feedback; it is surprising how many teachers lecture for an hour or more without pauses for questions or discussion.
2. Any instructional message should be adapted to a unique audience

of learners. The message-centered teacher prepares a speech in isolation from the students and asks them to adapt; the receiver-centered teacher recognizes the unique capabilities of a particular class and adapts each presentation to that uniqueness.

3. Develop good visual aids, like objects for demonstration, slides, and a list of available films. Unlike some one-time-only speeches, many classroom presentations need the same type of visual support each time they are given, and the aids may be used many times.

4. Always encourage two-way communication.

5. Try *mini-lectures*, short (10–15 minutes) instructional messages that are combined with other learning techniques during a class period.

6. Avoid manuscript speaking in classroom settings.

7. Use techniques to enhance interest and attention (see Chapter 9). Instructors considered the "best teacher" or "the person I learned the most from" are often simply the most interesting speakers.

### Short Speeches in Small Groups

When the 12-member Board of Directors of the Summer Recreation Program met to prepare their annual budget request, none of the participants expected to have to make a speech. But as the discussion developed, three points of view emerged. Some people thought that the bulk of the budget should be allocated to competitive team sports like Little League baseball and basketball. A second faction argued strongly for noncompetitive, instructional programs in sports like archery, gymnastics, swimming, running, tennis, and golf. A third position developed around arts and crafts and other learning activities like nature and wildlife hikes. As the group moved toward votes on various items, arguments became more complex and the individual comments became more lengthy, some lasting several minutes. Perhaps without realizing it, participants had begun to give brief impromptu speeches with introduction, body, and conclusion. Imagine what they might have thought had they been told beforehand, "Oh, by the way, at the meeting tonight you will have to give three or four public speeches on various topics that may arise." Yet, in effect, that is exactly what happened!

These impromptu presentations are typical of small group decision-making. Perhaps because we don't think of group participation as a "performance," we feel more relaxed in the small group setting and give little thought to the mini-presentations we make. Yet the people who seem to have some of the greatest influence on group consensus are frequently those who are effective as public speakers.

These discussion groups often have a lengthy history and participants know all the members well and can often predict their behavior and points of view. Yet decisions usually emerge spontaneously, a result of the unique and unpredictable events that occur during deliberations. Therefore, this speech context is one for which planning of specific "speeches" is difficult. Further, if we were to enter the discussion with a prepared speech, we might be guilty of one of the greatest crimes of small group interaction—having a closed mind toward alternate ideas.

Can we improve our presentational speaking in the small group context? The following might help.

1. Listen carefully, and seek clarification whenever necessary. We habitually close out others while we mentally prepare our remarks; our resulting comments may thus ignore what has just been said.
2. Jot down key ideas. As discussion progresses, we may discover a quick, neat way to organize our message. For example, "I'd like to mention three arguments. First, . . ." This helps prevent digression.
3. Be brief. Some mini-speeches will last less than a minute, and 2 or 3 minutes may be about the limit after which others will stop listening. Try to follow implied group norms; if everyone else has spoken for no longer than a couple of minutes, do not launch into a 10-minute statement.
4. Avoid becoming involved in extended, two-person debates that monopolize the discussion.

### The Exceptionally Large Audience

Ron Allen joined the Society of Mechanical Engineers when he was still in college, and as he advanced in his professional life he became especially active in the Society's committee work. As chairperson of the Goals Committee, he was asked to address the assembly at the national convention about the committee's conclusions. He was given a time limit of 30 to 45 minutes. The audience consisted of about 2000 people in the huge convention center auditorium.

Speaking to such large audiences is rare for most people. But when the situation does arise, it can be especially intimidating even for experienced speakers. Whether at conventions, large banquets, college lecture classes, or special programs, this communication context poses unique problems. The speaker can rarely interact with the listeners, and audience participation of any kind is awkward. The effective use of visual aids and demonstration is more difficult. Subgroups within the audience may respond differently throughout the speech; people close to the speaker may see and hear easily and respond enthusiastically, while those farther away may become impatient and surly. Audience members are much less likely to share common backgrounds and interests to the extent that members of smaller groups do. The greater the number of people, the greater the chance that the level of information will be too complicated or too simple, depending on the listener. A raised platform, podium, and loudspeaker system may keep the speaker locked to a tiny presentational area. The speaker must develop materials with the "average" listener in mind, and that typical listener's identity must be based on a subjective guess. Obtaining representative post-speech feedback can also be much more difficult than with smaller groups.

The following suggestions may be helpful:

1. Pretest loudspeaker equipment.
2. Try to interact casually with audience members beforehand to learn their attitudes, levels of interest, and background on the topic.
3. Electronic projections will be the most effective visual aids, because size and sound can be more easily varied.
4. Manuscript speaking may be more acceptable in this situation than with small audiences. Accurate presentation is more crucial because speaker-audience interaction is more difficult.
5. If audience questions are sought, it is better to get them *in writing*, collected by assistants or ushers, and selected by the speaker or a moderator.

## The Multi-Speaker Presentation

Each election year, the local chapter of the League of Women Voters
sponsors a "Meet the Candidates" night. This year, they decided to ask
each of the four candidates for mayor to focus on just one issue—problems and policies regarding the city's rapid population growth. Each
candidate would have no more than 10 minutes to deliver a prepared
message and would then be open to audience questions.

This example is sometimes called a *symposium*, in which two or
more speakers present differing viewpoints on the same topic. Variations of the multi-speaker communication event include the *panel*, a
group of knowledgeable people on a particular topic who discuss it with
each other and the audience; and a *debate*, in which two people argue
the pro and con sides of a specific proposition according to agreed-upon
rules and time limits. These situations pose special problems, because
in addition to adapting to a specific audience, the speaker must also
adapt fairly spontaneously to other speeches, some of which may directly refute his own position. Further, elaborate visual aids are rarely
used in these presentations; the focus is on the *interaction* between
people and their ideas, not on the specific content of a particular
presentation. Finally, an *adversary relationship* often develops between speakers (it always develops in a debate), and the speaker may
find himself in an atmosphere of attack and defense.

What can a speaker do to optimize this special context?

1. Be well prepared. It is easy to look foolish if other speakers appear
   to have better information.
2. Stick to the time limits. Audiences are usually aware of the time
   allocation and may become impatient and inattentive when a
   speaker exceeds the limit. And more assertive moderators may
   actually cut the speaker off in mid-sentence!
3. Take notes while others are speaking; use these notes in delivering
   impromptu responses to other speakers or to audience questions.
4. Be willing to make last-minute changes in prepared remarks;
   previous speakers may preempt your material or make comments
   that need to be refuted. Manuscript speaking is not advisable in a
   multi-speaker situation, because rapid adaptation is difficult.

## The Broadcast Media

The city council, a local utility company, and a television station decided to cooperate in developing a series of programs about energy and water conservation in the region. Their purpose was to obtain greater public commitment to reducing waste and lowering energy costs. Jim Hanley, a utility-company "consumer information" employee, was asked to develop a presentation on home insulation for one of the programs. The presentation would be taped and was to last exactly 27 minutes. Jim was to speak about 15 to 20 minutes, and then answer questions from a news commentator for the remainder of the time. The tape could be edited if the presentation went overtime.

In this type of context, even if a live audience is present, the public speaker should recognize that the target audience is that large and somewhat vague group of people who happen to tune into the broadcast. Over time, media people can begin to predict some of the characteristics of that audience, but since most broadcast speeches are one-time-only messages of a political, instructional, or public service nature on local stations, such reliable data are usually not available. More important, since a live audience in these broadcasts is rare, the speaker can get no immediate verbal or nonverbal feedback to help guide his presentation; the speech seems to be delivered in a vacuum. The program director, using the narrow eye of the camera, decides which tiny portion of the total communication event the viewers will see on their screen, meaning that some of the speaker's intended "message" may be lost. Finally, some speakers report greater speech anxiety when confronted with a microphone and camera.

An entire book can be written about speaking on television, but the guidelines below are a starting point for adapting to the medium.

1. Seek advice from station personnel about preparation of visual aids. Many types do not broadcast well (too small, bad coloring, etc.).
2. Discuss with director and camera operators ahead of time any planned movement, demonstration, or visual displays. Don't "surprise" them with unexpected action that the camera cannot follow.
3. Let the technicians worry about sound levels; do not try to talk louder or move closer to pre-set microphones.

© Howard Harrison 1972

4. If an audience is present, maintain eye contact with them, not the camera; if there is no audience, then regular focus on the camera lens is necessary.

## The Ceremony or Ritual

The University Honor Society had made its annual selection of outstanding students for membership in the organization. It then sponsored a formal initiation ceremony for candidates and their families. The ceremony typically lasted about a half-hour, included memorized recitations and readings by Society officers, and required the candidates to take a formal oath to continue the quest for truth and scholarly excellence. The middle of the ceremony called for a 10- or 15-minute inspirational message to be delivered by an invited speaker. This year the Society asked a campus minister, Ruth Lockhart, to present the message. They also asked her to speak on the general (and vague)

topic, "The Quest for Excellence." Ruth's task was a difficult one: to say something interesting, useful, creative, and inspirational in a fluent and relatively formal way.

While it may be that we have fewer rituals today in what has perhaps become a more casual, less ceremonial society, formal communication events like the one above are still fairly common. They include weddings, funerals, other religious services, awards presentations, dedications, initiations, graduation exercises, and many others. These events vary in form and style, but key factors in all of them tend to be *structure*, *order*, and *formality*. Both speakers and listeners usually have a cultural history of participating in rituals, and they therefore bring with them to each new event a set of expectations about what should occur. That is, they have more rigid attitudes about what should or should not occur. Probably for this reason, many speakers report that they find speaking in rituals more intimidating than in other contexts. And they also report a tendency to polish their speeches more and to deliver them less conversationally and more formally.

The purpose of ceremonial speeches is certainly persuasive (the speaker attempts to influence the beliefs, values, and attitudes of the receivers), but does not involve the practical policy issues or seek specific behavioral responses typical of most persuasive speaking. It can be argued that in some contexts, the message *content* (factual information, ideas, opinions) is not as important as the *process*, the fact that a message is being delivered. The argument goes this way: "No one remembers what the speaker said at the graduation ceremony, but they knew that a speech was presented and they would have been disappointed had there not been one. It does not matter so much *what* was said, but rather that *something* was said, consistent with their expectations about the ritual event."

We do not deny that the process of speaking at ceremonial events is a time-honored custom that we have come to expect. But we disagree with the notion that the verbal message is irrelevant. We believe that the speech content can and should be received, understood, and appreciated, that it should elicit particular responses which speeches in different contexts would not elicit. The speaker should be just as concerned about developing a stimulating and convincing message as would be expected in any other context. The fact that many ceremonial speeches are so easily forgettable should not deter us from trying to say something important and useful.

Several suggestions can help improve the quality of ceremonial speaking.

1. In pre-speech negotiations, find out *exactly* how the ritual will proceed, where your presentation fits in, and what you should be doing during other portions of the event.
2. Consider the ceremony as one of the few communication situations in which you might rely more heavily on manuscript, or at least use a more detailed outline.
3. Rehearse the speech more rigorously than usual, paying special attention to the time limits.
4. Strive for creativity and uniqueness. Try to avoid the trite generalizations that are so typical of the ceremonial setting.
5. If a primary purpose is to inspire, to stimulate emotionally, consider the use of specific examples and illustrations of real people in real events.

## SUMMARY

The *context* is the situation or setting in which the public speech occurs. Each context is unique, and the speaker's adaptation to it is a chief factor in speech effectiveness.

One important variable of the context is the seating arrangement, which often determines how people interact; it can elicit spontaneity, formality, various types of interaction, and determine the comfort of the receivers. The podium is another variable; it is not always necessary and, if used, should not become a crutch or barrier. Temperature and lighting are not only important to audience comfort and receptivity, but can also help establish the appropriate mood. Mechanical and electronic equipment, the fourth variable, is a blessing in most cases, but can become a curse if it malfunctions or is not used efficiently.

Many public speaking contexts do not conform to the traditional public speaking class model. The business conference occurs among insiders, and the speaker must conform to the receivers' norms, especially in terms of style, content, and length. The briefing is usually a short, informal instructional session, one that should be organized carefully for accuracy and brevity. It should also include open question-and-answer periods. Classroom instruction gives the speaker more time, but also encourages laxity in preparation; it should be carefully adapted to a unique audience of learners. Short impromptu speeches occur frequently in small task groups. They require careful listening and spontaneous organization of brief responses. The exceptionally large audience context places more constraints on two-way communication, speaker mobility, and adaptation to unique receivers. Support equipment like a public address system is usually needed. The multi-speaker event, like symposiums, panels, and debates, requires an excellent grasp of the topic area, along with efficient, spontaneous refutation of opposing arguments. Finally, the broadcast media may reach the largest audiences but obviously restricts face-to-face interaction. This type of speaking demands special equipment with which most of us are unfamiliar; the speaker must rely on the expert advice of radio and television professionals.

## QUESTIONS FOR STUDY

1.  Why is the public speaking class, though an important learning method, somewhat atypical in comparison to many communication contexts in everyday speaking? On the other hand, what special adaptations are necessary to deliver a speech for a class project?

2.  How can seating arrangement affect the speaker's ability to achieve the speech purpose? Give some examples.

3.  Of the "Special Communication Events" discussed in this chapter, which would be the most difficult for you to adapt to? Which would be the easiest? Why?

4.  Return to the chapter's opening example of Will Denton. For each of the contexts listed there, how would you have adapted a persuasive speech appealing for funds?

5.  Return to the example of the historian's ill-fated lecture (in "The Physical Setting" section). What things could he have done to eliminate some problems and manage others as they arose?

# chapter 12

# EFFECTIVE LISTENING

**LEARNING OBJECTIVES**

After reading this chapter, you should be able to:
1. Explain why good listening is important in public speaking.
2. Assess your own listening habits, especially in important communication situations.
3. List suggestions for improving your own listening skills.

# 12

When Marilyn Hazelton finished her Ph.D. and became a lecturer in European history at a state university, she was not prepared for the "television generation" that would make up most of her classes. These students were the most passive audience she had ever faced. Perhaps as a result of having watched dozens of hours of television for most of their lives, the students would sit back, stare passively at their instructors, and seem to be saying, "O.K., I'm waiting. Get my attention, pull me along through the material, and fill me up with information." To Marilyn, getting them to respond to her attempts at two-way communication was like "pulling teeth." She went to uncommon efforts to organize her lectures and to make them interesting. But the results of the exams told the story. Her students knew little more about European history at the end of the semester than they had known at the beginning. Marilyn Hazelton was to some extent the victim of an audience that had never learned how to listen.

Michael Cohen had been on the debate team in college and had achieved great competitive success as a fluent and persuasive speaker. He had experienced the intoxication of impressing audiences and receiving their praise. Now a junior-level supervisor in a large company, he sought out opportunities to make presentations—to employees, to colleagues in business conferences, and to public audiences as a company representative. Michael had only one problem as a communicator. He preferred being on the sending end of any transaction. In a receiver's role, he was frankly bored by others' presentations and usually let his mind wander or, worse yet, thought of ways to make the sender's message more stimulating. The result was that over time Michael missed significant amounts of important information. For example, during conferences he would be thinking so deeply about his eventual contribution to the decision-making process that he was unaware of what others were saying. His comments were thus redundant or even irrelevant. In casual conversations, he would cut people off and then expound at length on his own viewpoints. Michael began to get a reputation as someone who was self-centered, overly impressed with his own abilities, and insensitive to the ideas and feelings of others. He soon discovered that some of his best ideas were being ignored. Michael Cohen had become a victim of his own poor listening habits.

## IMPORTANCE OF GOOD LISTENING SKILLS

Although the public speaker has many responsibilities, one that is frequently ignored is the need to be a good receiver as well as sender of messages. And of all the factors that affect the outcome of a communication event, the one over which he has relatively less control is the listening habits of his audience. Thus, while a good speaker may make his presentation as interesting and imaginative as possible, he is still unable to command his audience to listen if they choose not to.

As noted in Chapter 1, communication is a two-way street, requiring the mutual effort of both sender and receiver. In the case of public speaking, listening is the counterpart skill necessary for effective communication. Listening is, in some respects, the most significant of our four verbal skills—reading, writing, speaking, and listening. Of the four skills, an estimated 25 percent of our communication time is engaged in reading and writing combined. About 30 percent of our time is spent talking, and about 45 percent of our time we are engaged in listening. Furthermore, common estimates suggest that as much as 85 percent of our total knowledge comes to us through the listening process.

### Benefits to the Listener

Good listening is important to anyone who interacts with others, but it is particularly important in the public speaking arena. First, it helps the *listener*. It does so by allowing us to gain maximum benefit from messages, to absorb, comprehend, and retain much more information. This material can usually be applied or adapted for later use. Good listening is also essential for effective evaluation of information which, in turn, is an important tool for effective decision-making. In addition, many speaking situations call for the listener either to respond actively to a speaker or to adapt to the speech content. Obviously, good listeners are more able to respond intelligently and articulately in such situations. In general, they are better equipped to enjoy, understand, and evaluate the messages they hear. The results of their efforts are often reflected in fuller appreciation of recreational experiences (such as movie-going, television viewing, concert attendance), better

© Howard Harrison 1969

job performance, more careful decision-making, and happier relationships with others.

### Benefits to the Speaker

Good listening also benefits the *speaker*. You may realize from your own experience that it is much easier (and more enjoyable) to speak to an audience that is attentive and involved, as opposed to one that is hostile, bored, or distracted. The very act of demonstrating interest provides impetus for a speaker to do a better job. Message delivery is often improved, and the feedback provided by an audience of active listeners generally helps the speaker adjust his message to the listeners' needs. For instance, an alert speaker might be able to tell when an idea or concept needs expansion or when the audience has sufficient information to move on to the next point. So an audience of effective listeners enhances the speaker's presentation by giving him valuable information that allows him to modify his message.

### Social Benefits

Good listening provides *social benefits*. The concepts of democracy and free enterprise are based on the notion of intelligent, critical decision-makers. The listener who can both understand and carefully evaluate a speaker's message is capable of making better social, economic, and political decisions. Furthermore, it is this kind of individual who serves as the conscience and watchdog for public speakers and message-senders in every sector of public life.

### Improvement of Public Speaking

Good listening *improves public speaking skills*. It does so in two ways. First, when we listen better to the speeches of others, we acquire a greater range of materials that we can use in our own speeches. Some of the most interesting public speakers are people who have themselves picked up facts, ideas, and anecdotes from listening to others. In Chapter 3, two techniques we suggested for gathering materials were "using one's own background" and "personal observation." Notice that both these resources assume that we have absorbed information from the people around us. And how do we perceive, comprehend, and retain this information? As noted above, a significant amount comes from listening.

A second way in which we improve our speaking skills is through critical listening—evaluating the message behavior of other speakers. Most speech instructors can attest to their personal improvement as speakers simply because they have heard and critically evaluated the speeches of others. Similarly, audience members who know that they will sometimes be in the role of speaker rather than listener should perceive the communication event on two levels: the *content* level, or the apparent meaning of the speaker's message; and the *process* level, or how the speaker is doing as a communicator.

## PROBLEMS OF POOR LISTENING

Despite the significance of listening in our lives, few of us listen well. Research shows that the average person retains only a portion of what he hears, perhaps about 50 percent of message content immediately after the speech. And this retention drops quickly after that. All of us, as listeners, have heard speeches about which we remembered almost nothing only a few hours afterward. Certainly such poor recall suggests equally poor comprehension, appreciation, and analysis.

One reason for poor listening is the fact that most people understand so little about the process itself. Our educational system has neglected the subject of listening almost entirely, and even those who have studied the process closely express uncertainty about some of its more complex aspects.

Another reason we know so little about listening is that it has only recently been recognized as a skill. In fact, many people still view the process as merely physiological, somewhat beyond our conscious control. This confusion has resulted, in part, from a misunderstanding of the role that hearing plays in the listening process. While the terms *listening* and *hearing* are often used synonymously, they in fact refer to quite different processes. *Hearing* refers to *the reception of aural stimuli (sounds)* and, as such, forms the basis of our ability to listen.

© Howard Harrison 1968

The term *listening* refers to *the total process of receiving, interpreting, analyzing, and retaining data.*

Although listening is based in part on hearing, we now recognize that listening involves more than reception of audible data, and often includes visual stimuli as well. Furthermore, there is little direct correlation between a person's hearing acuity and the ability to listen. One indication of the distinction between the two concepts is seen in the fact that it is very difficult to "turn off" our hearing and tune out loud, abrasive noises, yet we find little difficulty in "tuning out" a speaker whom we consider boring, uninformed, or irrelevant.

Ignorance of the listening process has resulted in at least two faulty assumptions. First, people have assumed that listening was largely out of their control, that it could not be taught or improved, and that they were therefore destined to a lifetime of poor listening. "I just can't seem to listen" (instead of "I just won't listen") has become an acceptable excuse to many people.

Second, a common belief is that since we all have essentially the same hearing apparatus, we all receive basically the same message. Actually, since listening is largely a psychological process, such individual factors as experience, education, beliefs, attitudes, values, and interests may so affect our listening that the message one person gets may be entirely different from the message received by the individual sitting next to him. As listeners, we should recognize what factors influence our listening so that we do not allow them to interfere with accurate message reception.

## SUGGESTIONS FOR IMPROVING LISTENING ABILITY

Fortunately, in spite of our individual differences, there are some things we can do about our listening ability. Educators have found that a number of factors bear directly upon our ability to listen. The following suggestions may help improve our listening efficiency.

1. *Be physically and mentally prepared.* Listening not only requires effort, but it demands a great deal of energy. It is not unusual for people who experience intense listening to become exhausted. Because listening is hard work, there is no way we can expect to listen effectively if we are physically or mentally unprepared. We cannot listen well if we are fatigued, hungry, or otherwise physically uncomfortable. Good listening is characterized by a general physical and mental alertness, including such physiological changes as a quicker pulse and a slight rise in the body temperature.

Because of the importance of the listener's role in effective communication, we cannot expect to lean back in our chairs and be "filled up" with knowledge without contributing our own effort. In order to be mentally prepared, it is sometimes necessary for the listener to bring to the event certain knowledge and information. One way to do this is to engage in advance reading for suitable background on a subject. This is particularly useful if we plan to listen to a message in which the speaker assumes that we have certain information, or in situations where time is limited and a subject cannot be explored thoroughly.

Quite often, listening to technical or unfamiliar material demands such preparation.

A second way to prepare for a listening situation is to be ready to take notes if necessary. Often people forget to consider the possibility that notes may be useful and find themselves wishing they had brought appropriate materials. Effective note-taking will be discussed in more detail below.

**2.** *Set listening goals.* One characteristic of many poor listeners is the tendency to confront listening situations without considering either what they hope to gain or how they might use the information they hear. A key to effective listening is determining general and specific goals for each listening situation. A general listening goal would be to decide whether you are listening for *pleasure*, *comprehension*, or *evaluation*. These three general goals can be viewed on a continuum, with listening for pleasure making the least demands on the listener and listening for evaluation requiring the most effort. Each of these listening situations can require different attitudes and skills.

Second, you might wish to determine specific goals (i.e., "I want to understand the causes of the French and Indian War," "I want to decide whether or not to support the upcoming referendum," or "I'd like to get really involved in this play, without becoming bored or distracted.") By consciously establishing goals, we are more aware of where to focus our attention, and by so doing, we are more likely to find our listening experience productive.

**3.** *Motivate yourself to listen.* Earlier we argued that speakers cannot command an audience's attention. While good speakers work to create interest and hold attention, they cannot force someone to listen if the person really prefers to daydream. Therefore, listening ultimately becomes an exercise in self-motivation by each receiver.

Good listeners develop strategies for motivating their own listening behavior. One of the most frequent complaints of ineffective listeners is that they can't make themselves concentrate, and concentration is the key to good listening. You may have had the experience of telling yourself to "listen better" or to "try harder to listen," only to find yourself focusing on your own behavior, missing the message almost entirely. Good listening requires focusing on the message, and the ability to concentrate usually begins with finding areas of interest or importance to you.

Good listeners are very selfish and very practical in that they aggressively seek information which interests them and which might be of later use. Bad listeners often conclude that a topic is boring or irrelevant after only a few sentences, or perhaps even before the speaker has begun. Good listeners may have the same initial reaction; however, they recognize the importance of productive use of time. By making the most of the situation, they generate their own interest and attention.

Another way to motivate listening is to reward yourself. Effective speakers often reward their audiences for listening—either subtly, by making the experience pleasant, or more obviously, by thanking the audience for their attention and responsiveness. Listeners can develop their own systems of rewards for times they have listened well.

**4.** *Focus on the message content and not the speaker's delivery.* One of the biggest listening traps is becoming distracted by the speaker's delivery. Many college students, for instance, have admitted to becoming so engrossed in counting the number of "uh's" or paces made by an instructor that they totally missed the content of the lecture. Other people have rationalized their way out of listening because of a speaker's monotone or some other unpleasant delivery characteristic. While good listeners may also identify delivery weaknesses in a speaker, they do not allow themselves to concentrate on them nor do they allow such factors to become an excuse for daydreaming.

**5.** *Avoid emotional reactions.* As noted earlier, psychological factors affect listening. Beliefs, attitudes, and values provide filters that can distort or inhibit message reception. Most of us have certain words, phrases or subjects which trigger our immediate emotional reactions. While a list of such emotional triggers might be endless, a few examples mentioned frequently are abortion, the defense budget, inflation, welfare, Affirmative Action, public utilities, and Richard Nixon. Whenever we hear one of our own set of trigger words, it is difficult to listen objectively; however, it is especially hard to listen when the speaker's remarks contradict our own opinions and feelings. In some cases, we may "tune out" the speaker. This selective listening results in incomplete and distorted information.

A common tendency among "overstimulated," emotionally charged listeners is to prepare a mental rebuttal, formulating argumentative responses or questions to be offered when the speaker finishes. While it seems that we are listening critically when we engage in mental rebuttal, actually just the opposite occurs, because we cannot objectively comprehend what the speaker is saying and at the same time develop arguments against his message. What generally happens is that we become so absorbed in preparing our own "speech" that we miss the speaker's message. In addition to losing valuable information, many people have discovered the embarrassment of having their inattention exposed publicly by asking a question or making a response to a matter which was already addressed in the speech.

A good strategy to avoid overstimulation is to assess the words and concepts which tend to evoke an emotional response. By focusing initially on comprehension (instead of evaluation), you can objectively note arguments and supporting material, ensuring a clearer understanding of the speaker's position. *After* comprehension and analysis are complete, *then* appropriate evaluation and response can occur.

6. *Look for the main ideas.* Most of us have difficulty discerning the main ideas in speeches. And there is frequently little agreement between listeners about which points appear to be most significant. Perhaps this problem stems from our preoccupation with facts in the United States. Most of us have been taught from an early age to "get the facts" or "look for the facts." Wiser advice is to "get the main idea" or "look for major points." What is wrong with looking for the facts? Facts by themselves have little or no use, but when coupled with ideas or principles, they take on value. Furthermore, it is difficult for most of us to remember facts in isolation. Ideas are the substance that give facts "sense." When we go about trying to memorize facts in isolation, we take on the added burden of trying to make sense out of them, and the result is that we are likely to fall quickly behind the speaker, losing valuable information and important ideas in the process.

Good listeners can find main ideas. They consciously remind themselves to focus on principles, asking questions like "What is the speaker getting at?" or "What principle does this information support?" Fortunately, some speakers give us clues to indicate the introduction of a major idea. Verbally, they often use such phrases as "First . . . ; second . . ." or "The point is . . ." or "We can conclude . . ." Main ideas are often previewed at the beginning of a speech and summarized at the end, so a careful listener watches for these clues. Speakers also employ a variety of nonverbal methods to suggest emphasis of an important idea. Vocally, a speaker may use pauses or a change in rate or volume to signal a major point. Other nonverbal clues include changes in body movement, gestures, or facial expression.

7. *Use note-taking to advantage.* Note-taking is often a useful tool for effective listening, though inappropriate note-taking can do more harm than taking no notes at all. While most of us need to take some notes in order to retain information, it is important that we use them to supplement good listening and not allow them to interfere with the listening process.

Many people get carried away trying to develop thorough, well-organized notes, often within a carefully structured outline format. Problems arise when the speaker does not follow an easily identifiable organizational pattern. Our experience has been that no more than one in three speakers carefully organize their material in such a pattern. If we try to reorganize their speech to fit our pattern, we sacrifice attention to the message. Effective note-taking means adapting to the speaker, not attempting to adapt the speaker to our style.

A second tendency among note-takers is to try to put too much down on paper. This is particularly true of people who get submerged in the search for facts. A strategy to avoid this trap is to listen for a few minutes, get a sense of the speaker's direction, and then begin note-taking. In many instances, fewer notes that are more concise and direct are more profitable than lengthy or detailed notes.

8. *Control the listening environment.* In most listening situations there are many potential distractions that can interfere with concentration. Such obstacles include noise coming through an open window,

people engaged in side conversations, poor lighting or acoustics, or a speaker who does not adjust his volume to the size of the room.

Often the problem can be solved by closing a window, asking the speaker to talk louder, or moving to a better seat. Sometimes it is necessary to concentrate harder. Effective listeners seem to recognize that while distractions are a normal obstacle, the listener should not permit them to become an excuse for poor listening. Furthermore, speakers often are not as aware of distractions. While a speaker might be very conscious of a loud siren outside the building, he is not as likely to notice noisy chatter in the back of a large room. For example, a speaker once addressed a group in a fairly large room that had no public address system. He asked if everyone could hear him clearly. Most people, including those in the back of the room, responded affirmatively. The speaker said, "If at any time you cannot hear me, wave a hand or speak up and I'll try to talk louder." At the end of his lecture, someone came up to him and said, "After the first few minutes, the noise in the hallway got so loud I couldn't hear a word you said." Our question is, whose fault was that? Certainly the responsibility of controlling the listening environment lies partly with the listener.

**9.** *Challenge your listening skills.* Many *poor* listeners are *inexperienced* listeners. They have generally avoided situations that involve extended listening time or difficult, unfamiliar material. Just as improvement in any sport requires not only practice but the confrontation of new and increasingly challenging situations, so does development of listening skill. If we confine our listening habits to half-hour situation comedies on television which are frequently interrupted by commercials, we are not likely to have the stamina to manage a 45- to 60-minute speech on a difficult, technical topic. Yet most of us must confront situations that require extended concentration. The development of listening skills requires stretching our powers of concentration and exercising the mind; it cannot be accomplished unless we are willing to seek out more challenging material.

**10.** *Ask questions and check perceptions.* If time is provided for a question or feedback session, take advantage of it. Too often that time is viewed merely as a chance for audience members to react with their opinions. Time can usually be better spent by probing for additional information or by seeking clarification. For instance, one might ask "Where did you get the statistics on rural growth?" or "How do you stand on the seniority system in Congress?" or "What is the basis for your conclusion that violent crime is decreasing?" These questions may take the form of a paraphrase of what the listener thinks he heard. For instance, "Do I understand you to oppose all forms of sex education in the public schools?" "Did you claim that there is irrefutable evidence to link crime with televised violence?"

**11.** *Capitalize on thought speed.* Nichols (1957) maintains that if we could measure thought in words per minute, we would find that people think at a rate of approximately 400 words per minute. Other estimates range as high as 750 words per minute. Yet the average rate of speech in this country is only about 125 words per minute. The impact of this differential bears directly upon the problem of effective listening. Since we can *think* four or more times faster than the speaker can *talk*, and since our mind does not "slow down" to adjust to the speaker's rate, we find other ways to use our surplus word-processing capacity. Daydreaming is perhaps the most popular pastime. Most of us are aware that it is quite easy to "check out" of a speech for a second or two, allow the mind to wander, and jump back in, picking up almost where we left off. The thought speed–speech speed differential makes this possible. Two problems arise from this activity, however. First, it is very difficult for our minds to handle effectively two entirely unrelated subjects for any length of time. We cannot do justice to both topics. Second, because daydreaming is much easier for us than listening, it almost invariably wins out. The farther we fall behind the speaker because of our daydreaming, the more difficult it becomes to listen, and eventually daydreaming takes over completely.

In spite of its pitfalls, our thought speed need not be a handicap. In fact, if used properly, it can become the listener's greatest asset. The most effective strategy is to *use extra thought capacity in ways which help rather than hinder the listening process.* Below are some specific strategies that will improve listening through the efficient use of thought speed.

## Listen for Comprehension

1. *Try to determine the speaker's purpose and direction*. What is the speaker's goal; what does he hope to accomplish? Where is he going with the point that he's making? What ground will be covered next?

2. *Recapitulate*. Mentally summarize the main points which have been made. How are the points related?

3. *Listen between the lines to get the speaker's total meaning*. Effective listening involves more than understanding individual words. We listen between the lines when we search for figurative as well as literal meanings, when we are aware of the speaker's use of irony, humor, or other creative devices. We also listen between the lines by noting nonverbal communication. The speaker's voice, posture, movement, and facial expression can, as we have noted, modify his verbal message. Thus, in using thought speed we consider things we *see* as well as *hear*.

4. *Note the speaker's supporting materials*. Does the speaker use evidence to support main points? If so, what kind?

5. *Relate the information to your own experience and point of view*. How does this new information apply to you? In what ways can you use it? Does it confirm or contradict your own experience and attitudes?

6. *Prepare some questions which you would like answered*. This list may include probes and paraphrases for the speaker to answer, but it may also include questions you will wish to check into later on your own.

## Listen for Evaluation

1. *Identify the speaker's general and specific goals*. Is the speech designed primarily to entertain, inform, or persuade? What specific response is intended from the audience?

2. *What are the main ideas expressed?* Do they seem to make sense individually? Do they seem to follow some logical sequence? As a unit, do they seem to provide a complete picture? Are there any gaps or hidden assumptions?

3. *How are the main ideas supported?* What kinds of support materials, if any, are used? Are the quote sources qualified and unbiased? Is the evidence verifiable? Does the evidence seem to be complete? Does it seem to support the conclusion the speaker claims? Is there variety in terms of the methods of support and the sources cited?

4. *What methods are used for motivation?* What values, attitudes, and needs are appealed to? Does the speaker as a person appear to be credible, both in terms of expertise and character?

5. *How does the speaker use language?* Is he clear, concise, imaginative? Is the choice of words appropriate to the audience in terms of understanding and taste?

6. *How does the speaker communicate nonverbally?* How effective is the use of movement, voice, facial expression, appearance, and visual aids for communication? In general, does delivery enhance or detract from the message presentation?

7. *Does the speaker use creativity to make his presentation more worthwhile?* What methods, if any, does the speaker use to gain and hold audience attention? Does the overall presentation suggest an imaginative approach to the structure of the speech, including the introduction and conclusion? Are creative devices used to stimulate the audience's imagination?

8. *What is the speaker's apparent attitude toward the audience?* Does he appear to be involved, congenial, adaptable? Is he responsive to feedback? How are questions and audience interaction handled?

9. *What is your general reaction to the communication event?* Do you feel basically positive, negative, or uncertain? How does this compare in terms of quality to similar events you have experienced?

10. *How does this event relate to the larger environment?* That is, what is the relevance or impact of the speech to other activities and issues in our lives?

## LISTENING BEHAVIOR AFFECTS THE SPEAKER

In conclusion, perhaps the most important single fact to remember about listening to a public speech is that *listening behavior affects the speaker's behavior*. It helps determine the degree to which audience members ask questions. It helps determine the kinds of nonverbal behaviors that they exhibit and that the speaker may perceive. And it helps determine the speaker's response to the feedback.

For example, in this chapter's opening example of the college lecturer, Marilyn Hazelton, how enthusiastic and committed to effective communication could she remain, semester after semester, if the poor listening behavior of her students remained the same? Could student listening habits be one reason why some teachers stop trying, why they just "go through the motions" because they are not being rewarded with positive student feedback? If so, then the result may be a vicious cycle. The teacher's lack of enthusiasm is perceived by students, who assume that the message is unimportant. They listen even more poorly than before, and the teacher responds with even less effort. The reciprocal effects that senders and receivers have on each other, a concept we have stressed throughout this book, suggest the responsibility that each listener must share when unproductive communication occurs.

On the other hand, consider what good listeners can do to improve a speech. Suppose they are determined to listen well. They ask questions that demonstrate their having comprehended the major ideas. Their eye contact is directly on the speaker, they nod attentively and jot down things the speaker says. The speaker perceives their behavior and becomes more enthusiastic and committed to do well. And the next time he gives a speech to this audience, he may be more inclined to think, "This is an important group of people. They are interested in what I have to say. I don't want to let them down, so I'll prepare especially well for this next speech." If he does well, or if he improves, the listeners may notice and continue to respond favorably. Thus, a cycle of positively reinforcing behaviors between speaker and listeners improves the productivity of each successive speech. In short, good listening rewards and stimulates good public speaking.

Similarly, good public speaking can reward good listening. Throughout this book we have provided suggestions to speakers that indirectly improve listening. For example, our suggestions for clear speech organization (Chapter 3) and for improving language and clarifying materials in informative speaking (Chapter 9) also facilitate a receiver's listening potential. Here we offer a final suggestion. *When good listening occurs, reinforce it directly*. The following comments, if sincerely felt and presented, provide such reinforcement:

> "Thank you for giving me your attention. Whether or not you agree with me, you certainly were the type of audience I enjoy speaking to."

> "The results of the exam tell me that you were listening carefully to the lectures. Good work!"

> "That's a very good question. It relates directly to the central point I was making."

> "Your constructive suggestions have been very helpful to me. I'm grateful that you were listening critically to my speech."

## SUMMARY

Listening is something we all do, but few of us do well. Its importance in public communication is fourfold. First, good listening helps the receiver, both in terms of responding to the speaker and in terms of using the information in practical ways. Second, good listening helps the speaker better achieve the speech purpose and adapt to receiver needs. Third, good listening has a social benefit, because people will make better decisions if they have received information accurately and critically. Finally, it improves public speaking skills, as receivers who listen well not only have more resources for their own speeches but also are more aware of good and bad speech habits.

*Hearing* is the reception of aural stimuli, but *listening* is the whole process of receiving, interpreting, analyzing, and retaining information. We may hear without listening. People vary significantly in their motivation and ability to listen well.

Suggestions for improving listening include: being physically and mentally prepared; setting listening goals; motivating yourself to listen; focusing on speech content rather than delivery; avoiding emotional reactions; looking for the main ideas; using note-taking to advantage; controlling the listening environment; challenging your listening skills; asking questions and checking perceptions; and capitalizing on thought speed.

In terms of thought speed, we know that people think more rapidly than a speaker talks, meaning that any listener has excess mental capacity to think about other things. This excess thought speed, rather than being wasted in daydreaming, should be put to use both to improve comprehension and to better evaluate the speeches we hear.

Speakers and listeners should realize that their behaviors are reciprocal—they affect each other. Thus, positive feedback from listeners can improve public speaking, and positive reinforcement by speakers of good listening behavior will improve receivers' future willingness to listen well.

## QUESTIONS FOR STUDY

1. In general, how good are the listening habits of students in your public speaking course? While students are giving speeches, what factors tend to detract from good listening?

2. How might some of the suggestions for improving listening skills be utilized in the public speaking course?

3. In what ways is the quality of public speaking today related to (interdependent with) the quality of listening behavior of both speakers and their audiences?

4. What is the difference between listening for comprehension and listening for evaluation? How might a listener's confusion about those two objectives yield negative results in a public communication event?

5. What are some situations in everyday living in which people usually listen well? What are some situations in which they often listen poorly? What are some reasons for these differences in the quality of listening?

# conclusion

# RESPONSIBLE PUBLIC COMMUNICATION

When James Armour decided to enter the ministry, he did so because of his religious beliefs and commitment to help others. But when he graduated from seminary and took a post as associate pastor of a large church, he discovered he had another important asset—the ability to preach in a way that kept parishioners interested and emotionally involved in the sermon. James began to get a good reputation, and church attendance began to increase on the days he was scheduled to preach. Other church staff noticed this trend and asked him to speak more frequently. As attendance increased, so did financial contributions to church programs. And so did James' popularity.

After a year of preaching, James pondered his success. He was frankly intoxicated with the experience of seeing the pews fill up with people, with their rapt attention to his message, and with the words of admiration that he received after each service. But he noticed something else. He had become less concerned with studying theology, with participating in other activities in the church, with counseling duties, with calling on the sick and elderly, or with the spiritual health of the parishioners. Most important, he had been selecting sermon topics on the basis of audience interest, sidestepping many relevant theological issues because they had less popular appeal. And in developing his messages, he had been arranging substantive information around the examples and illustrations that had strong emotional appeal. That is, instead of using emotional appeals as supporting materials to the main ideas, James built the main ideas around the emotional appeals. This technique, combined with his ability to add dramatic vocal inflections, were primary reasons for his success. But church attendance, membership, and financial giving were up, people appreciated his efforts, and his growing reputation would probably bring him offers for a head minister's position at another church. *Question*: was James Armour engaging in responsible public communication?

The Sierra Investment Company sells lots for vacation and retirement homes. Its latest project is several thousand acres of choice mountain property in Northern California that are for sale as half-acre home sites. The sales team consists of six members of Sierra Investment who have developed a carefully orchestrated sales program. *Phase One* is to obtain an audience of potential buyers. Generally this consists of offering free dinners to people who are willing to hear a presentation about "investment opportunities." *Phase Two* is the actual presentation, consisting of a film, colorful brochures, tape-recorded testimony of previous customers, and a polished speech by the most fluent and attractive member of the team. *Phase Three* is closing the sales, as the team members engage in semi-private table conversations with each individual or couple attending the dinner. These potential customers complete a brief questionnaire at the beginning of the dinner so that the sales agents can adapt closely to each person.

The campaign is based on three primary strategies. The first is an appeal to one's desire to make money, beat inflation, and live comfortably with a minimum of risk. The second is to achieve a series of "yes responses" to many preliminary questions, so that the person is more likely to say "Yes" when it comes time to sign on the dotted line. The third strategy is based on guilt, as the potential buyers who hesitate are made to feel that much time and money have been spent on the dinner and the presentation and that their refusal to buy is somewhat unfair.

The Sierra Investment Company has had great success with this sales strategy. While several buyers later felt that they were "taken in" by a slick sales gimmick, and while others realized too late that the investment was a financial burden, no one who kept up payments has ever lost a penny in the land investment. The company has operated for more than 20 years and has never been accused of fraud or unsupported claims about the developed property. *Question*: Does Sierra's sales presentation represent responsible public communication?

We cannot answer the two questions above for anyone else. Each person must make an independent judgment. But we do argue that *the public communicators in those examples should accept at least a portion of the responsibility for the results of their communication behavior.* Had they decided not to speak in the ways they did, the outcomes in the lives of the receivers would have been different—not necessarily *better*, but *different*. The speakers intervened in the lives of others, and their intervention had effects. We believe that the issue of responsible communication is a relevant one for any person who speaks publicly and who thus intervenes in and affects the lives of others.

## PUBLIC SPEAKING AS A TOOL

This textbook, like courses in public speaking in which it is used, teaches techniques and skills that become *tools for achieving results.* If we have done our job well in writing this book, if you have in fact improved because of materials we have presented, then we also share some responsibility for your subsequent public speaking behavior and the results you achieve. We think it is our responsibility to provide some discussion about how those tools ought to be used. For textbook authors to omit this analysis is, we believe, irresponsible.

We shall not explore in depth the problem of *ethics*, the study of good or bad behavior, of right or wrong. We shall not delve into personal morality to any great extent. For one thing, such topics are better left to studies in philosophy and religion. For another, we should be presumptuous to suggest that we know, in specific situations, what is good or bad behavior for public communicators. But we do think that everyone should give some thought to the implications of communicative responsibility.

We base our views on the premise that *speech is behavior; it is action.* Our society often tries to deny this premise. We hear phrases like: "Actions speak louder than words." "Talk is cheap—what can you deliver?" "I believe in deeds, not in words." "It's not what you *say* that counts, but what you *do*." "Sticks and stones may break my bones, but words will never hurt me." People will often refuse to accept an oral agreement and instead force others to behave more actively, to "sign on the dotted line," for example.

© Howard Harrison 1971

We regret this cultural tendency to minimize the significance of oral behavior. Some cultures, such as those of native American or Asian peoples, place a much higher premium on spoken words. But general American culture—business, politics, and even interpersonal relationships—tends to separate other physical acts from speech acts. We think this separation is meaningless. Behavior is behavior is behavior. Action is action, whether it is verbal or nonverbal. For example, hitting someone with your fists and criticizing him with your speech may be different in form, but they are the same in content. Both are behaviors that *you initiate*. Both are perceived and given meaning by another person. And both are actions that have some sort of result.

Remember that every so-called nonbehavior, or inaction, has effects. Try *not* answering an exam question or *not* paying your taxes to find out whether others notice, interpret, and respond to your passive behavior. As we've indicated before, you cannot *not* communicate and you cannot *not* behave. Both religion and law recognize this principle by including sins and crimes of *omission* as well as *commission*. We once heard an interesting discussion on whether there was any real difference between stealing food from a hungry person (*active*) and refusing to give food to a hungry person (*passive*). Similarly, is there any difference between saying something that hurts someone's feelings and failing to say something that could have soothed hurt feelings? How about making unsupported assertions in a speech that damages someone's good reputation, or refusing to speak out with evidence that would restore someone's good reputation?

Throughout this text we have argued that public speaking behavior, if noticed by others, will have some effect or response. The response may be important or insignificant, overt or unnoticeable, positive or negative, clear or ambiguous, permanent or short-range, conscious or unconscious. But a response will occur. And that response may then prompt further behavior by the initiator. Thus, we see the *interdependence* of communicative interaction and, by extension, the mutual, ongoing impact we have on each other. In essence, then, ethical or moral judgments are inevitable. We cannot escape them. Consciously or unconsciously, we make them each time we speak. (Even the person who says "I shall not concern myself with ethical problems" has already rendered an ethical judgment.)

We suggest that *responsible public communication* occurs when *a speaker develops awareness of his interdependence with others, of the kinds of message choices that are available, and of the possible results those choices might have.* The responsible communicator welcomes the personal accountability that goes with interpersonal conduct, especially public speaking behavior.

## Issues and Problems in Responsible Public Speaking

Once we realize that our public speaking has practical and moral consequences, we still must answer for ourselves several difficult questions. Our answers should then help determine how we speak, which choices we select. Below we list a few of these questions. We suggest that you not try to answer them with a simple yes or no, but instead think of possible justifications for either point of view.

*Do the ends justify the means?* Are we justified in saying things that may temporarily hurt or deceive, if the long-run impact of those messages is beneficial? Or should we always justify our communication on a short-range basis as well as a long-range one? For example, is an infantry officer in combat, during a briefing, justified in holding back information about the enemy's strength because he thinks it may demoralize his men and impede their ability to fight well and save their own lives?

*Should we use the self-reference criterion when we advise others?* Should we determine what is best for an audience according to what we think is best for us? For example, should we try to convince others that our beliefs and behaviors will help them because they helped us? Or should we encourage others according to what we guess their personal interests to be? Perhaps the speaker inevitably and unconsciously imputes his own values and attitudes to the audience when he tries to adapt his message to his receivers' backgrounds and interests. Is it advisable, or even possible, to avoid altogether the process of trying to persuade others?

*Should our messages be based primarily on rational, objective grounds?* Are we irresponsible if we urge others to behave according to their feelings, passions, sentiments, sensations? For example, are advertisers justified in pushing a product because it may "make us feel

young, alive, and exciting"? Should politicians use appeals to fear to get our vote? Does the discussion in Chapter 10 about nonrational appeals violate standards of responsible public speaking if they are instrumental in affecting a receiver's behavior, even if that receiver has not been asked to think deeply or logically about his response? Is it justifiable to use suggestion, even though this persuasive technique is designed to encourage an essentially "unthinking" response?

*Is responsible public speaking situational?* Does a speaker's ethical liability, his determination of what is good or bad, rely primarily on the unique situation? If so, does that mean that we cannot develop for ourselves a reliable yardstick or set of standards that will guide the moral decisions we make in public speaking? Or are there some hard and fast rules that should never be broken, regardless of context? For example, if we decide that one guideline is that our receivers should know all of the reasons why we are advocating a particular policy, including our personal reasons or motives, there might be times when frank disclosure of these reasons would detract from persuasiveness, from the response we seek. It might clutter an already complicated speech, or make the receivers unduly suspicious. In other words, there might be times when we would prefer, strategically, to reveal only some of our reasons for speaking persuasively. Can we make this determination, along with many other ethical judgments, according to predetermined rules? Some people argue that those who practice so-called "situation ethics" really operate *without* moral guidelines, since it is possible to justify any behavior on the basis of the unique elements of any particular situation.

*May we send messages that were created by another person?* If we use an idea originally phrased by another and perhaps lead others to believe that it is our own, are we irresponsible? Is a politician justified in delivering a speech that has been *ghost-written* by a staff of experts? If politicians or any other communicators truly *believe* what they say, does it matter who originally thought it up? It is physically impossible for some public officials, political candidates, and busy executives to spend the time necessary to prepare good speeches and still fulfill their many other responsibilities. What choices are open to them?

*Does "intentionality" make a difference?* If an audience responds to a speech in unexpected or unintended ways that are harmful to themselves or others, is the speaker's responsibility lessened if he did not realize what he was doing? If it was not his *intention* to hurt others? What if the speaker was simply naively unaware of the potential consequences? Must he accept full responsibility for his behavior, regardless of intent? For instance, suppose an audience follows a persuasive speaker's investment advice, information in which the speaker sincerely believed and that he thought would earn money for him and his clients. And suppose his persuasive efforts were successful; the listeners responded by doing as he urged. Finally, suppose the investment was a bad one, leading to devastating losses for many people who followed his advice. Their losses were a partial consequence of the speaker's communication behavior. Is that fact the "bottom line" in assessing ethical responsibility, or can the speaker be partially excused because he never intended to hurt anyone?

*Does listener receptivity make a difference?* If potential receivers do not seek my comments or do not prefer to hear them, am I justified in initiating those comments anyway? Does a responsible public speaker have any special obligations with an *involuntary or "captive" audience*, or are there some things that others *need* to hear, regardless of whether they *want* to hear? For example, if a speaker is convinced that she is speaking for an important cause that benefits people, can she ethically justify giving a speech with a public-address system in a public park or a college quad? What about renting a sound truck and presenting the speech as she drives through residential neighborhoods? Or what about a recent Academy Awards telecast, in which one of the award winners chose to make a political speech on the Israeli-Palestine issue? The audience voiced its disapproval with scattered boos but were powerless to do much else, as the actress said what she wanted to say and what she certainly thought it was justifiable to say. In what ways, if any, should listener receptiveness affect a public speaker's ethical judgments?

*Is secrecy justifiable?* Is it irresponsible to "talk behind someone's back"? To communicate secretly about other people? To make policy decisions in private—decisions that will eventually affect others? Are there times when more open communication could actually be irresponsible and dangerous? If a speaker is making a presentation to an "insider" group that will eventually render a decision, is it justifiable to exclude all "outsiders," including the press, from the audience? What if this presentation includes damaging information about particular people? What if it involves national security matters? The "open meeting" laws that have been enacted in many states have forced many speakers in public agencies to get used to an expanded audience of outsiders. But these laws, though they can dictate legal conduct, do not necessarily solve the moral issue of whether secret presentations that may affect people's lives can be justified as responsible communication.

*Can free speech ethically be restricted?* The classic prohibition against a person yelling "Fire!" in a crowded theatre suggests that our society does not condone unrestricted free speech. Laws against slander (telling lies about a person which cause him harm) affirm this point. But generally our legal system has gone far to protect free speech. A severe test occurred in the summer of 1978 when a court reluctantly agreed to permit the American Nazi party to march and make speeches in the predominantly Jewish town of Skokie, Illinois, despite the Nazis' odious racist philosophy and despite the chance of violence erupting. Our culture seems to be saying: "People with power to restrict public speaking act irresponsibly, and often illegally, if they use that power." Our legal system tends to agree with Voltaire: "I disapprove of what you say, but I will defend to the death your right to say it."

But the issue may not be the right of free speech *per se*, but rather the right of a speaker to say things to a particular audience at a particular time. The point made earlier about involuntary audiences applies here as well. May we ethically restrict a speech in a public place that, in our judgment, disrupts public order and tranquility? At what point does such a speech infringe on the rights of the unwilling audience? Is it responsible for the owner of a private company to set down rules against certain kinds of speeches on company premises, like a membership pitch by a union organizer? Is it ethical to ask voluntary members of a club or association to give up certain rights of free speech as a precondition of membership? Is it necessary for military organizations to control rigidly the narrow range of communication behaviors in which members may engage? How do we determine whether a restriction of free speech is unethical?

In summary, your answers to all these questions are a product of your beliefs, attitudes, values, experiences, and many other factors. These unique characteristics are one cause of the frequent disagreement that we find on difficult moral or ethical issues. Though we may be unable to achieve consensus on what are good or ethical communication behaviors, we can become more responsible public speakers when we think more carefully and consciously about our decisions on these issues.

## Guidelines for Responsible Public Speaking

As mentioned, we shall not prescribe specific ethical behaviors for specific communication situations. However, we think it is our responsibility to suggest general guidelines that we believe public speakers ought to use. They are not intended as absolutes. We assume that others may find equally convincing reasons to disagree with them. Therefore, these guidelines should be read carefully and critically.

1. *Responsible communicators attempt to be truthful.* They are honest. They avoid intentional deception. They frankly recognize the self-interest that motivates much of their message behavior, and they willingly disclose such motives to others. When attempting to persuade, they try to be empirically accurate and logically valid; they recognize that half-truth or partial distortion is really a kind of lie.

2. *Responsible communicators are accommodative; they are receiver-centered.* They compose messages according to the comprehension abilities of receivers, and they encourage open feedback—authentic two-way communication—to enhance shared meaning. They try to display empathy, to understand and appreciate the interests and feelings of an audience.

Even more important, the receiver-centered speaker respects the time and energy that listeners must expend in a public speech. To participate in a public communication event is, by definition, to forgo other activities at that particular time. Is it worth the trade-off, and in some cases the sacrifice, for a listener to be here rather than someplace else? The responsible speaker prepares messages with thought and care so as to justify the receivers' time and attention.

Most crucial of all, the receiver-centered speaker does not try to offend or injure people with his remarks. His own motives are important here. If a speaker is critical of one or more receivers, is it for a constructive purpose? Is the criticism based on a speaker's sincere interest and positive regard for the listeners as people? Or does he instead want to use his public communication skills as a weapon to get revenge, to attack, to embarrass or humiliate others? Responsible communicators consider the well-being of their receivers. They do not exploit or harm others for personal gain.

3. *Responsible communicators are also effects-oriented.* They are concerned about the *results* of their communication behavior. They acknowledge their interdependence with others and willingly accept responsibility for the outcomes of their transactions.

4. *The responsible public speaker affirms the right of listeners to make critical choices.* He has faith in receivers' abilities to act in their own best interests, to "make up their own minds." Therefore, while a speaker may be strategic, forceful, and aggressive, he avoids coercion and threats. He also avoids emotional tricks or techniques designed to elicit primarily nonrational audience responses. He lets his ideas be accepted or rejected on their own merits, not on factors unrelated to the inherent value of the ideas and proposals in the speech.

5. *Responsible public speakers try to develop listening skills and improve two-way communication.* They welcome questions and seek information from audience members and try to respond nondefensively. They try to listen carefully and attentively. They use probing and paraphrasing responses to assure that they have *understood* the audience member (established shared meaning) before they evaluate that message or provide new opinions and information. Most important, they recognize two-way communication as a legitimate process in all public speaking events.

6. *Responsible public speakers think about the moral or ethical implications of their communication behavior.* They recognize that it is impossible not to decide ethical issues, that in avoiding an issue they

have in fact made a decision. They ask the question: "Regardless of my skill in eliciting an audience response through public speaking, is this the way I *should* be communicating? Is it *good* for me to do this?" That ethical issue cannot be answered with certainty, but it can be answered. We believe that when more speakers consider ethical issues more often, public communication and our society in general will improve.

## SUMMARY

In conclusion, we cannot justify teaching people to develop physical strength if they use it to brutalize others. We cannot justify teaching people to write, if they use their skill to flood the market with pornographic literature. We cannot justify teaching people how to work skillfully with firearms and explosives, if they use this information to become thieves, murderers, or terrorists. We cannot justify teaching surgical techniques, if doctors use them to perform gruesome medical experiments on human beings, such as occurred in the Nazi death camps.

We cannot justify teaching any competence unless it is tempered with a moral sensibility of what is good or bad. That is why we are concerned that our efforts to improve communication skills can lead to an abuse of what has sometimes been an awesome ability to deceive and exploit. The better each speaker becomes, the greater the potential for both good and bad effects. If, indeed, "the age of public speaking is just beginning," then it must evolve with the firm belief that communication is not just a tool, but also a weapon.

# references

Andersen, Kenneth. *Persuasion: Theory and Practice*. Boston: Allyn and Bacon, 1971.

Baker, Eldon. "An Experimental Study of Speech Disturbance for the Measurement of Stage Fright in the Basic Speech Course." *Southern Speech* 29 (Spring 1964): 232–243.

Berlo, David. *The Process of Communication*. New York: Holt, Rinehart and Winston, 1960.

Bormann, Ernest, and George Shapiro. "Perceived Confidence as a Function of Self-Image." *Central States Speech Journal* 13 (Spring 1962): 253–256.

Brandes, Paul. "A Semantic Reaction to the Measurement of Stage Fright." *Journal of Communication* 17 (June 1967): 142–146.

Buehler, E. C., and Wil Linkugel. *Speech: A First Course*. New York: Harper and Row, 1962.

Clevenger, Theodore. "A Synthesis of Experimental Research in Stage Fright." *Quarterly Journal of Speech* 45 (1959): 134–145.

———, and Thomas King. "Visible Symptoms of Stage Fright." *Speech Monographs* 28 (November 1961): 296–298.

Foulke, Emerson. "Listening Comprehension as a Function of Word Rate." *Journal of Communication* 18 (September 1968): 198–206.

Freeley, Austin. *Argumentation and Debate*, 3rd ed. Belmont, Calif.: Wadsworth, 1971.

Friedrich, Gustav. "An Empirical Explication of a Concept of Self-Reported Speech Anxiety." *Speech Monographs* 37 (March 1970): 67–72.

Giffin, Kim, and Bobby Patton. *Fundamentals of Interpersonal Communication*. New York: Harper and Row, 1976.

Gilkinson, Howard. "Social Fears as Reported by Students in College Speech Classes." *Speech Monographs* 9 (1942): 141–160.

Howell, William, and Ernest Bormann. *Presentational Speaking for Business and the Professions*. New York: Harper and Row, 1971.

Klee, Bruce. "The Myth About Stage Fright." *Today's Speech* 12 (February 1964): 20.

Knapp, Mark. *Nonverbal Communication in Human Interaction*. New York: Holt, Rinehart and Winston, 1972.

Lohr, J., and M. McManus. "The Development of an Audio-Taped Treatment for Systematic Desensitization of Speech Anxiety." *Central States Speech Journal* 26 (1975): 215–220.

Lomas, Charles. "The Psychology of Stage Fright." *Quarterly Journal of Speech* 23 (February 1937): 35–44.

McCroskey, James. "Measures of Communication-Bound Anxiety." *Speech Monographs* 37 (1970): 269–277.

———. "The Implementation of a Large-Scale Program of Systematic Desensitization for Communication Apprehension." *Speech Teacher* 21 (1972): 255–264.

———, J. Daly, V. Richmond, and B. Cox. "The Effects of Communication Apprehension on Interpersonal Attraction." *Human Communication Research* 2 (1975): 51–65.

———, D. Ralph, and J. Barric. "The Effect of Systematic Desensitization on Speech Anxiety." *Speech Teacher* 19 (1970): 32–36.

Mingler, B., and J. Wolpe. "Automated Self-Desensitization: A Case Report." *Behavior Research and Therapy* 5 (1967): 133–135.

Monroe, Alan. *Principles and Types of Speech*. Chicago: Scott, Foresman, 1939.

Mowrer, O. Hobart. "Stage Fright and Self-Regard." *Western Speech* 29 (Fall 1965): 197–200.

Nichols, Ralph. "Ten Guides to Effective Listening." *Nation's Business* 56 (July 1957): 56–60.

Paul, G., and D. Shannon. "Treatment of Anxiety Through Systematic Desensitization in Therapy Groups." *Journal of Abnormal Psychology* 71 (1966): 124–135.

Phillips, Gerald. "Reticence: Pathology of the Normal Speaker." *Speech Monographs* 35 (1968): 39–49.

Ray, Jack, and Harry Zavos. "Reasoning and Argument: Deduction and Induction." In Gerald Miller and Thomas Nilsen (eds.), *Perspectives on Argumentation*. Chicago: Scott, Foresman, 1966.

Robinson, Edward. "What Can the Speech Teacher Do About Students' Stage Fright?" *Speech Teacher* 8 (January 1959): 1–10.

Sieberg, Evelyn. "Confirming and Disconfirming Organizational Communication." In James Owen et al. (eds.), *Communication in Organizations*. St. Paul, Minn.: West Publishing, 1976.

Sticht, Thomas, and Douglas Glasnapp. "Effects of Speech Rate, Selection Difficulty, Association Strength, and Mental Aptitude on Learning by Listening." *Journal of Communication* 22 (June 1972): 174–188.

Weaver, Andrew, and Ordean Ness. *The Fundamentals and Forms of Speech*. New York: Odyssey, 1963.

Winterowd, W. Ross. *Rhetoric: A Synthesis*. New York: Holt, Rinehart and Winston, 1968.

Zimmerman, Gordon, James Owen, and David Seibert. *Speech Communication: A Contemporary Introduction*. St. Paul, Minn.: West Publishing, 1977.

# Index

## DATE DUE

| | | | |
|---|---|---|---|
| | | | |
| | | | |
| | | | |
| | | | |
| | | | |
| | | | |
| | | | |
| | | | |
| | | | |
| | | | |
| | | | |
| | | | |
| | | | |
| | | | |
| | | | |
| | | | |
| | | | |
| | | | |
| GAYLORD | | | PRINTED IN U.S.A. |